DOWN-TO-EARTH WOMEN

DAWN MACLEOD

Down-to-Earth Women

THOSE WHO CARE FOR THE SOIL

WILLIAM BLACKWOOD
Edinburgh

William Blackwood
32 Thistle Street
Edinburgh EH2 1HA

First published 1982
© Dawn MacLeod 1982

ISBN 0 85158 158 7

Printed by William Blackwood & Sons Ltd

Remembering Mairi Sawyer of Inverewe, who cared for fifty acres of West Highland soil with its wealth of fine plants, and found time to cultivate human friendships as well.

Acknowledgements

Thanks are due to the Reverend Mothers and Communities of Stanbrook Abbey, Worcester; St Mary's Abbey, West Malling; St Mary the Virgin, Wantage; and Our Lady at Burford.

To Lady Eve Balfour, Flower, Lady Furness, the Countess of Haddington, the late Lady Meade-Fetherstonhaugh, and the late Mrs Mairi Sawyer of Inverewe.

To Rene Clayton, N.D.H., Carola Cochrane, Florence Craggs, Doreen Dennis, Madge Elder, Valerie Finnis, V.M.H. (Lady David Scott), Madge Hooper, Sybille Kreutzberger, Mary Lutyens, Elsie Matley Moore, Nigel Nicolson, Betty Prentice, Pam Schwerdt, Graham S. Thomas and Algy Villiers.

To the late Margaret Brownlow, B.Sc., N.D.H., Margery Fish, Beatrix Havergal, V.M.H., and Cecily Mure.

To Charles and Judy Clive-Ponsonby-Fane and to the Boyd-Carpenter family; to Mary Knox Finlay, V.M.H., Mrs Sheila Graham, Lady Holden, Anne Scott-James, Mrs Elizabeth Sherriff, and to my friend since we were very young at the Croydon High School, Doris Pring, for her recollections of Eleanour Sinclair Rohde.

To the National Trust and the National Trust for Scotland, the Royal Horticultural Society, the Herb Society, the Soil Association and the Women's Farm and Garden Association.

To Messrs George Allen & Unwin, G. Bell & Sons, Ernest Benn, Crosby Lockwood, Darton, Longman & Todd, Faber & Faber, the Faith Press, the Hogarth Press, Hamlyn Publishing Group, Michael Joseph, Longman's Group, the Medici Society, for quotations.

To Robert Adam, *Amateur Gardening*, Jane Bown, the British

Museum, *Country Life*, S. J. Clarke, the Cement & Concrete Association, J. E. Downward, R. Eudall, *The Field*, *Home and Country*, Royal Botanic Gardens, Kew, 'Julian', Nicholas Meyjes, Stephen Mitchell, Arthur Mould, the *Observer*, Peter Reason, Harry Smith, Adam Tegetmeier, L. S. Thompson, Sir George Trevelyan, the National Trust for Scotland and the National Portrait Gallery, for pictures.

I am particularly grateful to my husband, Alfred Wilson, for constant support and encouragement and for his careful examination of proofs.

So many people have kindly offered information during a long period of research that I fear some may have been omitted. If so, I apologise and ask forgiveness.

Dawn MacLeod

Preface

To a publisher who wanted an 'impersonal, objective book about gardening' I replied that gardens were of little interest to me unless they were personal and subjective – an opinion which helps to illumine a major difference between male and female attitudes to this ancient art and craft of horticulture. Man likes to dominate and impose his own will upon the smaller fry of existence (at times on his own kind too), whereas woman through centuries of motherhood has learned to appreciate life in all its manifestations, curbing and controlling the unruly subject only when such intervention is deemed necessary for the well-being of the individual and his family.

There is nothing artificial in distinguishing between the sexes in connection with gardening, or in attempting to evaluate the lives of some notable women who have cared for the soil here in the British Isles. In varied careers these women have nearly all shown one dominant trait – a strong love of the earth and its growing plants, a devotion in which desire for personal power and prestige has had very little place. There are exceptions. One of them, Ellen Willmott, was obviously a highly ambitious woman, rich, attractive, spoilt and proud of her ability to compete in the rarefied atmosphere of the highest ranges of horticulture and botany, until then almost exclusively a man's world. That was still largely true when I began to collect material for this book over ten years ago. Only recently have women begun to take their rightful place in horticultural circles as elsewhere.

There have been some celebrated men who gardened for love rather than money or fame. The late E. A. Bowles and Dean Hole, who worshipped roses, spring to mind immediately. Would it be unfair to suggest that they were exceptions to the rule? One highly skilled woman, the late Phyllis Reiss, the creator of the splendid garden at Tintinhull, was described by a close friend as having 'gardened like a man, ruthlessly expelling any plant that did not please her'. For this behaviour to be spontaneously labelled 'masculine' suggests that others too have perceived that there are male and female attitudes to gardening, even if these attitudes may be separated by a ha-ha rather than an iron curtain.

Certain gardens could have been made only by a woman. I cannot conceive of a man who would have dealt with plants as Margery Fish did at Lambrook. Her so-called ground-coverers, such as lamiums and vincas, rose up into shrubs and adorned walls; jasmines, clematises, akebias and stauntonias climbed trees; self-sown teasels, spurges and ornamental thistles placed themselves on paths; and if such unconvential efforts proved pleasing, the trespassers were left undisturbed. Another kind of exuberance appeared with striking effect at Vita Sackville-West's garden, Sissinghurst. This garden is not so much a permissive environment for the happy accidents of nature as a gorgeous floral opera, whose scenery and players were grouped on the stage to satisfy the opulent taste of its producer through the twelve acts of the year. Sissinghurst is aristocratic and aloof, like its maker, screened from the outer world by high walls and yew hedges – a sharp contrast to the cottage-type garden of Mrs Fish, which is securely integrated into its small village.

That mid-Victorian pioneer, Jane Loudon, who by her writings persuaded innumerable contemporaries to do so much more in their gardens than just gather spoils grown there for them by men, would no doubt have been astonished to see what green-fingered women have managed to create in this century. To Jane Loudon's influence, and to that of her even greater successor, Gertrude Jekyll, we probably owe the delights of Sissinghurst, Tintinhull and Lambrook. It was women, too, who bestowed skilled direction on the larger conceptions, originally man-made, at Inverewe and Rowallane. The knowledge and tact required to maintain the character of two such individual gardens are akin to the qualities required of a first-class accompanist – an art where instrumental technique is used to complement and not obscure the soloist. Until her untimely death in 1953, Mairi Sawyer of Inverewe gave a life of unpublicised devotion to the sub-tropical oasis created by her father, Osgood Mackenzie, in the wilds of Wester Ross; also, the Hon. Mrs Terence O'Neill (now Lady O'Neill) has supervised with conspicuous success the late Mr Armytage Moore's lovely Irish garden, Rowallane.

Because ownership of many of our finest gardens is now vested in trustees and because the gardens are open for everyone to explore and enjoy, it seems inevitable that a most far-seeing woman, Octavia Hill, co-founder of the National Trust with Canon Rawnsley and Sir Robert Hunter, should creep into these pages. Not herself a gardener, she served as a kind of midwife between the makers of famous gardens and the enormous public which now has access to their handiwork. In this motorised age few of us would care to forgo visits to houses and gardens, woods, fields, moorlands and mountains preserved by the Trust; yet the name of Octavia Hill is in danger of being forgotten.

At present living quietly in the background, although in future years she may rank among the most famous, is Lady Eve Balfour. Her persistence and energy in pursuing for nearly half a century experimental work with organic methods of farming and gardening has at last gained a hearing. Her study, once derided as 'muck and mystery', is now acknowledged to be of immense importance to mankind. This is indeed a down-to-earth project. The voice of the Soil Association, for whose formation in 1945 Lady Eve was chiefly responsible, is increasingly heard in the councils of those who care for the land, and a compost heap is found in every garden.

Education of another sort was the province of Beatrix Havergal, one of the very few women whose work in the first half of the twentieth century earned her the Royal Horticultural Society's Victoria Medal of Honour. Her Waterperry Horticultural School near Oxford was the creation of a woman pioneer against tremendous odds. It became one of the best training grounds for young women desirous of making careers in practical gardening, rather than in scientific, administrative or teaching posts, and throughout its history commanded the respect of horticulturists all over Britain.

Long before the time of Jane Loudon or Gertrude Jekyll, it had been customary for women to cultivate herbs for use in cookery and medicine and to provide fragrance in the home. Many herb gardens were attached to convents, where nuns can still be found working at the cultivation of herbs, vegetables and flowers. Between the wars of 1914/18 and 1939/45 herb gardening was revived in the outside world as a career for emancipated young women. One of the best-known herb-growers, Eleanour Sinclair Rohde, gardened in

Surrey and became famous for her many books about herbs, their history and culture.

In 1926 Dorothy Hewer, inspired by Miss Rohde's work and by her friend Mrs Grieve, author of that standard book of reference *A Modern Herbal*, founded the Herb Farm at Seal near Sevenoaks in Kent. She was succeeded as Director by her pupil, Margaret Brownlow, whose books and lectures, for nearly thirty years until her death in 1968, spread the knowledge of herbs and their culture to a wide range of gardeners in this country, most of them women. In Herefordshire Madge Hooper of Stoke Lacy still carries on the skilled cultivation of herbs which she learned from Dorothy Hewer at Seal. Another ex-herb farm student, Mrs Barbara Keen, has been running a herb-growing business since 1932.

A vast number of unpublicised women now tend their own gardens, often creating little oases of singular charm in or near built-up areas. Such gardens range from the tiny plot of Kensington planted exquisitely by Cecily Mure and the town garden made by Elsie Matley Moore behind the famous house of Greyfriars in the heart of Worcester, to a larger cottage garden designed and planted by Enid Money in the Cotswolds and a mill-house garden created by Betty Prentice in Berwickshire.

And what of humble gardeners in earlier times? Those weeding-women who were paid threepence a day for removing charlock, nettles, convolvulus, dodder, thistles, dandelions and groundsel from the gardens of Hampton Court (heaven knows how many hours they worked for that pittance!); the country wives who not only grew the flax, but prepared the fibre, spun the thread and wove their linen (according to Thomas Tusser, the good housewife in 1557 was busy out of doors 'in March and April from morning to night'); the herb-wives who peddled their wares from door to door; the nuns who laboured in garden, farm and vineyard. Of their stories only a few fragments remain. I wonder what became of that stone effigy of a weeding-woman which Celia Fiennes saw in a cherry orchard at Woburn in 1697 and described as being so lifelike as to persuade many visitors that it was real.

The famous John Gerard, who had a herb garden hard by London's Holborn, published his popular *Herbal* in 1597, helped by his wife, who provided information of particular interest to women, thus ensuring a large circulation. In the seventeenth century we must remember 'Mistress Bugg of Battersea' who raised a fine purple auricula – the first mention, to my knowledge, of a woman plant-breeder in these islands.

Among the ladies of noble, sometimes royal, birth, Queen Henrietta Maria who made her gardens at Wimbledon outstanding in Stuart times; the Duchess of Beaufort who developed a fine garden at Badminton; Elinor Mordaunt, whose marriage to the eldest son of the Duke of Gordon in 1706 was so greatly to benefit the estates of Gordonstoun and Invergordon; Lady Luxborough, gardening friend of the poet and 'landskip' expert William Shenstone; and the Dowager Princess Augusta, mother of George III, whose flair for plants helped to inspire Kew Gardens – all made their mark on the horticultural world of their day. In this century the Dowager Countess of Westmorland with her lovely Lygrove garden, the Countess of Haddington at Tyninghame and Mellerstain in Scotland's Borders, and Queen Elizabeth the Queen Mother at her northern retreat, the Castle of Mey, carry on the tradition of green-fingered royalty and aristocracy.

During the nineteenth century, women worked at garden projects as oddly various as that of an 'Alpine rockery designed in the form of the Savoy Alps around Chamonix', designed by Lady Broughton; the raising of a superb cooking-apple, the Bramley's Seedling, in a cottage garden at Southwell by Miss Brailsford (first fruited between 1819 and 1823, the apple tree is still living); and the cultivation of unusual (and then unfashionable) foliage plants by Miss Frances Jane Hope, a Scotswoman of Edinburgh. She took great delight in placing variegated broccoli between bedding plants in her flower borders, and published many articles and a book about the planning of gardens and cultivation of plants.

In England, Mrs Theresa Earle, a well-informed and very practical gardener, made herself suddenly famous at the age of sixty by writing her first book, *Pot-Pourri from a Surrey Garden*. This striking success, issued in 1896, was followed by several other 'pot-pourri' books, which are said to have made a profit of £30,000 for their publisher. The author stated that she had made very little money out of her writing, a complaint which has not changed with the years.

In a period dedicated to the cult of youth, it is cheering to notice that in the horticultural world age and experience come into their own. Vita Sackville-West was nearly forty before she took up gardening seriously, and her well-known articles on the subject for the *Observer* were begun at the age of fifty-five. Mrs Margery Fish took no interest in gardening until she reached late middle age, with a newspaper career behind her; and Mrs Cecily Mure, whose work in a small Kensington plot was described as 'miracle gardening' by Fred Whitsey, was well into her fifties when she worked her small miracle.

Some of the women pictured herein have recorded their gratitude to others who helped them by generously sharing their own knowledge of plants. Among these benefactors were Mrs Clive of Brympton d'Evercy, Mrs Norah Lindsay and her daughter Nancy, and Miss Raphael, owner of a lovely woodland garden at Kingston Bagpuize. All may be classed as gifted amateurs.

Reference must also be made to some modern women who work professionally in spheres connected with horticulture. Heading the list are the distinguished landscape architects Sylvia Crowe and her former partner Brenda Colvin, both past presidents of the Institute of Landscape Architects. Dame Sylvia, who was awarded the C.B.E. in 1967 and created D.B.E. in 1973, is the author of several books, including *Garden Design* (Country Life, 1958) which has been reprinted. In addition to designing and remaking private gardens and those of certain Oxford colleges, she has served as consultant to the new towns of Harlow and Basildon and to the Forestry Commission.

Among the many women who have taken up market gardening, Miss Carola Cochrane, author of *Two Acres Unlimited* (Crosby Lockwood, 1954) made an outstanding success of her land at East Brabourne in Kent. In the same county Mrs Rene Clayton developed a lively and prosperous Garden Centre at Hollingbourne near Maidstone. Other nurserywomen of note are Miss Hilda Murrell, who restored the fortunes of the Portland Nurseries near Shrewsbury after World War II; Mrs Desmond Underwood of Colchester, who until 1977 drew crowds to her charming exhibit of pink and silver plants at the Chelsea Show; Mrs Mary McMurtrie of Balbithan House near Kintore in Aberdeenshire; and Beth Chatto.

We must not overlook those invaluable women employed as practical gardeners. Would there were more of them! Miss Pamela Schwerdt and Miss Sybille Kreutzberger, the Waterperry-trained girls who were described by the late Vita Sackville-West as her 'treasures' have become, since her death and the transfer of Sissinghurst to the National Trust, the first professional women to take charge of an important Trust garden. The story of Madge Elder, the deaf Scotswoman who managed the Duke of Buccleuch's gardens of Bowhill during World War II, is a brave one to inspire other handicapped people.

Although plant-hunting in distant lands cannot of itself be classed as gardening, a remarkable Scotswoman who became involved in both activities deserves mention. Betty Sherriff was a daughter of the Rev. Dr John Graham who founded some well-known children's homes in Kalimpong, where Betty was born. After 1942, having married George Sherriff – of the Ludlow-and-Sherriff partnership which so enriched Britain with Himalayan species of plants – she took part in many of her husband's expeditions to remote regions of Northern India, Tibet and Bhutan.

Probably the only woman of her time to have tracked down a particularly fine 'Blue Poppy' (*Meconopsis grandis*, No. 20671) growing in its native soil, Betty retired to Scotland with her husband in 1950. At Ascreavie, 900 feet up in Angus, she laboured alongside him to create a Himalayan garden from the overgrown hillside, and for ten years following his death in 1967 she skilfully maintained this lovely place single-handed.

Standard histories of gardening are concerned largely with the work of men. Until recently the library of the Royal Horticultural Society in Vincent Square could produce disappointingly sparse material about even the most famous of women gardeners, and such names as Phyllis Reiss, Mairi Sawyer of Inverewe and Beatrix Havergal are still too little recognised.

It is hoped that this book will be found as companionable as the women themselves. To make reading a pleasure, the subjects have been limited to some fifty individuals. Otherwise this might have become a mere catalogue. Although each choice is a worthy representative of her genre, there are in this rich field many other skilled and creative gardeners working in Britain, to whom I can only pay tribute in general terms without names. Let us honour all those green-fingered women who care for the soil with unremitting devotion.

Dawn MacLeod

Contents

Illustrations

xix

1

Early Gardeners and Nuns

A garden book written in the nineteenth century by a woman, the Hon. Alicia Amherst's *A History of Gardening in England*, states that nothing worthy of being called a garden existed in Britain before the Norman Conquest. 'Britons revered the oak, held the mistletoe sacred, and stained their bodies with woad, but of horticultural effort we know nothing,' she says. Like most categorical assertions, this one invites queries.

First there is woad. It takes a lot of this plant to produce enough blue dye to stain even one's hands, so that users of body paint would have needed a large supply. Was it found in the wild or cultivated by primitive gardeners? That is a query nobody is ever likely to answer with certainty. After the Conquest there were fairly early references to woad-growing in Kent, although in later medieval times Lincoln, Cambridge and Somerset were the chief centres of the woad industry. With the importation of indigo from the East, woad was superseded as a commercial dyestuff. Small remnants of woad cultivation are still be be found in one or two localities in England.

Then there is the apple. In his book *The Speaking Garden* Edward Hyams wrote:

> In Britain the culture of the apple is prehistoric, for those mysterious characters the Druids cultivated orchards, if only because mistletoe favours the apple-tree as a host plant. I have, it is true, read that only when parasitic on the oak was it sacred. Strict scholars dismiss the tale that Avalon was so called after its abundance of apples, for they do not believe that any such place existed, and even deny existence to the sixth-century poet Merddin, who wrote of apples. This Merddin was not the Merlin of South Wales, but a Scot, and his poem is called *Avallenau*.

Only a visionary could in the sixth century have seen an orchard of so many identical trees – as are described in the poem – for identity of size and habit is a modern development. But then the Celtic peoples have always had second sight; and, it would seem, foresight. For when, driven out by Saxons, St Brieuc and his monkish band landed in Brittany, almost the first thing they did was to plant apple trees, which no doubt they had brought with them.

Most authorities now seem agreed upon beyond doubt that the Romans developed the art of gardening in Britain to a standard which in some respects may be called 'modern'. They were concerned not only with utilitarian branches of horticulture, but with the purely decorative as well, their favourite flowers being the rose, lily, hyacinth, violet and narcissus. The Romans were adept at the topiary art – in Pliny's day hunting-scenes and fleets of ships were fashioned from clipped evergreens – and they practised pruning, budding, grafting and fumigating. They also made hothouses, with windows of talc; and Martial refers to an apple tree which had greater comfort in cold weather than some human guests in the villa bedchamber.

After the dissolution of the Roman Empire in the fifth century, the horticultural arts must have suffered a decline. The early Christians kept small pockets of cultivation alive, around their humble cells at first and in larger monastic gardens later. Probably most of this gardening entailed vegetables for the pot and herbs for the infirmarian, although Roman custom of using flowers for such festivals as the Ambarvalia was adopted by the Church. Garlands were used in England for Rogationtide processions, and the clergy wore crowns of blossom on feast days until the Reformation put a stop to these pleasant habits.

There is some argument as to which of the plants introduced into Britain by the Romans survived the Dark Ages, and which were re-imported at a later period. It seems likely that lilies, poppies and roses did survive, together with vines, pears, figs, plums, mulberries and some vegetables and herbs. The Saxons liked colewort, or wild cabbage, cultivating this plant in plots near their houses, so the English 'boiled greens' have a long tradition behind them.

The Saxons also used the paeony – for flavouring purposes in the main – and carried around paeony seeds as a charm against evil spirits. This custom lasted for at least ten centuries and may not be dead yet. In the Gloucestershire village of Filkins between 1879 and 1912 the local Benefit Society marched through the lanes on Whit Tuesday to the sound of its own band, preceded by stewards bearing staves decorated with bunches of the old double red paeony. My good friend George Swinford, famous as a stone mason in the Cotswolds, remembered the custom vividly, but knew nothing of the Saxon belief in the plant's power. Since the Saxons had names for kale, beet, radish, onion, leek, lettuce and turnip, they must have cultivated all these vegetables for the pot.

This is a study of women who have cared for the soil, and references to gardening women in the early centuries are very scarce in Britain. Due no doubt to the wholesale destruction of records at the Dissolution of the Monasteries, we have less knowledge of the work of medieval monks and nuns than may be found in most countries on the Continent of Europe. In France there is the story of Radegond, queen of the Frankish king Clothair, who fled from the court to Poitiers. Here she founded a nunnery and laid out a garden on the sunny slope beneath the city walls, where she and her nuns toiled with their own hands. Bishop Fortunatus composed poems there in the sixth century.

The first gardening book dating from medieval times was written by a tenth-century monk of St Gall. In his *The Little Garden* he wrote: 'The gardener must not be slothful but full of zeal continuously. Nor must he despise hardening his hands with toil. . . . I plant my seeds and the kindly dew moistens them. Should drought prevail I must water it, letting the drops fall through my fingers, for the impetus of a full stream from a water-pot would disturb my seedlings. Part of my garden is hard and dry under the shadow of a roof; in another part a high brick wall robs it of sun and air. Even here something will at last succeed!' His name was Walafred Strabo.

In the time of William Rufus – who died in 1100 – an English nunnery garden provided a story which Eadmer heard from Archbishop Anselm and wrote down. The Abbess Christina of Romsey Abbey had taken her twelve-year-old niece Maud (Matilda) to be educated by the nuns. William Rufus wanted to see this child, but chose to mask his aim by pretending that all he wished for was a glimpse of the convent roses and herb garden. The prudent Abbess, mistrusting the king's purpose, dressed the girl in a nun's habit and veil, and let her pass through the garden in the company of other nuns. So well-hidden was she that the king left her in peace. Later she became the wife of Henry I.

From nuns we may move on to another group of female gardeners, composed of that very humble class of employee known as the 'weeding-women'. Weeders in the orchard at Hampton Court in July 1516 were listed as Agnes March, Alice and Elizabeth Alen, Elizabeth Anmun, Joan Smeton, Annes Lewes, Jone Abraham, Margaret Cookstole, Katherine Wite, and Agnes Norton. Their wages were threepence a day for clearing the ground of charlock, cockles, convolvulus, dodder, thistles, nettles, docks, dandelions and groundsel.

The standard list of hand tools has varied very little through the centuries. The spades and rakes in use today are similar to those used in Tudor times, although stainless steel is new and the prices have gone up at least fifty-fold. One curious aid to weeding which we have discarded was seen by John Loudon in 1823 at Aubrey Hall, where a weeding-woman wore gloves whose forefinger and thumb were tipped with sharp wedge-shaped thimbles of steel. These could be re-pointed when worn down. Victorian women gardeners appointed to Kew in 1896 were kitted out rather more sensationally in bloomers, which 'brought hordes of Cockneys out on the tops of buses to see the bold young ladies at work'.

Although queens, princesses and other great ladies of Europe have disported themselves in gardens for at least a thousand years, there is little evidence of the high-born female having gardened for herself. In 1250 Henry III commanded the Bailiff of Woodstock to 'encircle the Queen's garden with two walls, well built and high, with a good herbary, in which the queen may disport herself'. The herbary may have been a herb garden, or perhaps an 'herber' or arbour. Sometimes these were of elaborate design with several compartments, made out of pleached trees and having floors of turf. At that time there were also gardens attached to the royal residences of Windsor, Westminster, Clarendon, Charing and the Tower of London.

Many illustrations of gardens may be seen in illuminated manuscripts, the finest being in Anne of Brittany's *Book of Hours*. It was painted by Jean Bourdichon and is in the *Bibliotheque Nationale*. Anne is depicted seated in a small garden, with a castle behind her, making a garland of flowers. Probably such women were more versed in the arts of the florist and flower-arranger than in gardening. The library of Trinity College, Cambridge, contains a

4

fourteenth-century treatise on rosemary, sent by the Countess of Hainault to her daughter Phillippa, wife of Edward III. It records several beliefs about this herb, including the curious notion that rosemary never grew above the height of Christ when he lived as a man on earth.

Lower in the social scale is Thomas Tusser, whose popular book *Five Hundred Points of Good Husbandry* (1557) gave much useful instruction to country housewives. Such women were expected in his day to 'sow and set a garden or other like plot'; to do the digging, weeding and watering themselves, and, when crops were ready, to harvest and store everything required for the kitchen, storeroom and medicine chest. They also had to sow, pull, ret, clean and dry all the flax needed in the home. This was followed by the breaking, beating, heckling, and spinning of flax fibres for the weaving of linen.

The Elizabethans paid great attention to garden walks, or 'allies'. 'The fairer and larger they be, the more grace your garden shall have.' Broad open walks were sanded or turfed, or planted with dwarf sweet-smelling herbs which released fragrance when trodden underfoot. The gardens were enclosed within the shelter of high brick walls, often covered with rosemary, and the ground between the walks was laid out in knot-gardens, raised beds, mazes, topiary work and cool, shady allies with trees, such as willow, lime, sycamore and whitethorn trained to meet in arches overhead.

A curious feature of Tudor gardens was the decorated statuary of carved, painted and gilded wooden beasts of heraldic origin, set up on pillars. Elizabeth I had thirty-four of these in her privy garden at Whitehall. That royal pleasaunce contained a tennis court, a bowling green, and a great sundial. The heraldic beasts held aloft vanes painted with the royal arms. Creatures of similar type were made in 1951 and used in the Festival of Britain.

The garden at Sion House near London, famous in Tudor times, was originally worked by monks and nuns of the monastery and convent of St Saviour and St Bridget, begun by Henry V, who endowed his foundation with the gift of the Manor of Isleworth. At the Dissolution, the Daughters of Sion had to leave their garden with its fine cypresses, bays, yews and mulberry trees. They took refuge in the Portuguese city of Lisbon.

In reply to inquiries about work done in convents, past and present, I received some interesting letters from the gardening nuns of our own time. St Mary's Abbey at West Malling in Kent is said to have owned thriving vineyards in the Middle Ages at East Malling, but it is not believed that these were worked by the community. 'We do know of present-day nuns in Jugoslavia who grow and tend their vines. Possibly on the Continent, with its large peasant population, these things would been have been more common'. My correspondent added that the Cistercian Order, which follows the Benedictine Rule, lays great stress on manual work – monks and nuns usually have farms and gardens which they work themselves.

'This Abbey was founded in 1090 by Gundulph, Bishop of Rochester, and nuns were here until the Dissolution. Our community came in 1916. We are members of the Church of England and we follow the Benedictine Rule. We care for our own vegetables, except for the heaviest work, and produce all we need for our Guest House and ourselves. We have a small herb garden for culinary herbs. We also bottle fruit juice, which the Infirmarian finds very useful when there is a cold epidemic.'

Another community, that of Our Lady at Burford in Oxfordshire, sent information about the land surrounding their priory, which was originally built in 1180 as a hospital for poor men in the care of four Augustinian brethren under a master.

In the little court outside the refectory, where one can imagine the old men sunning themselves on stone seats that line the walls, figwort and caper spurge grow to tremendous heights, and digitalis springs up in unlikely places, but refuses to grow in the wood where it would be appropriate.

We have twelve acres of woodland, looked after by a firm of competent men who remove trees that are over-age and replace them with young beech, oak, larch and fir. The real joy of the wood, from our point of view, is the pleasant vista of the Costwolds with the little river Windrush winding among its rushes. One of the Sisters planted waterlilies, arrowheads, marsh marigolds and other water plants in or beside the old monks' fishpond, where there is a boathouse and steps to the water's edge. There baptism by immersion used to take place.

The whole property is surrounded by a high stone wall built in the 'dry' manner usual in this locality. The garden is quite beautiful. We are indeed grateful to God for having given us so exquisite a home. It slopes down the hillside in terraces of varying width, enclosed by an inner wall of mellow Cotswold stone, of which the Priory itself is built. All the enclosed garden is looked after by the nuns, each having her allotted piece to dig and weed and plant.The kitchen garden is cared for by a gardener who also mows the lawns. The Sisters look after chickens and earn quite a bit from the sale of eggs. Our Sister Infirmarian has started a herb garden for making pot-pourri. She also looks after the roses, whose petals are dried and used.

Who loves the land must love birds. We have a resident family of kingfishers down by the fishpond. We sit very quiet so as not to frighten them away. When we first came to Burford a chaffinch used to come to tea whenever we had recreation out of doors. His mate was less friendly, but he brought their young ones to be introduced. Now the robin who frequents the kitchen does the same. If the Sisters practise plainsong out of doors, the robin perches on the arm of the seat, unafraid, and shows them how it should be sung, with beak open wide and head well raised.

The Community of St Mary the Virgin at Wantage also has some keen horticulturists. Sister Penelope, who gardened there all her life and helped to produce much fruit and many hampers of vegetables for the kitchen, not to mention chapel flowers, was well past her seventieth year when she sent me her picture, and was still caring for the soil. She gave permission to quote from her book *Meditations of a Caterpillar* (Faith Press, 1962).

Some four years before her birth in 1890 her father was appointed to the living of Clent in Worcestershire.

It was the first birth for a hundred years in that queer old house, and there has been none since. Clent became all my world; all the world there was for me at first, so of course it seemed the place where everything had happened. The shepherds, for instance, on that first Christmas night had watched their flocks in Mr Boucher's field adjoining our orchard. Joseph was cast by his exasperated brethren into the old disused manure pit near the stable, and David danced before the Lord in the stable yard.

Clent remained the centre when my world grew bigger, and pictures of it line my memory still. One is of the garden in late May or June. The view is from a strip of lawn that slopes down to the pool, the vivid turf dotted with cuckoo-flowers, and one clump of marsh marigold just at the water's edge. A few yards to the right of where I stand, an enormous yellow azalea is in full bloom. Exquisitely fragrant, it leans out over the water, and on my left a great white rhododendron does the same.

As a septuagenarian I look three ways: back over my remembered life, around, and forward, meditating on what I see. One of the nice things about getting old is that by then, when you look back, you see a pattern in your life and see it whole. From looking around me looking forward follows of itself. First there is dying to look forward to; then, when the change has been effected, being dead. And lastly, the great final metamorphosis at the Last Day, the corporate change of form and mode of life of the whole human race, and the whole universe.

Only a lover of the soil and a close observer of nature could have written like this; one who has watched delicate petals fall, great plants wither and die, and a little brown seed, hidden in dark earth and apparently lost, reproduce all that beauty again. From Walafred Strabo to Sister Penelope, over a thousand years have been spanned, and still the mark of the gardener is hope.

A meditative Indian friend domiciled in Scotland, Marjorie Queyrayne, sent me a letter, unaware that I had just set down those words. 'Of course gardening is essentially a spiritual activity,' she wrote. Although I have been growing steadily more aware of this truth as the decades pass, I had hitherto followed the generality of garden writers in leaving it undeclared. Some younger, more physically obsessed gardeners may dismiss the idea. Ageing is itself a spiritual process, and so the years nourish our wonder at the power buried in a small seed.

The Lady Julian of Norwich, a fourteenth-century anchoress, wrote in her *Revelations of Divine Love*: 'He showed me a little thing, the quantity of an hazel nut, in the palm of my hand. I looked thereon with the eye of my understanding and thought What may this be? And it was answered generally thus: It is all that is made. I marvelled how it might last, for methought it might have fallen to naught for littleness. And I was answered in my understanding: It lasteth and ever shall last, for God loveth it. And so all thing hath the Being for the love of God.'

In recent years there has been some speculation as to the power of human beings to influence plant growth by talking to garden subjects – a recondite matter which has even reached the radio programme *Gardener's Question Time*. While keeping an open mind on this aspect of horticulture, I cannot help attaching more importance to the influence exerted upon me by the plants I serve. Anyone who has gardened alone in remote woodlands, as I did at Inverewe, can hardly fail to be conscious of silent messages coming from all the companionable green growths around one, a truly peaceful persuasion which penetrates the hard surface of worldly preoccupation and stimulates deeper levels of thought. Lest it be assumed that nuns spend all their time plumbing spiritual depths, I will turn now to my recent visit to the gardening nuns of Stanbrook Abbey in Worcestershire. Sister Margaret Mary wrote explaining that, as the great convent at Callow End is the home of an Enclosed Order, the nuns were not allowed to show their garden to visitors, but would be pleased to discuss their work with me in the parlour. 'In any case our herb garden is a mess, because builders remodelling our kitchen have been using it as a refuse tip. Sister Ethelreda, a cook, and I planted it several years ago and we hope to clear it up soon, but there is nothing to see at present.'

The two young nuns who received me must have felt some natural dismay at having their laborious work disrupted, but their smiling confidence was undiminished. All would be restored in God's good time. Their original work on this herb garden had involved hours of tough physical labour. The ground was thickly infested with 'scutch' or 'couch' grass, one of the worst weeds to eradicate. Sister Margaret, a farmer before she entered the convent, felt less daunted by it than Ethelreda, who came from an office background.

Gradually the pair managed to dig out the grass – many barrow-loads of the stuff – but disposal of the material then posed a problem. Mr Wix, who has charge of the main vegetable garden, would not have it dumped on his compost heap, for couch did not rot down, he said. He had more than enough of his own, anyway. Sister Margaret had an idea. She wished to try an experiment with the unwanted waste, so together they piled it in an isolated corner, separate from their ordinary compost, in a very dry spot beneath a chestnut tree. There it remained through one fairly hot summer and another of prolonged drought. After two years it had desiccated rather than rotted, forming a fine friable soil suitable for herbs. Given the right amount of heat and drought, this unorthodox method of making compost worked extremely well.

Meanwhile the ground had been dug over twice, and levelled. Brick and stone excavated in the process served to make paths, for nuns have to be thrifty and nothing goes to waste. Among the weeds some ancient roots of lemon balm and spearmint came to light. Friends brought presents of other herb plants, including lovage, peppermint, chives and thyme. A venerable rosemary elsewhere in

9

the grounds provided cuttings which took well in the open garden. Soon the herb plot was alive and flourishing. The couch, well and truly transformed, never again caused trouble.

In spite of being shaded by buildings on the south and east, this plot of land proved to be very productive. Before long there were surplus crops of herbs to be dried and sold in the Stanbrook Abbey shop. Herb teas became an acceptable drink in the community, particularly when brewed from lemon balm and served with milk and brown sugar.

Sister Ethelreda wrote an article about the project for the magazine *Popular Gardening* (20th October, 1976), so one more creative activity has been added to those for which Stanbrook is already well known: literature, printing, music and art. A former Lady Abbess, Dame Laurentia, corresponded with G. B. Shaw about fifty years ago – a correspondence preserved in print. Dame Felicitas Corrigan recently published a biography of the poet Siegfried Sassoon, who became a Catholic. The Abbey printing-press is always at work, turning out distinguished examples of letterpress and illustration.

Before I took leave of the two nuns, they told me a little more of their daily lives. Their herbs are valuable in the kitchen, because diet in such a community is restricted to food that is in season. 'When there is a glut of something, we have to eat it each day until it is finished. We never have anything out of season. So the variety of flavours obtained from the herb garden is particularly welcome'. When food is scarce, their diet becomes more abstemious. In 1978 they had a splendid crop of fruit and vegetables, and a special mass of thanksgiving was held.

The community's attempt at fish-farming has been less successful. The still, deep pool seemed just right for carp, so a few were put into the water. Nuns passing by watched over them, and bestowed offerings of food. One carp became very tame and grew apace. Carp have been known to reach twenty pounds in weight; the community was not being unduly optimistic in hoping for a fine fish dinner, enough to go round. Nuns are patient people, so a long wait did not worry them.

They had not anticipated a marauder from outside. One fine day a heron swooped down and snatched the carp away before the horrified nuns could do anything about it. This episode became no more than an entry in the book kept all the year round for notes on every flower, bird and beast observed within the convent walls.

10

Information about the locality is also preserved. I learned that a lane alongside one of the walls, known as Jennet-tree Lane, is believed to commemorate a local variety of apple which once grew there. Before the development of synthetic dyestuffs, damsons were also cultivated hereabouts and sold for dyeing to firms in Worcester.

2

Gardening for Ladies in the Nineteenth Century

Jane Loudon and Caroline Hamilton

A London house, No. 3 Porchester Terrace, Bayswater, bears a blue-and-white plaque affixed to it by the London County Council, now the Greater London Council:

HERE LIVED
JOHN AND JANE
LOUDON
1783-1843 and 1807-1858
Their
Horticultural Work
Gave New Beauty to
LONDON SQUARES

John Loudon hated the gloomy evergreens which used to spoil so many public squares in the capital, so he set about trying to improve matters. In 1803 he published an article in *The Literary Journal*, 'Observations on laying out the Public Squares of London'. Yews and firs always looked dirty, from the effect of smoke on their foliage, and he wanted to replace them with certain deciduous trees. He named the oriental and occidental planes, sycamore and almond 'ornamental' trees which would survive the soot. His proposals were adopted, and these, together with later introductions, may be seen in a great many London squares to this day. He also selected some of the fine trees in Kensington Gardens, designed little stone lodges at the entrance gates, and suggested the bandstand near the Round Pond.

Jane, born the daughter of Thomas Webb of Birmingham in 1807, arrived at this Bayswater house in 1830 as the bride of John Claudius Loudon, and under her husband's tutelage became a pioneer of gardening 'for ladies'. She wrote some twenty books and achieved with her husband the dignity of an L.C.C. plaque.

It is worth noting that, although down-to-earth ladies were uncommon in the early nineteenth century, another Jane and her mother carried out manual work in their garden nearly thirty years before Mrs Loudon produced her epoch-making book *Gardening for Ladies*.

When the novelist Jane Austen, with her mother and sister, went to live at The Small House at Chawton after the death of the Reverend George Austen, she took time off from writing to redesign the garden. How much spade-work she carried out herself is not recorded, but it is well known that her mother, then in her seventies, handed over the domestic details to her daughters and toiled hard in the kitchen garden, dressed in a labourer's green smock.

The Austens were too modest to claim recognition as gardeners; Jane Austen managed to keep even her great literary talent hidden for a large part of her life. In her time, of course, women were not expected to write novels. Jane Loudon, who later became known as a garden writer, also began her literary career in the field of fiction, without disclosing her sex. Her novel, *The Mummy*, published in 1830, was an amazing flight of fancy, eligible for inclusion in a collection of science fiction. The story is centred on an Egyptian Pharaoh who came alive again, not in the author's own period, but in the twenty-second century A.D. He finds himself in England, where something like our Welfare State operates but with greater efficiency than we currently enjoy. There is cheap space-travel within the reach of everybody, the medium of transport being a kind of balloon. People, surfeited with giddy jaunts around their universe, are beginning to stay at home for a change. Jane Webb foresaw, or invented, many of our modern conveniences, such as air-conditioning, interior-spring mattresses and milking-machines.

John Loudon read this book when it came out and was so impressed that he reviewed it with enthusiasm in his paper, *The Gardener's Magazine*. Apparently he assumed that its scientifically-minded author must be a man. When he met the demure, ringleted Jane Webb he was astounded to discover her to be the inventor of

The Mummy. It was a case of love at first sight. Within seven months they were married.

As Mrs Loudon, Jane put away her wild imaginings and became a dutiful down-to-earth partner for John. He was a glutton for work, and saw to it that his wife followed his example. 'It would be difficult to find anyone more ignorant of plants than myself,' she said. Although her husband was anxious that she should learn as much as possible, he was a little too erudite to have patience with an absolute beginner. Leaving aside botany, he decided to let her work with the soil. A specially light spade, made to his design, and gauntlets designed by Jane herself were provided, as well as clogs and an overall.

An extract from her book *Gardening for Ladies*. published in 1840, obviously recalls her own initiation.

It must be confessed that digging at first sight appears to be a very laborious employment, one peculiarly unfitted to the small and delicately formed hands and feet of a woman. But it will be found that by a little attention to the principles of mechanics and the laws of motion, the labour may be very much simplified and rendered comparatively easy. The operation of digging consists in thrusting the iron part of the spade, which acts as a wedge, perpendicularly into the ground by the application of the foot.

It must be remembered that all operations which are effected rapidly by exertion of great power may be effected slowly by exertion of very little power if that comparatively feeble power be applied for very much greater lengths of time. A lady, with a small light spade may, by repeatedly digging over the same line, and taking out only a little earth at a time, succeed in doing all the digging that can be required in a small garden; and she will not only have the satisfaction of seeing the garden created, as it were, by her own hands, but she will find her health and spirits wonderfully improved by the exercise, and by the reviving smell of the fresh earth.

The necessary implements for digging being provided, the next thing to be considered is the easiest way of performing the operation. By inserting the spade in a slanting direction and throwing the body slightly forward at the same time, the mass of earth to be raised will not only be much less than if the spade were inserted perpendicularly, but the body of the operator will be in a much more convenient position for raising and turning it, which may thus be done with perfect ease. The time for digging should always be chosen if possible when the ground is tolerably dry; not only on account of the danger of taking cold by standing on the damp earth, but because the soil, when damp, adheres to the spade and it is much more difficult to work. Every lady should be careful, when she has finished digging, to have her spade dipped in water and then wiped dry; after which it should be hung up in some warm, dry shed or harness room to keep it free from rust; as nothing lessens the labour of digging more than having a perfectly smooth and polished spade. Should the earth adhere to the spade while digging, dipping the blade in water occasionally will be found to facilitate the operation.

Jane Loudon's book covers a long list of garden skills, from manuring and making hot-beds to 'Rock-work, Moss-houses and Rustic Baskets'. Her husband had already published the illustrated *Encyclopaedia of Gardening* (1822) which laid the foundation of his fame as a horticulturist, and he had been 'Conductor' of *The Gardener's Magazine* since 1826. Some years before his marriage he had suffered badly at the hands of incompetent doctors, who, in attempts to alleviate chronic rheumatism in his right arm, had caused damage that eventually led to amputation.

Although he managed to continue writing and illustrating horticultural books, together with supervising work in his garden, he was glad to have his wife as helper on the spot instead of being entirely dependent on secretaries and other hired labour. It became their rule to work every evening in the well-equipped library, and while engaged in this devoted service to John, Jane rapidly increased her own knowledge.

As we have seen, her training was by no means confined to theory. In addition to learning how to dig, she watched John as he directed the planning and planting of an arboretum in their own garden – a miniature containing about sixty trees and shrubs which he hoped to control by means of root-pruning. He also made a collection of roses and paeonies. These projects were carried out for experimental purposes but also served to exhibit to his clients what he proposed to plant in schemes designed for their gardens.

He was very particular about tidiness. Eveything had to be accurately and neatly labelled. Jane spent much of her time removing dead flowers, withered leaves and seed-pods from his plants, and when bad weather prevented this she sat in a garden shed, writing long botanical names on labels in Indian ink. These were later varnished to preserve the lettering. She also weeded the

15

beds – John detested the sight of weeds – and learned how to plant bulbs and pot up rare and delicate plants sent to her husband from abroad.

The potting-shed at Porchester Terrace was a model of order and efficiency. It contained stocks of potting material, loam, sand, leaf mould, chalk, soot and lime, together with pots of every size. There were cupboards for storing bulbs, corms and tubers, and a shelf of tins containing seed. As Jane worked among these things she developed a craving for knowledge. She found existing books on gardening too advanced or too specialised, and her husband was too busy to answer the endless questions of a beginner. The problems of her own early years as a gardener made her understand the needs of others in like circumstances, and inspired her to write the down-to-earth books which became widely known and popular.

Her first book, *Gardening for Ladies*, opens with a clear description of her motive.

> I write this because I think books intended for professional gardeners are seldom suited to the needs of amateurs. It is difficult for a person who has a lifetime's acquaintance with the subject to imagine the ignorance of those who know nothing of it, and so the expert often finds it impossible to impart the knowledge he possesses. Although it may appear presumptuous of me to teach an art of which for three-quarters of my life I was entirely ignorant, it is in fact that very circumstance which is one of my chief qualifications for the task. Having been a full-grown pupil myself, I know the wants of others; and having never been satisfied without grasping the reason for everything that had to be done, I am able to impart these reasons to others.

John Loudon was fond of saying that to be a really good gardener one must be a good botanist. The Royal Horticultural Society, wishing to attract more women into its membership, announced that Mr Lindley would deliver a course of six botanical lectures. This opportunity came at the right moment for Jane. She attended the lectures, took careful notes, and became a prize pupil. John, delighted by her progress, planned to make her the foremost lady gardener in Europe.

He wrote, 'the most artistical flower gardens may be laid out by ladies'. This theory he expanded in his book *The Suburban Gardener and Villa Companion* (1838), in which he compares the skill required to design a garden with that of the dressmaker who is able 'to cut out and assemble the different parts of a female dress'. His ambition – to turn every lady into a landscape gardener – may not have met with very marked success; but he certainly taught his wife to be a good practical flower gardener – one who, by her writings, helped many women to follow suit.

Pruning was not then considered suitable work for female gardeners, but Jane managed to overcome that prejudice. She wrote of dealing with 'quite large branches', having procured from Mr Forrest of the Kensington nursery 'a pair of small and elegant pruning shears'. She had a tender heart for plants, which caused her to shudder when her husband poured nearly boiling water over a box of hyacinth bulbs to bring them forward. A certain Dutch florist had a curious bulb garden at Shepherds Bush in London, where thousands of spring bulbs flowered under a sort of canvas marquee. Jane described the show as a blaze of beauty.

Early in 1832 Jane Loudon became pregnant. Refusing to take to a sofa in the then fashionable manner, she continued to work out-of-doors, and even accompanied her husband on one of his garden tours. He made many such journeys, mainly to gather material for his books and articles. The couple returned to Porchester Terrace in good time for the birth of their daughter Agnes on 28th October. The devoted Jane was soon up and about, ready to help John as usual with his major work, *Arboretum Britannicum*.

This vast undertaking required heavy expenditure of both energy and money. Realising that all the drawings of trees must be made from nature he employed seven artists to carry out the work. He was constantly out in the open air with them, from seven in the morning until dinner-time at night, going without food and drink all day.

After dinner he resumed the literary part of the task and continued, with Jane at his side, into the small hours. He had been a very strong man, but constant overwork began to wear down his powers.

By the time the young Queen Victoria was crowned in 1838, John Loudon had completed his comprehensive study of British trees; but he had exhausted his strength, overdrawn his assets to the sum of £10,000 and was in considerable pain from an arthritic condition in his legs. Jane, no doubt wishing to help in the financial difficulties, planned to expand her literary work. She had already

17

published articles in *The Gardener's Magazine*, and now set herself to prepare *The Ladies' Flower Garden*, for issue in monthly parts. This had some success, but her first work to come out in one volume surpassed it. *Gardening for Ladies* was the first to deal with this subject since Charles Evelyn wrote *The Lady's Recreation* in 1707. John Murray issued the book in 1840, and it turned out to be a winner.

There is no doubt that the rapid expansion of trade, the rise of an affluent middle class, most of whom built large suburban houses with sizeable gardens, and the novel fever of feminine ambition, provided the golden moment for Jane's book. Her encouragement was irresistible. 'Whatever doubts may be entertained as to the practicability of a lady attending to the culture of culinary vegetables and fruit trees, none can exist respecting her management of the flower garden. That is pre-eminently a woman's department. The culture of flowers implies the lightest possible kind of garden labour; only, indeed, enough to give an interest in its effects.' Those of us who have created a flower garden on heavy clay soil may not agree that it is light work, but the interest taken by women in gardening has certainly grown with their overall involvement in practical aspects, and for this Jane Loudon deserves much credit.

In the same year Miss Louisa Johnson published *Every Lady Her Own Flower Gardener*. Written in stilted language, her book made the suggestion that gardening might be taken up by single women 'as a distraction from the disappointments of life'. Such glum words could not achieve the popularity of Jane's cheerful prose, the fruit of a happily married young woman with a little girl to complete the family. Although spinsters abounded in the early nineteenth century, and few were trained for careers, none wished to be reminded of her disappointments or to have it supposed that she took up gardening when all hope of matrimony was gone.

Even the pictures in *Gardening for Ladies* are designed to show that practitioners of the art will be contented matrons. The frontispiece shows a demure lady in bonnet and ringlets, a pair of scissors protruding from her apron pocket. She holds a long-handled rake and gazes fondly at a little girl in frilly frock and pantalettes, who is clasping a hoe and leaning against a wheelbarrow. This happy pair stands beneath a vine-covered arch, surrounded by all the tools of their craft.

The success of her first book led Jane to have the parts of her

Ladies' Flower Garden which dealt with bulbs collected under the title *Ornamental Bulbous Plants*. The new volume had coloured plates of lilies, gladioli and irises, many of them old varieties now lost. Jane wrote poetically of her favourites. One gladiolus has 'petals which at sunset take a curiously shifting hue like shot silk'. This flower was very fragrant, particularly at dusk, which made it ideal for window boxes or veranda tubs. Another kind, known as the Viper Gladiolus, was introduced into England in 1794. It suffered an eclipse and was reinstated in 1825, but seems to have died out.It had green-and-brown striped petals and resembled the head of a snake. It, too, possessed a delightful scent.

Ornamental Bulbous Plants was issued in 1841, and in the same year Jane collaborated with her husband for the first time. Their venture, a dictionary of vernacular and botanic names of flowering plants commonly found in gardens, was called *The Ladies' Companion to the Flower Garden*. The dedication to Mrs Lawrence of Ealing Park in Middlesex, describes her in glowing terms: 'A zealous patron of floriculture, an excellent botanist, and one of the first lady gardeners of the present day.' This lady was the wife of William Lawrence, an eminent surgeon who had treated John with some success.

The Loudons had many well-known friends, including Charles Dickens and Thackeray. Mrs Gaskell, author of *Cranford*, was a close friend of Jane, and her father, Mr Stevenson, had been known to John Loudon before his marriage. As a young man John had been something of an artist. He used to exhibit landscapes at the Royal Academy, where he became acquainted with the Landseers (Charles and Edwin), Daniel Maclise, Edwin Freeth and others. As the fame of John and Jane Loudon spread – they were described as 'the foremost horticultural writers of their time' – so their company became sought after in the social world of London.

During the summer of 1841 the Loudon family travelled to Leeds, Manchester and Liverpool, where the Botanic Gardens were examined thoroughly in spite of drenching rain. Although Jane and little Agnes came to no harm, John caught a severe chill. He refused to give in, taking a ship as planned from Liverpool to Scotland. He spent the voyage in his bunk, with a high temperature, and had to remain in bed for six weeks after landing. As soon as he was able to walk he carried out the rest of the programme, visiting every garden of note in southern Scotland and paying visits to friends in Newcastle, Durham and Darlington on the way home.

By the autumn he seemed fully recovered. That winter the first
number of his *Encyclopaedia of Trees* appeared, followed by
Hortus Lignosus Londinensis in ten parts, while Jane was at work
on her *Botany for Ladies*. In the spring of 1842 her husband again
fell ill, this time with inflammation of the lungs. By April he was
allowed to convalesce in Brighton for a week or two, after which the
family made another garden tour – visiting Somerset, Devon and
Cornwall. Subsequently Jane and Agnes returned to London while
John stayed behind in Barnstaple to lay out a garden for Lord
Clinton. His wife had noticed that he coughed a good deal but as he
seemed in excellent spirits she thought little of it.

During the summer Jane had again to nurse her husband with
serious lung trouble. While she watched over the patient, she
prepared for publication in book form another section of *The
Ladies' Flower Garden*. It was now the turn of herbaceous
perennials. Although John seemed weak, the doctors let him
accompany his wife and child for a holiday in the Isle of Wight. He
He managed to do a little work in Southampton and Bath, but
returned to London in a state of collapse. The surgeon William
Lawrence diagnosed his illness as an incurable disease of the
lungs.

All through the autumn and winter Jane nursed the invalid and
tried to keep him in good spirits. Through painful days and nights
she kept at her writing, producing a story for young people called
Glimpses of Nature during a Visit to the Isle of Wight. The book is
dedicated to 'My little daughter, the Agnes Merton of the story'.
This description of the family's summer tour in an open carriage,
sampling the island's charm, is a happy tale, betraying nothing of
the strain with which its author had to cope.

Her husband, growing visibly weaker day by day, carried on
with his writing and advisory work to the end. During his last night
he dictated pages of a new book, *Self-instruction for Young
Gardeners*, to Jane until midnight when he went to bed. Unable to
sleep, he was up again at dawn, looking so ill that Jane hastily
dressed herself, prepared for emergency. He told her that he felt
unable to complete the book, asking her to arrange for a friend to
do this instead. An hour or two later, at the age of sixty, John
Claudius Loudon died in the arms of his wife.

So Jane was left a widow at thirty-six. She had been happy in her
marriage and fortunate to have a partner who believed, ahead of his
time, in the right of a woman to develop her gifts to the full and to

work as a professional in the arts or in any other career, in addition to being a wife and mother. Although she was still comparatively young and had many friends, including the handsome Charles Landseer – who escorted her to theatres and other entertainments – Jane does not appear to have been attracted to the idea of remarriage.

There was the pretty little daughter Agnes to be considered – Agnes who in later life said she had been badly spoilt by her parents and all their friends. Like most spoilt children, she was demanding. She grew up with a love of clothes and gaiety on a grand scale, which her mother found increasingly difficult to satisfy. Jane was now the breadwinner and responsible for the maintenance of her husband's garden. Debts weighed her down. Soon even the jobbing gardener had to be dismissed for lack of money to pay his wages. The award of a small Civil List pension came at an opportune moment, relieving the pinch and allowing Jane to resume her writing. Her first task was to compose a foreword to John's last book, a brief memoir of him which is still the only published biography, so far as I know.

In 1845 Jane published *The Lady's Country Companion*, a book in the form of letters to a young girl who had recently married and moved from the city to an old country manor house. The recipient of Jane's letters is advised to busy herself with the improvement of room decorations, the arrangement of furniture, and then to redesign the overgrown garden. Gloomy trees are removed from the ground near the windows, and Jane gives a choice of three different plans for replanting this space. The bride selects an arrangement of formal bedding, the plants being sweet-scented roses, petunias, calceolarias, pelargoniums and mimulus. She then adds to these clumps of phlox, double rocket and auricula. Jane advises her to include violets, heliotrope and mignonette, for she always advocated fragrance. She herself grew mignonette in pots indoors to give perfume within the house, an idea copied from the Empress Josephine.

When this work had been completed, Jane took her daughter for a holiday at a French chateau belonging to some old friends. Agnes was so delighted with the collection of clever pets, four dogs and a parrot, owned by their hostess that on her return to London she set to work writing a story about them. This became *Tales for Young People*, and by permission of the Queen, was dedicated to the young Princess Royal. The publisher paid her fifty guineas for

21

the copyright – a cheque which Agnes unselfishly handed her 'dearest Mamma' for use in paying bills.

Her Mamma continued to labour at her desk and in the garden. She issued *British Wild Flowers* in 1846, a work intended to encourage the study of botany by young people. It was followed in 1846 by *The Amateur Gardener's Calendar*, a book which the famous William Robinson so much admired that he edited it twenty years later and had it republished.

In 1848, when Agnes had grown into a well-developed girl of sixteen, her mother decided to resume entertaining. In spite of their reduced income, parties were held again in Porchester Terrace with charades and amateur dramatic performances in which Agnes shone. With her fair hair and blue eyes she was much sought after by the young men in her circle, but was too flighty to choose one among the many admirers. Her carefree existence continued happily until 1849, when her mother was summoned to the offices of Longman the publisher to hear the grim news that six years after his death John Loudon had been almost forgotten by a fickle reading public. His royalties had shrunk, until the total income expected from his major works, added to Jane's books, would not amount to more than three hundred pounds a year.

This reduction, coming at a time when Agnes required clothes and the housekeeping bills were greatly increased by entertaining, gave Jane an almost unbearable shock. She had felt of late that her creative life was over. She had said all that was in her to say. She was very tired. Now she had to pull herself together and flog her pen into action in the hope of restoring the financial position. Fresh horizons opened out before long, in the shape of a new journal for women, to be called *The Ladies' Companion at Home and Abroad*. Jane Loudon was appointed editor of this venture. Her literary life had been bound up with 'companions'; this one looked as if it might become her best friend.

For the next seven months Jane enjoyed her strenuous experience as an editor, while the salary put an end to monetary worries. The journal was aimed at the serious-minded women now emerging in Victorian society; those sufficiently well-educated to take an interest in the problems of their day, and too intelligent to care for the trash hitherto provided for women by journalists. The big library, which had seen so much of John Loudon's literary work in progress, now filled up with manuscripts submitted by hundreds of authors, all agog to find a place in the latest periodical.

Every time the publishers – Bradbury and Evans, who also issued *Punch* – wished to communicate with Mrs Loudon, they sent a messenger down to Porchester Terrace. Sometimes a Mr Mayhew, the sub-editor, arrived on the doorstep. Jane made no tiresome journeys to an office, such as 'career' women do today. The first issue was very well received. It cost threepence, and according to the *Spectator* it offered better value than other journals costing more than twice as much.

Jane gave a big Christmas party to celebrate the success, decorating her rooms with simple arrangements of fresh-cut flowers, a novel idea in those formal and rather stuffy days. It was the first time that she had put flower decorations in their home since John's death. For a while her life seemed to take a smoother course, but this improvement was short-lived. During 1850, sales of the new publication declined, – and in June Mr Evans asked for Jane's resignation from the editorial office. Her post was immediately given to a man. No reason for the summary dismissal was offered, and her distress was intense. Bewildered, hurt and humiliated, unsettled by sudden termination of regular duties which she enjoyed, the shock made worse by loss of the essential salary, Jane did not know what to do.

She sat alone in the library, thinking of her late husband, whose spirit seemed very near her, boosting her courage. If she trusted in God, He would provide. Her immediate task was to compose something first-class for her last appearance in print as editor of *The Ladies' Companion*. The column she wrote in that dark hour ended like this: 'Real and vital happiness depends only on ourselves. If once the mind can grasp this truth, and with firmness and courage resolve to draw happiness from sources whence alone it springs, no storms from without will permanently shake us, no fears depress, no trials overcome us.'

There is very little else to record. Money worries and the emotional entanglements of Agnes absorbed Jane's last tired years. She wrote three unremembered books for the young between 1851 and 1853, but did no more truly creative work. She died in July 1858 and was buried beside her husband in Kensal Green Cemetery. Today, fifty-one years of life is considered to be unusually short, but in mid-nineteenth-century terms it was a fairly good life-span.

*   *   *   *

During the years of Jane Loudon's activity as practical gardener and writer, an Irish lady was quietly discovering for herself the many delights of horticulture. Caroline Hamilton's *Garden Notebook*, a small, handwritten, leather-bound volume in the National Library of Ireland, was never seen by Jane, and if one may judge from Caroline's book lists in her diary, she had not read any of Jane's published works.

Caroline Hamilton, born a Tighe of Rosanna in County Wicklow, married Charles Hamilton of Hamwood in County Meath in 1801. According to her descendant, Major C. R. F. Hamilton, the young couple were responsible for making the garden of this late eighteenth-century mansion, built by the bridegroom's father in 1760. Together they laid out the grounds and put in the great hedges of yew and beech which still flourish there, alongside a climbing rose planted in 1817 by their friend Lady Isabel Chabot. That may be one of the oldest roses yet recorded in these islands.

The *Garden Notebook* covers a later period, from 1827 to 1846, and was begun when the diarist had reached the mature age of forty-seven. Although there are passing references to 'Charlie', there is no mention of shared activity in the garden. In middle life, it appears that Caroline Hamilton had become a practical working gardener, unaided by her husband, at a time when ladies as a rule did little more than snip off dead flowers.

Some of the earliest entries concern the herb garden. Caroline evidently liked culinary herbs, for she sowed 'Balm, Chervil, Borage, Angelica, summer and winter varieties of Savory, Purslane, Tansy, Marigold, Thyme, Mints, Scorzonera and Salsify'. She also kept bees, which would have appreciated many of these herbs. This note ends her entry for the herb garden: 'Get seeds from England whenever I can.' Apparently the Irish ones were less reliable. Of her favourite annual she writes 'Irish Mignonette always bad'.

On New Year's Day 1829 she listed the work to be done in her garden: 'Trim the gravel walk in the wood. Dig border on right hand going towards the flower garden, border opposite Morella Cherry and opposite Caroline's garden. Clean back alleys near the Beech hedge. Dig the square where the Red Cabbage is.'

Neat rectangular plots for vegetables and fruit, shown on diagrams amid the notes, are always referred to as 'the squares'. Unfortunately she did not attempt to sketch the rest of the garden

24

lay-out. From the comment that it took Nicholas three days to clip the box edgings, it is clear that the flower beds covered a large area. Many of the compartments were enclosed within high beech hedges, forming what in this century has been called a 'room garden'.

One of Caroline's pages is headed 'Observation from long experience of the garden at Hamwood'. She notes that 'the tall Beech hedges are invaluable, affording protection to the apple trees, which have often borne apples when other gardens have none. A garden intersected by hedges gives many a snug corner for plants. Frost never has been close to a Laurel hedge, it is found to have so much warmth in it. Even the earliest summer fruits in our garden have always been plentiful, from the protection given by hedges, when in other gardens they have been blasted by high winds. The height of the trees protects the apples from pilferers, should any chance to be among the farm boys'.

Varieties of apples are listed as 'Captains, the earliest, picked in August, Pearmains, Lemon Pippins, Crabs, Tankards, and Codlings'. In good years the surplus apples were sold. The method was unusual; without weighing or measuring in bushels, the fruit was counted and receipts entered as '300 for 2/6 a 100; 600 Codlings sold'; and so on.

Caroline always had male helpers of some kind, even though her husband (once the initial lay-out had been done) seems to have dropped out of the picture. 'Gardiners' gave her a good deal of trouble. Then, as now, the charming characters were seldom very efficient, whereas more capable men could be awkward. A certain Mr Fox told some curious tales to his employer. In the summer of 1837 the Hamwood cabbages were infested with caterpillars. 'Fox throws these off by shaking the plants. He says they fall never to rise again. Nothing else destroys them, neither lime water nor brimstone nor anything else he has ever heard off.' Shaking is easy, but the caterpillars I have come across would promptly rise again from the ground. Possibly the large bird population at Hamwood obliged Fox by snapping up most of the fallen pests.

Roses were a feature of the flower garden. Named in the notebook (in Caroline's spelling) are 'Tuscan Rose, *Rosa plicca*, Cherry Rose, Purple Scotch Rose, *Rosa incomparabilis*, *Rosa celeste*, Striped Mignonne, *Rosa grandi purpurea*, and the Macartney Rose'. Cultural hints include 'cut back the Macartney Rose to two eyes in spring, that it may be well covered with blossoms in autumn. The time for trimming Scotch Roses is just after they have gone out of blow'.

Caroline's 'Macartney Rose' was introduced into Britain in 1793 by Sir George Staunton, Lord Macartney's secretary, who brought it from Peking and named it after his chief. The botanical name is *Rosa bracteata*. Kingdon Ward records having seen it scrambling over rocks in Upper Burma and Tibet. Our modern Mermaid Rose is a descendant, probably crossed with a yellow tea rose. It is already over fifty years old, having celebrated its jubilee in 1967. In his *Manual of Shrub Roses* G. S. Thomas gives his advice for dealing with *Rosa bracteata* and Mermaid: 'No pruning.'

Among the herbaceous plants grown in the flower borders at Hamwood, many now neglected or even lost, were 'Soapwort, Pink Cockle, Astrantia, several varieties of Spurge, Yellow Flax, Teucriums, Thalictrums, Hawkweeds, Gaultheria and Lady's Mantle'. Caroline calls her *Yucca filamentosa* 'Superior Adam's Needle'. She shows particular affection for her 'sweetest Heliotrope with a white flower', and notes that her hollyhocks have their top shoots nipped off 'to prevent them from being drawn up too high'. To make her agapanthus 'blow' she mentions the necessity of watering them plentifully during spring and summer. I remember great banks of agapanthus growing out of doors at Inverewe. They bloomed profusely. As the rainfall of Wester Ross is about sixty inches a year, these plants were kept moist without any exertion on our part.

Caroline Hamilton was extremely fond of carnations, including the old-fashioned 'cloves' with their pungent scent. She raised a great many plants herself, sending for seed to the famous firm of Vilmorin – Andrieux in Paris, naming varieties *Double Ordinaire, Jaune, de Fantaisie* and *Flammand*. At this period the firm had a woman as Directrice, Madame Elisa Vilmorin, an expert breeder of the strawberry.

Perhaps the main interest of Caroline's *Garden Notes* for today's gardeners lies in the lists of plants which were popular in her time. Some shrubs grown at Hamwood were named in her own spelling, as '*Eccremocarpus scabra, Deutzia scabra, Deutzia floribunda*, White Persian Lilac, *Pyrus spectabilis*, Pyrus Scarlet American, *Jasminum wallschianum, Leycestria formosa, Cotoneaster microphylla, Cotoneaster affinis*, Broad-leaved *Euonimus*, new Double-Flowering Cherry'.

Long before the time of garden centres and chemical pesticides gardeners had to manufacture their own. A home-made wash for fruit trees was concocted at Hamwood to this recipe: 'Boil a gallon of clear rain-water. Pour it on a pound of camomile flowers. Cover it down, but not too close, Stir it occasionally, and when cold pour off the water and put another gallon of water on the flowers. To these two gallons add seven gallons of clear unboiled rain-water. The trees to be brushed down several times with this decoction.'

Among other deterrents, Caroline notes: 'Onions in drills between the drills of carrots keep off the grub which eats them. Celery ground is apt to be full of the worm which eats the carrots. To catch the red worm, bring a potatoe near the plant and you will find it after a little time eating the potatoe.'

The bird population is regarded with favour. 'Birds should be encouraged rather than destroyed in a garden, provided that the fruits are protected by nets, and cherry trees. They pick up not only caterpillars but the seeds of weeds. Peafowl too, not scratching, pick up more insects than they do mischief. Ducks and cats are very useful in a garden.' (Some of us have reservations about the last-named.)

Among her many friends, the writer numbered the Ladies of Llangollen, John Wesley, Mrs Felicia Hemans, Edmund Burke, and Lady Mornington, mother of the Duke of Wellington. Besides being a dedicated gardener, she was also a competent artist and caricaturist, as specimens of her work still hanging at Hamwood prove. She died in July 1861, in her eighty-first year.

In this study of women gardeners a sharp division has been noticeable between attitudes. In the nineteenth century they had no hesitation, particularly at moments of stress or elation, in referring to their spiritual beliefs. Caroline Hamilton closed her *Garden Notebook* for 1846 with these lines:

> Live while you live, the epicure would say
> And seize the pleasures of the present day.
> Live while you live, the sacred preacher cries
> And give to God each moment as it flies.
> Lord, in my heart let both united be;
> I live in pleasure when I live to Thee.

With the exception of nuns dedicated to the religious life, no woman gardener of the twentieth century has been found making any reference to spiritual matters in her writing. Some, like my late friend Margery Fish, have been practising Christians with deeply sincere faith; but in her view this was a purely personal belief, never to be made public in her work. Such reticence may be a reaction from what is often regarded as 'preachifying' by the Victorians. It is also possible that secrecy is adopted as armour against the thrust of materialistic ideas which Marxism and modern technology combine to nourish. Some effort to redress this imbalance may be due, for the anti-God campaigners are far from silent, and younger people are now sufficiently remote from the nineteenth century to accept gentler Victorian sentiments without undue prejudice.

A religious of C.S.M.V. in her gardening overall – photograph by 'Julian'.

Woman at work in a medieval vineyard (British Museum).

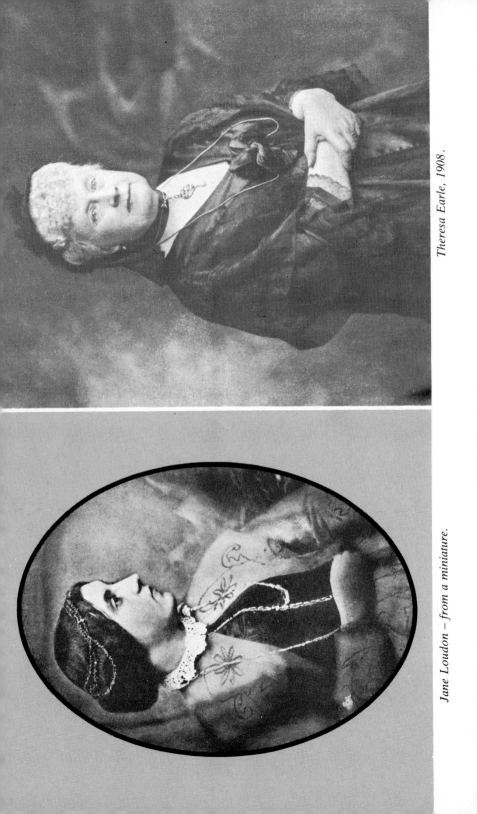

Theresa Earle, 1908.

Jane Loudon – from a miniature.

3

Lady Gardeners in the Early Twentieth Century

Theresa Earle, Gertrude Jekyll and Ellen Willmott

Although by birth an Early Victorian, Theresa Earle soon developed ideas far in advance of her time. The well-known series of 'Pot-Pourri' books, which brought her fame after the author's sixtieth birthday, were issued from 1897 onwards. So she is suitably grouped with Gertrude Jekyll and Ellen Wilmott, whose names appeared alongside hers as Patrons of Viscountess Wolseley's School of Gardening for Ladies, believed to be the first of its kind.

Born in 1836 of aristocratic parents – her father, the Hon. Edward Villiers, was a great-grandson of the second Earl of Jersey, her mother, the Hon. Elizabeth Liddell, a daughter of the first Baron Ravensworth – Theresa lost her father from tuberculosis when she was barely seven years old. After this shock her widowed and very beautiful mother had to bring up three girls and a boy in a modest country house in Hertfordshire.

Finances were severely limited, so the eldest daughter learned to make do, fitting herself, as she said later on, to be a good poor man's wife. Her younger sisters, twins as good-looking as their mother, both married well-known men. Edith became the wife of Edward Bulwer Lytton, later Viceroy of India, and Elizabeth became Lady Loch. Theresa, who was short, plump and somewhat homely of countenance, loved to show off her lovely mother and sisters, doing so without the least trace of jealousy. She herself was presented at court in 1854, 'from a humble lodging over a baker's shop', she wrote. She was just eighteen.

Two years afterwards she was invited to serve as Maid of Honour to Queen Victoria, an honour declined without hesitation. Henceforth she was known in court circles as 'radical Theresa', or 'T'. She took great pride in the work of her uncle, Charles Pelham Villiers, who, as Member of Parliament for Wolverhampton during the Hungry Forties, pledged himself to a total repeal of the Corn Laws.

Few people are aware of the reason why Theresa's Christian name was shortened to 'T' by all her family and close friends. In a recent letter to me, Mary Lutyens related this amusing little story. Theresa's charming and beautiful mother once wrote a letter to her eldest daughter which began as follows: 'Dearest T (I have not got time to write Theresa). . . .' After that, Theresa was obliged to answer to 'T' for the rest of her life.

While staying with friends in Florence, the radical 'T' met a Captain Charles Earle. He made little impression on her, and was almost immediately posted to India for six years. During that time he corresponded regularly with Mrs Villiers, making no secret of his interest in Theresa, but she condescended to write only one letter to him. She had thrown herself into the serious study of art at the South Kensington School (later the Royal College of Art), and, like most girl students of the period, took little interest in men of her own age. John Ruskin on his artistic and literary pedestal was in a different category; but her admiration for the great man and his work was not reciprocated. He said she paid too much attention to detail and finish, losing sight of the broad effect. Nevertheless, Theresa received a National Medal from the School of Art. This was some five years before Gertrude Jekyll joined it as a student.

The faithful Charles Earle had his wish. He married Theresa in 1864, and although she wept copiously at parting from her mother and sisters, she admitted to feeling quite happy and confident. The next fourteen years were spent in nursing her husband through various illnesses and bearing him three sons. They lived on small means in a little house at Watford, which 'T' managed with cheerful efficiency.

In 1878 everything changed – for the better, most of us would have thought. A large legacy from a relative enabled Captain Earle to take a London house in a fashionable neighbourhood, to entertain lavishly and to keep a carriage. Theresa now complained for the first time in her life. She said her talents were no longer used, for she had ceased overnight to be a poor man's wife, and as her husband completely recovered from his ailments, he had no further use for her nursing skill. Her liberal conscience was troubled, making her feel ashamed to drive in a smart turn-out when so many Londoners around them existed in squalid conditions. She also thought that money added to the problems of bringing up their sons.

The Earle's circle of friends now included George Eliot, Oscar Wilde, John Morley, the Gladstones and the Huxleys. When Theresa sought the advice of T. H. Huxley on the question of teaching religion to the boys (both parents having become agnostics), he said that they should be brought up in the mythology of their age and country.

That Theresa had great understanding of young people is shown by the number of so-called 'nephews' and 'nieces' who swarmed around 'Aunt T' in her later life. One of the adopted nephews, Eddie Marsh, described her in his book of reminiscences as being memorable as an *English Worthy*. Of her writings he had no great opinion, but of her character and kindness he was in no doubt. He also said that she possessed 'that perfecting dash of tartness which saves benevolence from insipidity'.

The tartness came out amusingly on one occasion when she met the composer Dr Ethel Smyth at the home of a 'real' niece, Lady Betty Balfour. The two redoubtable women did not see eye-to-eye, and as both were equally forthright the conversation grew very acid indeed. Finally Ethel Smyth rose from her chair, saying stiffly, 'Well, Mrs Earle, as we do not agree on any subject there seems no point in continuing our conversation.' Instantly Theresa responded. 'On the contrary, you consider yourself to be a very remarkable woman, and so do I' – cryptic words which could be interpreted as the hearer chose.

The acquisition of a country home, *Woodlands* at Cobham in Surrey, changed the course of Theresa's life again. With sons fully grown and her husband perfectly well, she now channelled her energy into the improvement of their garden, and from gardening she developed into a writer. Much of her knowledge came from regular attendance at shows of the Royal Horticultural Society in Westminster.

She wrote: 'I think all amateurs who are keen gardeners ought to belong to the Society – partly as an encouragement to it, and because the subscriber of even one guinea a year [increased to £14 in 1982] gets a great many advantages. He can go to fortnightly exhibitions, as well as to the great show at the Temple Gardens in May [now held in the grounds of Chelsea Hospital] free, before the public is admitted. He has the run of the Society's library, he receives the yearly publications and he is annually presented with a number of plants.'

Of the Temple Gardens Show she remarked, 'How odd it seems that for years and years I never went to a flower show, or knew anything about them, and now they have become one of the interests of my life!' She took particular notice of the herb plants, both for use in cookery and for scenting the house, and influenced her readers to take up the cultivation of many herbs some years before Eleanour Sinclair Rohde spread her wide knowledge of such plants through her books and articles.

That Theresa Earle should promote the growing of fresh vegetables and herbs seems highly appropriate, for she was a life-long vegetarian. Her eldest great-nephew, Mr A. E. Villiers, the grandson of her brother Colonel Ernest Villiers, has written to me about his great-aunt 'T' and the delicious vegetarian meals he enjoyed at Woodlands when in his teens. She did not force her ideas on the family; meat was allowed for anyone who preferred it, but she knew how to make meatless food attractive to eye and palate.

Between the ages of twelve and fourteen she had suffered from mysterious recurrent ailments which the orthodox medical practitioners were unable to relieve. In the end, homeopathic treatment, with cold water substituted for tea and coffee, brought about a complete cure of her condition. For the rest of her long life she was remarkably strong and free from illness. Her belief in 'natural' treatment would have formed a bond with her great-niece, Lady Eve Balfour, had she lived long enough to hear of the pioneer work of the Soil Association (see Chapter 8). Although Theresa did not practise gardening until well into middle age, she had greatly loved the garden of her childhood in Hertfordshire.

> I was brought up for the most part in the country, in a beautiful, wild, old-fashioned garden. This garden had remained in the hands of an old gardener for more than thirty years. Almost all that has remained in my mind of my young days there is how wonderfully the old man kept the place. He succeeded in flowering many things year after year with no one to help him, and with frost in the valley to contend with in

32

spring. An ever-flowing mill stream ran all round the garden; and hedges of Chinaroses, Sweetbriar, Honeysuckle and White Hawthorn tucked their toes into the soft mud and throve. The old man was a philosopher in his way, and when on a cold March morning my sisters and I used to rush out after lessons and ask him what the weather was going to be, he would stop his digging, look up at the sky and say: "Well, Miss, it may be fine and it may be wet; and if the sun comes out, it will be warmer." After this solemn announcement he would wipe his brow and resume his work, and we went off, quite satisfied, to our well-known haunts in the woods to gather violets and primroses for our mother, who loved them.

All this, you will see, laid a very small foundation for my knowledge of plants; yet, owing to the vivid character of the impressions of youth, it left a memory that was very useful to me when I took up gardening later in life. To this day I can smell the tall white double Rockets that did so well in the damp garden and scented the evening air. They grew by the side of glorious bunches of Oriental Poppies and the on-coming spikes of feathery *Spiraea aruncus*. This garden had peculiar charms for us because, although we hardly realised it, such gardens were already begining to grow out of fashion, sacrificed to the new bedding-out system, which altered the whole gardening of Europe.

An old gardener in her youth and the Royal Horticultural Society in later life provided all the instruction she required to keep her constantly interested in the care of her garden, and enabled her in her early sixties to write the book *Pot-Pourri from a Surrey Garden* (Smith, Elder, 1897) and its sequels, which brought her considerable fame. Sales of the first were greatly helped by a whole army of friends and relations, who gathered in Hatchard's Piccadilly bookshop and caused one of the salesmen to exclaim that he called it 'more of a social success than a literary one' – a story which the author liked to tell against herself.

To everyone's surprise the unique amalgam of garden lore, cookery hints, reminiscences, suggestions for further reading, and much else, proved so popular with English book-lovers that most country houses had one or more of the 'Pot-Pourri' series on bedside bookshelves. I can remember as a child looking around in every strange guest-room for Mrs Earle's books. It became a ritual, although I have no recollection of reading them until I grew up. Her later publications, *Letters to Young and Old* and *Memoirs and*

Memories, are of period interest; but both would be improved by some editing, and the second of them by provision of an index. I am inclined to think that Theresa Earle's books, which are said to have made £30,000 for the publisher, were successful because of the vivid portrayal of her warm personality rather than the knowledge they imparted. She had enormous zest for life, which even the tragically sudden death of Charles Earle could not quench.

Her first book came out in 1897. Charles read it and seemed very pleased. Then he went for a bicycle ride with his son, and, losing control on a steep hill, was thrown on his head and died without regaining consciousness. Theresa lived on at Woodlands for nearly thirty years and died in 1925 at the age of eighty-nine.

In 1967 at Sidmouth in Devon, I met Ethel Case, who in her youth had been Mrs Earle's assistant and in 1914 collaborated with her in the last published work, *Pot-Pourri Mixed by Two*. Ethel, a lively ninety when I saw her, recalled how deeply involved Mrs Earle had been with younger people, right to the end of her life. She always advised her contemporaries to make friends with later generations; and although some of the affiliations of her own nieces were scarcely to her taste – the acts of militant suffragettes, for example – she offered house-room to Constance Lytton for suffragette meetings.

When Theresa Earle wrote of her 'longing for the United States of Europe', that wish had a stunning novelty to those who heard about it seventy years ago. Eddie Marsh summed up his adopted Aunt 'T' in these words: 'She had a brilliant, singularly modern mind, a most racy humour, and boundless generosity of nature'. Whatever niche she occupies in the literary hall of fame, she shares with Gertrude Jekyll the distinction of being an ideal aunt.

*   *   *   *

Gertrude Jekyll (it rhymes with 'treacle') was born in Grafton Street close to Berkeley Square in London's West End, in the year 1843. Although a London child, she was able to enjoy making traditional daisy chains in the Square garden and to play at dandelion clocks in Green Park. When she was five her family moved to Bramley House near Guildford in Surrey, a county which from that moment became the place she loved best. With a sister seven years her senior and four brothers away at school, she spent much of her time as the only child in the house. In her old age she described herself as having been in many ways more like a boy than a girl, adding that she could still – when nobody was looking – climb over a five-barred gate or jump a ditch.

The gardens surrounding Bramley House had been well planted with interesting shrubs and trees, which Gertrude learned to name at an early age. There were several varieties of magnolia, specimens of ailanthus, known as the 'Tree of Heaven', cut-leaved beeches, some hickories and cypresses. In the flower borders were moss roses, old-fashioned herbaceous plants and, among the annuals, her favourite blue cornflower. She used to ride the local lanes on a small pony, accompanied by her dog, and when a governess gave her a copy of *Flowers of the Field*, by the Reverend C. A. Johns, she brought home specimens to identify from its pages.

The Jekyll family tree traces them back to the sixteenth century, which caused Gertrude in the last year of her life to describe herself as belonging to the 'armigerous class', entitled to bear arms. This was said with a chuckle, and as a challenge to the highly erudite Logan Pearsall Smith, a regular visitor off whom she liked to score when the opportunity arose. Apparently he had no claim to such grandeur. When asked how armigerous persons could be identified, she said with a mocking smile that an armigerous gentlemen would never take a lady to the dress circle of a theatre, but always to the stalls. She loved words. On one occasion she objected to a plant-breeder because he named a variety *robustus elegans*. She said it was a contradiction. 'For example, I should call *you* "*robustus*" but not "*elegans*"!' By this time she weighed fourteen stone, so it was cheeky of her to abuse another heavyweight. No doubt that was her intention, for she was given to leg-pulling.

Artistic interests ran in the Jekyll family. Joseph Jekyll, born in 1753, was well known as a Fellow of the Royal Society of Arts, a witty politician and barrister, founder of the Athenaeum Club. Gertrude was reared in a home where artistic pursuits were encouraged. Her mother played the piano well. She had been a pupil of Mendelssohn, and her musical evenings at Bramley House became a feature of the social life of West Surrey.

In her teens the future gardener used to reap a long hedge of lavender, a plant she loved all her life. The task, she said, was made particularly pleasant owing to the bushes of ripe gooseberries within easy reach of the lavender plants. We are not told at what age she began her gardening, but in her book *Children and Gardens* she wrote of her great pride and delight when she was first given a piece of soil to cultivate as she liked.

In 1861, when she was seventeen, Gertrude persuaded her parents to permit the unusual step of enrolling her as a student at the Kensington School of Art, which later became the Royal College of Art. In refined circles at that time it was considered coarsening for a young lady to work in studios with young men, and even worse to draw from nude models. It was very rare for a girl not the child of a professional artist to be given such freedom. But Gertrude was a determined character and her parents wished her to develop her talent. She had shown considerable promise as a painter, with a fine sense of colour.

After two years of full-time training in fine art, Gertrude apparently discovered a greater feeling for applied art, the design and handcrafting of brass and silver objects, of embroidery and woodwork. She became a highly-skilled craftswoman, making such things as brass scutcheons, corner cupboards, appliqué work and a silver paten for Witley Church. As a child she had found pleasure in her father's workshop at home, where she first learned to handle tools and appreciate the intrinsic nature of materials. Personal contact with William Morris and study of his books probably led her to concentrate on making useful and beautiful articles. When her student days in London came to an end, she took lessons privately in Italy and elsewhere.

During her first visit to Italy in 1868, she took up carving and gilding; writing of the experiences later, she said, 'I have never missed an opportunity of learning from good workmen, especially when I have spent the winter or some months in any one foreign place. The most consecutive of these slight apprenticeships was to a carver and gilder in Rome. The kindly *padrone* put me through a piece of work from beginning to end. Any Italian who has "Carver and Gilder" over his shop really does carve and gild.'

Soon after this the Jekyll family moved to a house called Wargrave Hill in Berkshire. The departure from her favourite county grieved Gertrude. She spent more and more time away from home in the artistic and musical circles where she had made many friends. The group included Brabazon the painter; Blumenthal the pianist and his wife; Barbara Leigh-Smith (later Madame Bodichon), the co-founder of Girton College; and H.R.H. Princess Louise, an accomplished sculptress whose statue of Queen Victoria may be seen near Kensington Palace.

In the winter of 1873, when Gertrude and Barbara were staying in Algiers, Gertrude befriended a young painter, Frederick Walker, and shepherded him back to London in a poor state of health. Whether this association might have proceeded to something deeper and more permanent will never be known, for the young artist died from lung trouble, and young women in those days did not wear their hearts on their sleeves. It is not surprising that many people attributed the fact that Gertrude remained Miss Jekyll to the end of her days to a 'broken romance' in youth.

She busied herself with painting, craftwork, study and travel, until in 1876, following the death of her father, it seemed that her mother needed her help. Wargrave Hill had now become too large, and the decision was made to return to Gertrude's favourite county. A house called Munstead at Godalming was built for Mrs Jekyll, and here for the first time we hear of Miss Jekyll the garden-planner. Her lay-out was admired by several competent judges; as it matured the Munstead garden was visited by well-known gardeners, including Wiliam Robinson of Gravetye, whose book *The English Flower Garden* became a classic, and Dean Hole of Rochester, author of *A Book about Roses*.

Almost by accident, Gertrude Jekyll found herself regarded as an authority on gardens. In 1881 she was asked to judge at the Botanic Show in Regent's Park, a horticultural event which developed later into the Chelsea Flower Show and allied exhibitions at the Vincent Square premises of the Royal Horticultural Society. Soon she had met G. F. Wilson, whose garden near Cobham formed the nucleus of what are now the famous R.H.S. gardens at Wisley. Her ideas, and the practical expression of them at Munstead, attracted Joseph Hooker, Alfred Russell Wallace, the Reverend Woolley Dod, Bennett Poe, W. G. Gambleton and Edward Woodall, all of whom were well-known in the field of horticulture. The latter wrote:

> My first memories of Gertrude Jekyll go back to the days when she returned to England from Algiers. The Reverend Reynolds Hole of Caunton (afterwards Dean of Rochester) introduced me to her. It was he who discovered the talents of William Robinson, and soon we all made friends. Gertrude did not specifically devote herself to gardening until, with Robinson and others, she revolted against the formal style of summer bedding then in vogue.
> Her special love of hardy shrubs and flowers was assisted by her neighbour G. F. Wilson at what is now Wisley, and her nimble pen put

37

forth a stream of garden lore which set us all thinking. Japan and China sent their wealth of azaleas, rhododendrons, lilies, richly-coloured maples and cherries, and she first showed us how to group and arrange them, planting in bold masses and not dotting them about.

At this time Gertrude began to contribute articles to William Robinson's paper *The Garden*, and in a letter to her friend Hercules Brabazon she wrote that she had been 'making living pictures with land and trees and flowers for home and for friends.' Among other visitors to Munstead she received in 1888 Sir Thomas Hanbury of La Mortola, the famous garden just over the Italian border near Mentone. When I saw this some years ago it instantly suggested a Jekyll garden to my mind. Osgood Mackenzie, who made the sub-tropical gardens of Inverewe in the north-west of Scotland, had a Hanbury mother who was cousin to Sir Thomas. Although I worked at Inverewe alongside Osgood's daughter, the late Mairi Sawyer, I cannot recall any mention of Miss Jekyll. Whether she directly influenced the gardening Hanburys or not, her spirit has undoubtedly been at work in their lovely creations.

By the time she reached middle-age Gertrude Jekyll had achieved recognition in more than one sphere, but her interests and talents were spread over too wide a field to bring her to the top. In 1891, when she was forty-eight, physical disability obliged her to specialise. As so often happens, a blow turned out to be a blessing. Eye-trouble had been worrying her to some extent for several years past; but when it became too painful to be ignored something had to be done – so, on the advice of friends, she consulted a famous German oculist in Wiesbaden.

After a thorough examination he could hold out no hope of a cure. Damage to the sight could probably be arrested and that was all. The patient was absolutely forbidden to continue her embroidery and other close work. She could still paint with plants, and she was allowed to write. The garden designer and author were now to take over her life and in time to make her famous.

Fortunately she was already self-trained to use what sight remained to the best advantage. In her own words, 'throughout my life I have found that one of the things most worth doing was to cultivate the habit of close observation. Like all else, the more it is exercised the easier it becomes, till it is so much a part of oneself that one may observe critically and hardly be aware of it. I know that the will and the power to observe does not depend on keen sight. I have sight that is painful and inadequate; short sight of the severest kind, painful and progressive; but the little I have I try to make the most of'.

Although she had no use for self-pity, the enforced adjustment to a new pattern of existence must have required steady determination over a considerable period. A lesser personality, approaching fifty and with failing eyesight, might have looked upon herself as a 'back number' and abandoned all creative effort. If such a thought ever crossed Gertrude Jekyll's mind, the advent of a new, young and stimulating friend put it to flight.

His name was Edwin Lutyens. A promising architect, just twenty-two, he bicycled over to Munstead and stayed to tea. Apparently he and Gertrude took an immediate liking to one another. For her, nothing could have been more opportune. She was always young at heart, and the young man provided plenty of high-spirited amusement. 'Ned' Lutyens had experienced ill-health in boyhood. This prevented him from playing games, and long spells in the care of nurses had accustomed him to female company. The association with Gertrude turned out to be of great value to his career. It is hard to tell whether Ned owed more to her, or she to him.

Lady Emily Lytton, who became Ned's wife, used to address Gertrude as 'Aunt Bumps'. The origin of the nickname is not recorded. It has been described as onomatopoeic: that is, derived from the sound of her hob-nailed garden boots on the oak floor of her hall. (Sir William Nicholson painted those boots.) On the other hand, Lady Emily wrote of her first visit to Munstead: 'Miss Jekyll is the most enchanting person. She is very fat and stumpy. Mr Lutyens calls her "Bumps".' So that word, some people think may have been rhyming slang for 'Stumps'. The significant thing is that the middle-aged Victorian lady had no objection to being addressed in this irreverent manner by her juniors.

The courtship of Lord Lytton's daughter by the impecunious – and at that date almost unknown – architect did not run smoothly to begin with; but it was a case of true love on both sides, and with 'Bumps' as an earthy and sagacious Fairy Godmother, it all came out happily in the end. A celebration before the wedding took the form of dinner at Munstead, to which the young couple invited themselves. They made a surprise entry with mutton chops, eggs, sponge-cake, macaroons, almonds and bullseyes. Emily described it as altogether a most heavenly evening.

Gertrude, who firmly believed in Ned's capacity from the start, was able to help advance his career in a number of ways. She introduced him to Princess Louise, Duchess of Argyll, who commissioned him to design some additions to the hotel at Roseneath. Ned also designed a new house for 'Bumps' – her own home, the Munstead Wood which housed her and her large collection of works of art and country crafts until the end of her life. Between 1896 and 1897 the building went forward for the most part in close and genial co-operation, although Gertrude recalled that once 'the fur flew' over some point. She had the last word in grand style, saying to Lutyens, 'My house is not to be built as an exposition of *architectonic inutility.*' Long words had their uses as 'engines of warfare', commented Miss Jekyll at a later date.

In October 1897, when the new house was ready, she moved in and felt instantly at home. This was the month of her greatest distinction – the award by the Royal Horticultural Society of its newly instituted Victoria Medal of Honour. In the midst of these excitements Ned was not forgotten. By introducing him to Edward Hudson, who founded the paper *Country Life* at this time, she gave his career a boost. Many of his buildings were featured in that influential journal, and before long it became the thing, for people who could afford the latest, to commission a Lutyens house with a Jekyll garden.

Gertrude had been in the fortunate position of owning her land before the builders began their work. She was able to plan the lay-out of her garden and prepare ground for planting well in advance, so the dream of most gardeners, a house built to order in an already-furnished garden, in her case came true. She was very pleased with her dwelling – a house of size, with the simple styling of a cottage – but there can be little doubt that the prepared setting made her feel contented from the first day. Later she wrote, 'Does it often happen to people who have been in a new home only a year and a half to feel as if they had never lived anywhere else? My own little new-built house is so restful, so satisfying, so kindly sympathetic, that so it seems to me.'

Her gardens and her writings were now well known and discussed wherever horticulturists met. Visits from experts of high repute were frequent, and articles signed 'Gertrude Jekyll' were sought after for William Robinson's paper *The Garden*, and for the *Edinburgh Review*, the *Manchester Guardian*, the *National*

Review and other publications. Within six years of the oculist's ban on her originial preocccupation with fine embroidery and other craftwork, she had triumphed over the handicap of poor and worsening eyesight.

In 1899 Longmans published her first book, *Wood and Garden*, which she modestly described as 'notes and thoughts of a working amateur, with photographs by the author'. Fourteen years earlier the then novel art of photography had been taken up with enthusiasm. Always very thorough in all she did, Gertrude had a proper darkroom fitted up for her new hobby, and learned to carry out her own developing and printing expertly. Already a large stock of original prints was available from which to select illustrations for her books and articles.

Wood and Garden had considerable success. Soon the publisher wanted a sequel, so Gertrude composed *Home and Garden* on similar lines. These are enjoyably discursive books, covering a wide range of useful ideas and information. Works of this type are no longer acceptable within the financial straitjacket worn by modern publishing houses. Mention has already been made of the twentieth-century ban on spiritual references in books not specifically classified as 'religious'. It seems worth noting that in Gertrude Jekyll's *Wood and Garden*, issued in 1899, I found what I believe to be the last mention of God in any gardening book. Gertrude wrote: 'The good gardener knows with absolute certainty that if he does his part, if he gives the labour, the love and every aid that his knowledge of craft, experience of conditions of his land, and exercise of his personal wit can suggest, that so surely as he does this diligently and faithfully, so surely will God give the increase.'

After that it seems as though the guillotine fell, cutting out mention of the Creator from books about his creation – something which had not occurred through all the centuries since the first account of Adam and Eve in the Garden of Eden. It is generally agreed that the twentieth century marked a watershed in many ways, but I have not yet seen the spotlight turned on the attitude to religion displayed by writers of garden books. Discoveries are always of interest to the discoverer, although it may be that other people will disdain them.

The death of Queen Victoria in 1901 and the beginning of the Edwardian period brought sweeping changes to life and thought in the British Isles. My own mother, at that time a young woman just three years married, told me how she and her contemporaries rejoiced in the wind of change associated with the accession of King Edward the Seventh. It blew away forever, they believed, what she described as stuffy Victorian conventions, giving men and women alike the freedom to think and act naturally. Fifty years after she told me this, I wonder uneasily if part of the baby may have gone out with the bath water.

For Gertrude Jekyll, quietly busy in her woodland retreat, life went on much as before. Her touching appeal in the preface to *Home and Garden* helped to preserve her peace. She had written: 'In thus again offering my suggestions to the public, it is but just to myself to say that, with my limited reserves of strength, it required some resolution to face the real fatigue involved in the execution of my task. May I go one step further, and say that, while it is always pleasant to hear from or see old friends, and indeed all who work hard in their own gardens, yet, as a would-be quiet worker who is by no means over-strong, I venture to plead with my kind and numerous, though frequently unknown friends, that I may be allowed to retain a somewhat larger measure of peace and privacy.'

I suspect that Gertrude Jekyll suffered not only from limited reserves of strength, but also from the trouble experienced to this day by those of us who use home as our workshop – the continual interruption caused by people who expect a woman to be willing to receive and talk to all and sundry so long as she is under her own roof. Away in a school, office, shop or hospital we are free to become completely absorbed in jobs without interference from relatives or neighbours; but any female who wishes to carry out professional work at home requires the patience of a spider, the cunning of a weasel and a sort of thick rhinoceros armour against reproof.

Gertrude was well supplied with the helpful company of expert horticulturists and designers when she needed stimulation, including Canon Ellacombe, whose garden at Bitton near Bristol she visited; Theresa Earle of the *Pot-Pourri* books; Edward Hudson, founder of *Country Life*: Harold Falkner, R.I.B.A., and Ellen Willmott, who also received the Victoria Medal of Honour at the time it was instituted by the Royal Horticultural Society.

Edward Hudson's own home, Deanery Garden at Sonning-on-Thames (open to the public under the National Gardens Scheme), was a Lutyens house in a Jekyll garden, and in 1905 he had the *Country Life* offices designed by Lutyens. Harold Falkner, himself an architect, said that Gertrude Jekyll's sensitive and informed craftsmanship and keen appreciation of materials so influenced Lutyens that he stood out with distinction from all the other architects of his time. People who might find difficulty in naming many of Lutyens's greatest architectural works – such as New Delhi and the Roman Catholic Cathedral in Liverpool – are usually aware that he also designed the cenotaph in Whitehall.

By that time knighted, Sir Edwin recalled an incident at Munstead Wood over twenty years earlier. He had built for 'Bumps' a garden seat, made from a substantial balk of timber resting on stone supports, and when it was completed a friend named it 'The cenotaph of Sigismunde', explaining that a cenotaph was an empty tomb erected to the memory of a person or persons buried elsewhere. When Lloyd George wanted a catafalque set up in London for the anniversary of the armistice each year on November 11th, to commemorate the dead of 1914-18, Lutyens remembered his earlier project and made use of the idea.

Before the war he had collaborated with his old friend on many occasions. She designed the garden of his own house, Folly Farm in Berkshire (open to the public under the National Gardens Scheme); another at Hestercombe in Somerset; and planned the gardens for the King Edward VII Sanatorium at Midhurst. Next, Gertrude bought a small piece of land near Bramley and commissioned Ned to build a cottage there, for which she made one of her best gardens. It is called Millmead, and is described in *Gardens for Small Country Houses*, which she wrote with Sir Lawrence Weaver in 1912.

Gertrude Jekyll was a good collaborator. *Country Life* in 1902 published *Roses for English Gardens*, which she wrote with Edward Mawley (a founder of the National Rose Society) and Edward Woodall. It contains many imaginative suggestions for the use of roses: climbing up into trees; trained along verandas; upon arches, walls and fences; made into hedges, or utilised as ground-cover on banks. Among its many fine illustrations there is only one of a formal rose-bed, the kind carved out of a lawn and crammed with bushes. Gertrude's title for this picture was 'A kind of rose-garden that may be much improved upon'. It is a kind still seen in some places which would still benefit from her ideas.

The art of the flower-arranger is now rivalling flower gardening as a popular creative pastime, sometimes a professional career; but in the early years of this century little was known about it in the west. Gertrude Jekyll's book *Flower Decoration in the Home* (1907) was not only a fresh subject for her but a novelty for most readers too. It expanded a few references to floral art which she had made somewhat tentatively in *Home and Garden* seven years earlier. She always spoke of flower arranging as 'a branch of gardening'.

Ned Lutyens, now the father of a family, suggested that Aunt Bumps should write a book introducing children to the delights of gardening. From his advice she developed *Children and Gardens*. It contains a great deal of practical information about the sowing, planting and care of flowers and vegetables, has some side-glances at botany and natural history, and includes (as only the down-to-earth Gertrude would have insisted upon) recipes for cooking all the edible things which children might easily grow and handle, together with delicious salad mixtures containing various herbs.

In spite of being looked after by excellent servants all her life Aunt Bumps had a sound knowledge of cookery. On one occasion, when entertaining her nine-year-old niece Pamela, this cordon bleu expertise was put to unorthodox use. Aunt and niece decided to give a cats' tea-party for the quartet of adult felines and two kittens then resident at Munstead Wood. A delicious meal of fish, rice, and sauce with butter and cream was prepared, a menu written out in French, and a table laid. Owing to the presence of kittens it was thought wise not to introduce floral decorations. In the end the kittens were allowed on the table, while their elders sat on stools.

The party went off in fine style. When every scrap had been eaten the guests purred their thanks very prettily. Such was the charm of this event that the hostesses considered sending an account of it to the social column of the *Morning Post*.

For the rest of her life Gertrude continued from time to time her collaboration with Lutyens. His restorations at Great Dixter, Lindisfarne and Lambay were complemented by her garden designs. Even the eccentric Sir George Sitwell called both of them in to assist him with grandiose schemes at Renishaw, as Sir Osbert Sitwell has recorded in his book *Great Morning*.

The lovely fifteenth-century Manor House of Great Dixter in Sussex is still occupied by the Lloyd family. When I stayed there in 1967 Mrs Nathaniel Lloyd, whose late husband commissioned Lutyens to restore the house in the 1920s, was still sprightly at eighty-seven; an adept at fine petit-point and other needlework, at gardening, and much else. She told me how her youngest son, Christopher, was taken to see Gertrude Jekyll, then a very old lady in a wheel-chair, when he was about seven. Miss Jekyll was

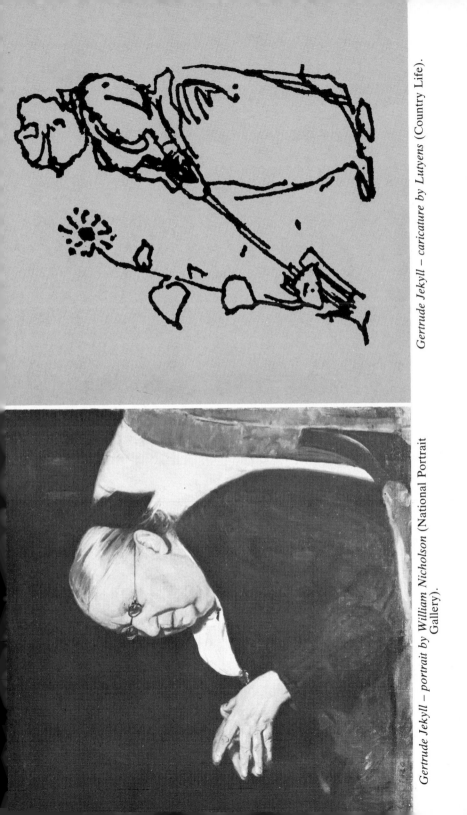

Gertrude Jekyll – caricature by Lutyens (Country Life).

Gertrude Jekyll – portrait by William Nicholson (National Portrait Gallery).

Ellen Willmott – artist unknown.

delighted when the boy asked why her Blue Poppies (*Meconopsis baileyi*) grew like cabbages.

Considering such acute observation worthy of her gardening secrets, she leaned down and confided to him that these plants were always given water twice a day. When her visitors were about to leave she kissed the child and told him to carry on the good work. Christopher Lloyd is now one of the best-known plantsmen in Britain, author of innumerable articles and proprietor of a specialist nursery at Great Dixter. Although the herbaceous borders planned here by Gertrude have been supplanted by a modern labour-saving mixture of herbaceous subjects and shrubs, with clematis climbing through them, the enduringly happy marriage between house and garden could not fail to please her.

She had written in 1900: 'The connection must be intimate and access not only convenient but inviting.' On the relationship of house and garden to its surroundings, she advised that 'natural conditions should first be studied. If they are emphatic or in any way distinct, they should be carefully maintained and fostered.' Of Munstead Wood she said, 'My house is approached by a footpath from a quiet, shady lane, entering by a close-paled hand-gate. There is no driving round to the front door. I like the approach to a house to be as quiet and modest as possible, and in this case I wanted it to tell its own story as the way in to a small dwelling standing in wooded ground' (from *Home and Garden*, Longmans Green, 1900).

A good deal may be learned about the design of gardens from that one sentence alone, for is not letting it 'tell its own story' the first and most essential principle to be observed? Elsewhere she wrote this about entrances: 'In many cases the manor-house entrances have recently been made into gardens, and one cannot but think that the gardening has been overdone; for the safest rule is to keep the entrance side quiet as to showy flowers, and to reserve the main display for the garden front of the house. This always works well in practice, and the use of such restraint involves no penance, for what is more delightful than Box and Bay and Rosemary, Skimmia and Alpenrose and the handsome ground greenery of Lent Hellebore, Megasea and Acanthus?'

From the many books and articles with their wide range of subject matter it is difficult to select short extracts to exemplify Gertrude Jekyll's basic ideas, but the following description in *Home and Garden* of how she set about planning a rock garden of fairly large dimensions is typical of her method.

On the lower part of a steep hillside, a little gorge or dell with its own stream and natural rock cropping out. . . . Such a picture shows what could be done with our own native plants and these alone. Some stretches of native Heaths, the pink Bell-heather and the white Irish Menziesia would not be out of place. I should wish the ground above the glen on both sides to be wooded: not with the largest forest trees, but mainly with Birch and Juniper. Some of these would be allowed to seed and spring up in the rocky banks, the seedlings being removed or retained so as best to suit the grouping of such a picture. As the dell descends it should widen out until it dies away into nearly level ground, and as it flattens the trees might fall away into thinner groups, or be altogether absent if the ground is heath or pasture.

This kind of gardening can only be done well and beautifully by somewhat severe restraint in numbers of kinds. The eye and brain can only take in and enjoy two or three things at a time in any one garden picture. The lessons taught by nature all point to this; indeed one thing at a time is best of all, but as all natural or wild gardening is a compromise, the nature-lessons must be taken mainly as the setting forth of principles.

If these principles are well taken in and digested and assimilated, we shall find no difficulty in rightly using that part of their teaching which bears upon gardening, and we shall know how to treat wild nature, not by slavish imitation, not by driving or forcibly shaping, but by methods that can hardly be described in detail, of coaxing and persuading into pictorial effect. I would have everything planted in longish drifts, and above all it should be planted geologically: the length of the drift going with the natural stratification.

One summer in late August my husband and I went out on foot to the fringe of Warleigh Wood in the lovely Avon valley near Bath. We chose our pitch near some fine beeches, and after a picnic lunch I settled down to continue my re-reading of *Home and Garden*. It was a perfect day, with a few light clouds skimming across a blue sky, and a fresh breeze from the south-west tempered the midday sun.

After a while I looked up from the book and began to study our surroundings in detail. Suddenly I realised that we were in the midst of a natural garden where most of Gertrude Jekyll's principles could be observed. Wild flowers were plentiful, but not of many kinds – I counted eight in bloom or seed – which made for a restful effect. They grew together in long drifts, not spotted about. Willow herb, hemp agrimony, thistle and sorrel made a harmonious colour scheme ranging from acid purple to rusty red. Here and there a stately burdock, covered with burrs like brown bees, supplied a focal point.

Patches of nut-brown earth beneath some trees were bare, or nearly bare of grass, and little trails of dwarf self-heal with claret-coloured autumnal foliage led up to mossy growths that close-carpeted the grey roots of the beech trees. Where grass grew, the blades had been gentled to a strawy tone by a swaying veil of dry stalks and seeds, and where shafts of sunlight touched the mosses they glowed golden olive, the richest colour in the picture.

The strong, smooth beeches were arranged in a loose drift, their lowest branches sweeping down almost to the bank. Miss Jekyll's trained eye would have rejoiced in the strong, clean 'drawing' of their lines. It has been said of her that she appreciated green and brown as colours at a time when most gardeners wanted a blaze of primary hues in their flower beds. I daresay she went even further. My own unforgotten art-master, Leslie Badham, R.B.A., used to say 'the more sensitive your eye, the more highly you regard the tertiary colours and are inclined to give them *first* place'.

Green is, of course, a secondary colour (mixed from the primaries blue and yellow) and brown a tertiary. The range of the latter, from beige and stone to chestnut and madder-brown, also bluish-nigger, brownish-black and plum-black – in a variety of textures which have an effect on colour – are some of the visual delights to be gained in gardens from foliage, barks and seed-heads; from rocky outcrops and lichens too, and, if you are lucky, the Guinness-coloured water, complete with froth, of a Highland stream.

In a chapter headed 'A Wood Ramble in April' it is easy to see how Miss Jekyll's art training influenced her outlook. 'I wish I had with me some young student of painting. The varying colours of the trees in this wood in today's light offer such valuable lessons in training the eye to see the colour of objects as it appears to be. The untrained eye only sees colour as it is locally. I suppose those who have never gone through this kind of training will scarcely credit the difference it makes in the degree of enjoyment of all that is most worthy of admiration. It enables one, even in greater degree than the other perceptions of form and proportion that the artist must acquire, to see pictures for oneself, not merely to see objects.' Some burdock plants are described in the words of an artist: 'Their leaves have almost the grandeur of the gourd tribe, but without their luscious weakness, and the vigour of rhubarb without its coarseness. I never cease to admire their grand wave of edge and the strength of line in the "drawing" from root to leaf-point.'

These paragraphs from her early books show how far-reaching were Gertrude Jekyll's studies of art and nature, the firmest of bases on which to found a garden designer's creed. Those of us who are confined to small plots of land may take heart from her opinion of size.

> The size of a garden has very little to do with its merit. It is merely an accident relating to the circumstances of the owner. It is the size of his heart and brain and goodwill that will make his garden either delightful or dull, as the case may be, and either leave it at the usual monotonous dead-level or else raise it, in whatever degree may be, towards that of a work of fine art.
>
> But the lesson I have thoroughly learned, and wish to pass on to others, is to know the enduring happiness that love of a garden gives. I rejoice when I see anyone, and especially children, inquiring about flowers and wanting gardens of their own, and carefully working in them. For the love of gardening is a seed that, once sown, never dies, but always grows and grows to an enduring and ever-increasing source of happiness.

After the end of World War I she was invited to prepare planting schemes for British war cemeteries in France. One of her ideas was for areas of white thrift, which the Imperial War Graves Commission adopted for setting above the flower of the Empire's youth. Was the irony of growing thrift in juxtaposition to such colossal wastage of human life apparent to her acute mind? Or did she, believing as did many optimists of the time that this had truly been 'the war to end all wars', not regard the holocaust as a vain sacrifice?

In 1920 Edwin Lutyens persuaded his old friend to sit for a portrait to Sir William Nicholson. At first she resisted the idea with great force, saying she was not in the least paintable, and in any case had no time to spend on sittings. In the end by a combined effort the architect and painter cajoled her into unwilling consent. As she insisted on using all the daylight hours for outdoor work in the garden, Nicholson was obliged to 'take her likeness' by lamplight. He filled in waiting periods by painting a pair of her old gardening boots. The portrait of Gertrude Jekyll, sitting in an armchair with hands aloft, palms together, in what was evidently a characteristic attitude, hangs in the National Portrait Gallery in London.

We are told that her everyday dress throughout the year was made of serge, with the addition of a strong apron for garden work, and a battered straw hat. I suspect that in warm weather the so-called 'serge' was really alpaca, a fine, lightweight material favoured by my own grandmother, herself an indefatigable gardener. With that uncrushable stuff for dresses, finest lawn for underwear, and the luxury of delicate woollen material called 'nun's veiling' for night-dresses, not to mention real silk crêpe-de-chine for blouses and evening wear, women of that generation had clothes which far surpassed any synthetic imitations of today.

In 1923, her eightieth year, Gertrude took part in plans for that exquisite toy, the Queen's doll's house. Lutyens, fresh from dealing with many square miles of grandeur in New Delhi, designed this miniature building while Bumps took care of its garden. She still got through a lot of work in spite of doctor's orders to spend one day each week in bed. In May 1925 Viscountess Wolseley (Frances Garnet Wolseley), who founded the School for Lady Gardeners at Glynde, of which Gertrude Jekyll, Ellen Willmott and Theresa Earle were the patrons, was informed by postcard that she and her friends would be very welcome any afternoon after 3.30, 'as I am *obliged* to have a complete rest in the early afternoon'.

Her articles still appeared in various journals – *The Gardener's Chronicle*, *English Life*, and *The Empire Review* among them – and she was regular in her attendance at local branch meetings of the National Trust. Octavia Hill, one of the Trust's founders, has as her memorial a tract of land not far from Munstead, which was laid out in 1914-15 by Gertrude Jekyll with help from a group of boy scouts.

While her physical powers slowly waned, ultimately confining her to a wheel-chair, the great Miss Jekyll's mind remained fully alert. Logan Pearsall Smith, a friend of her brother Sir Herbert Jekyll, now living near his sister at Munstead House, described in *Life and Letters* a visit he paid to her in the last year of her life.

Across the road from Munstead House a high fence-like barrier shuts in and secludes from the world Miss Jekyll's house and garden. But in this barrier there is a little door, carefully locked; a secret key hangs on a secret nail which, if one knows where to look, one can find by reaching over and groping for it. I was initiated into this mystery, I was shown the key, allowed to open the gate . . . and so found admittance into the great wood. Walking along shadowy paths, I came at last on a glade of lawn, and saw Miss Jekyll's house before me.

All was hushed in silence; there was not a soul about; the house stood there in its hidden glade like the abode of some admirable august and kind-hearted ogress, inspiring awe but as good as gold, dwelling in the midst of the garden she had charmed into existence by her own white magic. It was really like something one reads of in old romances – the locked gate and secret key, the walk through the wood to the beautiful house which its venerable inhabitant had built for herself so long ago, and over which brooded the silence and solitude of exteme old age.

But when, after knocking at the door, I was admitted into the silent house, I found myself in the presence of the Gertrude Jekyll I had known before. She seemed more feeble in body, of course, but her mind was as alert as ever; her eyes twinkled behind her heavy glasses with their old gaiety of welcome, the sound of her deep chuckle was quite as rich with the tones of friendship, mockery and fun. . . .

It was on this occasion that she teased her erudite visitor by referring to herself as an armigerous person.

As I took my leave I said 'Now, Miss Jekyll, what would you advise a *non-armigerous* person like myself to say or do? Would you advise me to keep to the usages of my own condition?' Miss Jekyll gave a snort or two; her friendliness seemed to be struggling with an unregenerate impulse derived from the first of lady-gardeners; and I am happy to say that the struggle ended as of old it ended in that other paradise. She snorted, she almost winked, and then she chuckled. 'Well, I think if I were you – yes. . . . I think if you insist upon an answer, yes, you had better stick to the ways of your own class.'

With this parting shot, which the armigerous old Amazon delivered from her bow with undiminished vigour, Miss Jekyll laughed her jolly laugh. 'Go and have a look at the garden if you like,' she added. 'There's a big patch of blue meconopsis behind the tool-shed you might like to see. I'm sorry I can't come and show it to you. Good-bye. . . .'

She had her eighty-ninth birthday that November, and nine days later, on 8th December, 1932, she died. She was buried at the church of St John the Baptist at Busbridge, the organ being played for the service by her niece Pamela McKenna, for whom the cats' tea-party had been held long before. Old William Robinson, ninety-four and paralysed, was brought thirty miles in his wheel-chair to attend the funeral.

Sir Edwin Lutyens designed the memorial for Busbridge churchyard, which was erected in 1934. On it is the simple inscription:

GERTRUDE JEKYLL
ARTIST
GARDENER
CRAFTSWOMAN

*   *   *   *

I think that Ellen Willmott's is the only unhappy story in this collection. She afflicts me with gloom. But life, even among the green-fingered, must have its dark patches. The trouble with Miss Willmott was that she possessed too much to begin with. Had this outrageous affluence remained constant, though she would never have known the satisfaction of gradually achieving some desired end through a long preparatory period of self-restraint, she would at least have been spared the terrible downhill regression which acted like a slow poison on her character in later years.

Ellen Ann Willmott was born on 19th August 1858 at Spring Grove, Heston, Middlesex, the elder child of Frederick Willmott, a solicitor, and his wife Ellen (*née* Fell), who was devoted to flowers and a keen gardener. When their first daughter was still an infant they moved to the big house of Warley Place in the same county, where Mrs Willmott could indulge her taste by making a splendid garden. She was far ahead of her time in disliking the Victorian ardour for carpet and ribbon bedding; she must have thought along similar lines to those which the genius of Gertrude Jekyll was later to develop, far-reaching 'natural' ideas that altered the whole pattern of gardening in England.

Soon there was a second little girl at Warley Place. This daughter was to grow up and marry Major Robert Berkeley of Spetchley Park in Worcestershire, where she, too, took up gardening and raised a well-known strain of primroses. Her son,

Captain 'Bob' Berkeley, inherited Spetchley Park and has written to me about his famous aunt, Ellen Willmott. But that is going ahead too fast.

Ellen remained single and, losing both parents while still quite young, inherited the great house of Warley together with a large fortune. She was beautiful, she was rich, she was highly accomplished, but she never married. Sir William Lawrence (President of the Royal Horticultural Society) said that she 'broke more hearts than lances', so it is clear that in her youth she was attractive to men. Did she experience a great sorrow or disappointment of which we know nothing? Was she burdened, as her acquaintance the distinguished botanist Dr W. T. Stearn appears to think, with a feminine counterpart of the Napoleonic complex? We know that she amassed a comprehensive set of books about Bonaparte and, more strangely, had a hut built in her Alpine garden that was an exact replica of one in which he slept when crossing into Italy. Her sex prevented her from being a Napoleon – did she console herself by identifying with the Empress Josephine?

Like the Empress, she developed a sound knowledge of botany, and she lavished money on new plants for her garden. We do not know how much Josephine spent on this hobby, but the late Louis Russell of Richmond said that Miss Willmott between 1890 and 1900 ran up annual accounts with his firm of £1,500 besides dealing with others. That was a large sum in late Victorian days.

Everything at Warley was done on the grand scale. Some authorities say she had eighty-six gardeners there; Captain Berkeley mentioned eighty-five. If you employ such a regiment of men, one here or there would hardly be noticeable anyway. In spite of all this hired labour, Ellen Willmott herself was described by her friend Gertrude Jekyll as 'the greatest of living women gardeners'.I find it hard to believe that Miss Jekyll would have said that unless Miss Willmott really took a spade in her hands. Miss Jekyll, honest and plain-spoken, would not have admired a cheque-book gardener. That solid face of hers was not created for flattery. So Miss Willmott must have been a good practical gardener in spite of her army; she also made a serious study of botany, becoming a Fellow of the Linnaean Society – the first woman to be elected (1904).

The Empress Josephine preferred roses to all other plants and engaged the celebrated artist P. J. Redouté to paint them for her, a set which he published in book form – the popular 'Redouté Roses'.

His Empress liked being associated with botanists, and sought the co-operation of Ventenat, Mirbel and Bonpland. Ellen Willmott also produced an imposing rose book, *The Genus Rosa*, illustrated sumptuously in colour by Alfred Parsons, A.R.A., and she obtained the services of that good botanist, John Gilbert Baker (1834-1920), some-time keeper of the Herbarium, Kew, to assist her with the text. He drew up the descriptions in Latin and English, but she contributed the historical and cultural notes. There was a certain resemblance between the two ladies in this respect.

Ellen Willmott liked to indulge her imagination. Although we find no clear evidence that she fancied herself in the role of the Empress, there are signs that she augmented a link with the great diarist John Evelyn to suit her own purposes. Warley Place had belonged to Evelyn for a short time – from 1649 to 1655 – so Miss Willmott pretended to suppose that he had written his *Sylva* there, perhaps in her garden. But Evelyn was mostly abroad until 1652, and there is no evidence of his having spent more than a few nights at Warley, so her theory is almost certainly a pleasant fiction. John Evelyn's gardening was done at Sayes Court, Deptford, and it is thought most likely that he purchased Warley Place as an investment, selling it again when it became profitable to do so. He lived another fifty years after that, and died in 1706 aged eighty-six.

If we discount the connection with Evelyn, and pass over the possibility of Napoleonic obsessions, we must come to grips with an appraisal of Ellen Willmott as a plantswoman. There can be no doubt that her garden at Warley achieved an international reputation as a collection of newly introduced and rare plants. It is also true that she had a flair for grouping her subjects, bulbs in particular, and, being skilled with a camera, took photographs of the best effects to illustrate her book *Warley Garden in Spring and Summer* (1909). This preceded *The Genus Rosa*, which was first issued in parts, 1910-1914.

But Warley, with its eighty-six (or eighty-five) gardeners did not satisfy Ellen Willmott. She acquired other gardens, at Ventimiglia and at Aix-les-Bains, with another seventy gardeners in Italy and a mere half dozen in France. It was her custom to attend the meetings of the Royal Horticultural Society in London with an unusual or puzzling specimen from one of her gardens in her lapel, and watch to see how many of the members of the Floral Committee were unable to identify it. Sir William Lawrence, in his articles in *Gardening Illustrated* used regularly to mention what Miss Willmott had worn in her buttonhole at the last show. I suppose she thoroughly enjoyed these occasions; she had her hour.

Among the horticulturists whom she knew well were L. R. Russell, W. T. Ingwersen, and the great E. A. Bowles. She gained a slightly wry reputation for extracting knowledge from the experts of her day to build up her plantsmanship, afterwards ignoring those who had assisted her. This may in part have been due to the realisation that it was very much a world of men, where women had a hard fight to be recognised, and perhaps she over-compensated by haughty behaviour when success did come her way. Gardeners are in the main kindly people, and it is pleasant to record that when, in declining years, Miss Willmott got into some trouble in a court action (she was charged with the offence of shop-lifting) her old friends all rallied to her support.

In her heyday she gave handsome financial help to some of the plant-hunters, notably E. H. Wilson; and she bought the novelties of Van Tubergen and others as soon as they became available. She fancied certain subjects: *Epimedium*, *Hedera*, *Iris*, *Narcissus* and *Rosa*, and acquired almost every variety that money or persuasion could achieve. Many of them were depicted by painters whom she commissioned; a few of her Iris paintings were bought by the Royal Horticultural Society for its Lindley Library in 1935, but most of that set and the entire collection of paintings (by Champion Jones) of the genus *Epimedium* have vanished. It is thought likely that the ageing lady, after losing her money, disposed of such possessions secretly to dealers – probably for sums far below their true value – because she did not wish her old associates, who would have paid more for them, to know how hard-pressed she was.

All her life Ellen Willmott had been musical; she was an accomplished violinist; after she inherited Warley Place she made a fine collection of musical instruments, many of them of great historical interest. Captain Berkeley kept at Spetchley Park, Worcester, a harpsichord from his aunt's collection which belonged originally to Marie Antoinette at the Trianon. Beatrix Havergal, founder and Principal of the Waterperry Horticultural School, apparently made friends with Miss Willmott when they were both members of the London Bach Choir (see page 146).

The plants that were named after Ellen Willmott or her Warley garden make an impressive list. The most popular of these today is possibly that blue-eyed darling, *Ceratostigma willmottianum* from Western China. The hybrid tea-rose 'Ellen Willmott', a large single pale creamy-yellow, pink-tinged rose raised by Messrs. Archer, is a lovely thing but seldom seen now. Then there is Narcissus 'Ellen Willmott', a garden hybrid yellow trumpet daffodil raised by Engelheart; *Paeonia willmottiae*, *Primula willmottiae*, and *Rosa willmottiae*, all from Western China; *Rosa blanda var. willmottiana* from North America; *Iris willmottiana* from central Asia; *Tulipa willmottiae* from eastern Turkey; and a number of subjects named after Warley: *Epimedium warleyense*, a garden hybrid; *Lilium warleyense* (syn. *L. Davidi var. Willmottiae*); *Lysionotus warleyensis*; and *Rosa X warleyensis*, a hybrid between *R. blanda* and *R. rugosa*. This is not a complete list, but should be correct so far as it goes, having been sent to me by Dr W. T. Stearn, V.M.H.

In *The English Rock Garden* (1919) Reginald Farrer, who seldom names the introducer of a plant, does so in the case of *Primula magaseifolia*. He describes the plant as 'not happy in the open although quite hardy. Its perverse habit of trying to unfold its rather ugly magenta stars in mid-winter is largely accountable for this, as in rich good soil it grows readily . . . unfolding one or two umbels of long-pedicelled large yellow-eyed flowers in a rather chilly and bitter tone of magenta-lilac (suggesting an acid old maid crossed in an unseasonable love-affair) and nipped by the winter frost of their belated appearance. . . . It was introduced by Miss Ellen Willmott in 1901.'

Poor Miss Willmott. It is so hard to find anybody who has said nice things about her. In a review of Betty Massingham's book, *Miss Jekyll – Portrait of a Great Gardener*, in the *R.H.S. Journal* for November 1966, Dr Stearn wrote:

As a boy I corresponded with Miss Jekyll; as a young man I knew Miss Willmott. They were cultured art-loving and artistic women united in friendship by an intense love of gardening and an intimate knowledge of garden plants. Both received the Victoria Medal of Honour when it was instituted in 1897. Both had the high compliment paid to them by dedication of a volume of *Curtis's Botanical Magazine*. There the resemblance ended. When about 1929 Nelmes was compiling his *Curtis's Botanical Magazine Dedications. 1827-1927*, Miss Willmott, now a waspish old lady embittered by the loss of her money and the ruin of her celebrated Warley garden, declined to state her age and provided a portrait made in her twenties, at a period, as Sir William Lawrence noted, when she broke more hearts than lances – which was certainly not true of her later.

Poor Miss Willmott she had become, in a material sense. All that extravagant expenditure in her youth could not be maintained after World War I, because the bulk of her investments had been in Germany and they disappeared in the holocaust. For twenty years she lived on, watching the once cherished Warley turn into a wilderness for lack of labour. After her death in 1934 the house had to be pulled down. Dr Stearn writes: 'It is hard to believe today in the present wild state of Warley Place that so much care, labour, thought and money had been spent upon the area, and it is also very sad, although the survivors among the trees, shrubs and bulbs indicate clearly enough the work long ago of a keen planter.'

I have not myself visited the wreck of Warley, for it seemed better to leave it to the birds and other wild things. They will not waste time brooding over the fate of a beautiful, accomplished lady who once had great possessions.

4

Herbalism in Modern Times

Mrs C. F. Leyel, Mrs Grieve and Eleanour Sinclair Rohde

The modern revival of interest in herbs in the British Isles may be traced mainly to two women, one of whom was a botanist and student of herbal medicine rather than a practical gardener. Mrs Leyel, born Hilda Winifred Wauton in 1880, started her botanical studies at the age of four. Her father, Edward Wauton, was a housemaster at Uppingham, the public school for boys; but this academic parent was not the little girl's tutor. No lesser person than the great Edward Thring, the headmaster, took her out into the school gardens and surrounding fields to impart the rudiments of botany.

Of these early years Hilda Leyel wrote: 'I still remember the pride I felt when he strapped the black, japanned tin lined with green to my tiny back. Although at the time I was only four, and much too young to enjoy searching in the heat for such rare plants as Ladies' Tresses and Green Hellebore, the names of the plants, like the dates of the English Kings, were impressed upon my mind so vividly that it has been impossible for me ever to forget them.' After the death of Mr Thring, his daughter Sarah continued the lessons in botany.

When she reached her late teens, Hilda Wauton thought of studying medicine. That proved to be a false start. After a brief period on the stage with Sir Frank Benson's company, she married a Swiss theatrical manager and bore him two sons. Carl Frederick

Leyel died in the late nineteen-twenties, leaving Hilda a widow of forty-six. Not for her a decline into middle-age idleness. In 1924 she had run a highly successful lottery in aid of ex-servicemen and hospital charities which produced the very large sum, for those times, of £350,000. It was known as the Golden Ballot, and brought her into collision with the Lottery and Betting Acts. The prosecution failed, and her acquittal made history, for it legalised lotteries held in aid of charitable causes.

After this *cause célèbre* Mrs Leyel became Life Governor of St Mary's Hospital, the West London and the Royal National Orthopaedic Hospitals, voluntary work which coincided with her original idea of pursuing a career in medicine. But again she deviated, to some extent, for she soon became caught up in a study of herbal cures, a branch of healing almost forgotten for a century or more. She gained a detailed knowledge of the work of herbalists in past ages, notably of Nicholas Culpeper, the seventeenth-century Londoner who combined herbalism with astrology. During this period she amassed the store of old herbals and manuscripts which Wilfrid Blunt later described as one of the finest privately-owned collections in the country.

These concentrated herbal studies brought Hilda Leyel into contact with Mrs Grieve, a practical horticulturist who ran a herb farm and school at Chalfont St Peter in Buckinghamshire. Her excellent series of monographs on a wide range of herb plants came to Mrs Leyel's notice at an opportune moment for both women – and for the development of public interest in a neglected subject. Instantly recognising their value, Hilda wrote to the author suggesting that an authoritative and much-needed modern herbal might be compiled from such material.

Together they worked on the project. Jonathan Cape agreed to publish the herbal, with Hilda Leyel as editor. The firm stipulated that details about American herbs were to be included. It was a large and important book, over which both author and editor expended a great deal of time and energy. The result was an enormous success. Mrs Grieve's *A Modern Herbal* has served as a standard work of reference for fifty years and was recently reprinted in both hardback and paperback editions.

Mrs Leyel's next venture, the opening of the first Culpeper shop in London on St Valentine's Day 1927, soon led to expansion of the idea all over England. The clean simplicity of design, a simple style invented by Basil Ionides, with all Culpeper shopfronts painted alike in green and white, brought people in surprisingly large numbers to sample herbs for culinary, cosmetic and medicinal use. The intention had not been anything greater than to supply wholesome still-room elixirs, distillations, lotions and creams made to recipes used by people of an earlier time, and to present them in an agreeable setting. For too long, in Mrs Leyel's opinion, herbalism had been relegated to dingy back-street premises and associated with dubious side-lines.

As she said of her new project:

Success was instantaneous. The good old traditions had not been wholly forgotten. The sight of an attractive herbalist's shop in the centre of London seemed to revive memories of childish colds cured by black-currant tea, of the healing properties of many herbs, and of walks in old physic gardens. It soon became clear that a belief in herbs and pure herbal remedies had survived the spate of patent medicines and much-advertised commercial cosmetics. There were still even a few people who had some definite knowledge of herbs and knew what they wanted.

I had anticipated that there might be a ready sale for the lotions, face creams, scents and tisanes; but what surprised me was the instant demand for medicinal herbs and herbal remedies. This demand increased rapidly. One early customer was a milkman who wanted a cure for his cough. A fortnight later he returned with the money for twenty-eight bottles of the same cough mixture, which he had recommended to people on his rounds.

Then there was the manager of the business in Bond Street who asked for an ointment for a very disfiguring skin complaint on his face. A few weeks later we heard that all Bond Street was speaking of Culpeper House, and of the wonderful cure of a man whose skin disease had caused acute suffering for years. From these small beginnings more and more ailing people came to the shop in search of herbal remedies.

It soon became obvious that medicinal herbs could not be sold over the counter without the purchasers receiving proper advice as to their use. The need of consultation with a person experienced in herbal therapy, so that the individual complaint should be carefully diagnosed and the right herb given seemed even more imperative. Herbs are not nostrums. They do not stop pain instantly, but work on its cause – and a pain may have several causes. I thus decided that it was impossible to continue this indiscriminate sale of herbal medicines, and started giving consultations. Although I had no intention of doing so, I now became a consultant herbalist. This work was to occupy my time and attention for the next twenty-seven years.

The first Culpeper shop opened in London's Baker Street in 1927, and was established by The Society of Herbalists Ltd – which at that stage had been formed solely to run the business enterprise. Sir Ernest Wallis Budge and Lady Simpson were Directors. The latter, better known as Lena Ashwell, had been cured by herbal treatment of a gastric ulcer which failed to respond to orthodox medicine. Her husband, Sir Henry Simpson, a gynaecologist who later brought the future Queen Elizabeth the Second and her sister Princess Margaret into the world, took a friendly interest in herbalism.

All good doctors know that healing is an art as well as a science, and realise that human beings have not been created to a standard pattern. Every general practitioner has on his records patients who cannot tolerate certain drugs, or react unfavourably. Such doctors also know that these people often get cured as a result of some different treatment which may have no place in the curriculum of the medical schools. For her part, Mrs Leyel tried to work in collaboration with doctors, not in opposition to them, and was grateful for consideration and kindness received from many orthodox physicians.

She has written (in *The Truth about Herbalism*) of her inherited interest in medicine and in aspects of natural history. Her great-great-grandfather on her mother's side, William Jones of Chelsea, was a celebrated lepidopterist whose paintings of butterflies are now in the Oxford Museum. Her grandfather, also a naturalist and keen student of birds and plant-life, was a friend of John Ruskin, who used to stay with him in Sussex. Her uncle, Dr Dartrey Drewitt, was a distinguished physician who served on the Council of the Zoological Gardens and as vice-chairman of the Chelsea Physic Gardens; he wrote of it in *The Romance of the Apothecaries' Garden*. No doubt the pioneering work done by Doctor Drewitt in recognition of the dietetic value of vegetables and fruit influenced his niece, and also helped to bring her sympathetic attention from other members of his profession. Herbs and medicine were in the family.

In his book *The Divine Origin of the Craft of the Herbalist*, Sir Ernest Wallis Budge, for many years Keeper of Egyptian and Assyrian Antiquities at the British Museum, wrote: 'When the

Sumerians began to compile their herbal – or record of herbs used for medicinal purposes – cannot be said, but a tablet which was at one time in the library of Ashurbanipal, King of Assyria 668-626 B.C. at Nineveh, and is now in the British Museum, has a note at the end which states that it was copied from a tablet which had been written in the second year of the reign of Enlil-Bani, King of Isin, about 2201-2177 B.C. The note refers to a tradition from the time of "The ancient rulers before The Flood". So it is clear that the Sumerian Herbal was in existence in the second half of the third milennium B.C.'

It contained the names of about a thousand plants. Remedies are divided into organic and inorganic substances, and among plants which have been identified are dates, figs, anise, juniper, caraway, coriander, colewort, willow, oleander and jasmine. Records of the early medical knowledge of the Indians and Chinese are less reliable, although there is some extraordinary evidence that Hindus taught surgery by operating on vegetables and other plants instead of on animals. The virtues of seven hundred and fifty plants were known to them, garlic and birch bark being particularly important. Opium, rhubarb and ginseng were used long ago in China.

In regard to medicine the position of women in ancient times and in eastern countries is too obscure to be guessed at; but in this country it is known that the art of healing was for many centuries looked upon as women's work. The tradition lingered on well into the seventeenth century. Gervase Markham in his book *The English Housewife* puts the knowledge of medicine first on his list of accomplishments expected of an ordinary woman. After that he names cookery, gardening and the art of distilling.

So Hilda Leyel was following a trail marked out by long-forgotten women in the privacy of their own homes, but she re-shaped the pattern to meet modern needs. Few women today have time or opportunity to grow and process a wide range of herbs for themselves. The Culpeper shops, which gradually spread all over Britain, provided the best quality prepared herbs and spices, guaranteed pure and attractively packaged. Customers have never been induced to try medicinal herbs by alluring advertisements or promises of miracle cures. Herb remedies as a rule work slowly – a fact that has always been honestly stated in those spheres where Mrs Leyel held sway.

A certain amount of confusion has been caused by the statement that she 'inaugurated the Society of Herbalists in 1936': this was a later, non-profit-making, association, completely separated from the Culpeper shops. It soon had some 10,000 members, most of whom had derived benefit from herbal medicines, believed in them, and wished to protect and further the interests of herbalism. For the nominal fee of two shillings and sixpence a year the members were entitled to visit the library of old herbals, early flower books, books on husbandry and wine, on gardening and cookery, and continental and English early Festival and Dancing books. As one who was fortunate enough to see this collection, I feel intense regret that in the 1960-70 period of rising inflation the Society felt obliged to break up this splendid bequest left by the Founder. No longer can such societies be run on a shoe-string, aided by voluntary helpers and donations from wealthy patrons.

The Society's committee listed in Mrs Leyel's *The Truth about Herbs,* which was issued by the Culpeper Press in 1954, resembles extracts from *Debrett* and *Who's Who.* A duke and two duchesses, a marchioness, five countesses, several baronets and ten 'ladies' are companioned by Edith and Sacheverell Sitwell, Wilfred Blunt, Sheila Kaye-Smith, and Eric Coates the composer. Mrs Leyel herself took the chair, and a prominent member of her committee, the Hon. Lady Meade-Fetherstonhaugh, was later to preside over the Society for nearly twenty years.

Her work with the herb saponaria (soapwort) must be mentioned. It began at her home, Uppark in Sussex, now a National Trust property. When Admiral Meade-Fetherstonhaugh inherited the house, his friends said that the shabby old curtains must be taken down and thrown away. Lady Meade, as she was affectionately known, described her own feelings in her book *Uppark and its People.*

> Those curtains were not going to be thrown away, though they hung like depressing wreaths of damp pink seaweed, for I was going to mend them. . . .There were over thirty curtains, each measuring 16 to 18 feet high and 6 feet wide, which could not be let down: the sight was too shocking. They were made of Italian brocade of 1740, and I knew of no other house which had them.
>
> Our family was blessed with two maiden aunts, and they brought to Uppark one day a little old lady who taught me how to make soap from a herb called *Saponaria officinalis.* She smiled at me kindly after she had taken in the magnitude of the restoration needed.

'You can do it, it only needs work,' she said. A bundle of herbs was sent for from Norfolk. Pascal, our chef, provided a cauldron in the old still-room kitchen. It was impossible not to think of Macbeth's witches as we watched muslin bags bobbing on the seething water in the cauldron. As the ritual proceeded the air became pervaded with the subtle unforgettable scent that filled my nostrils for the first time, and proved to be my novice introduction to the miracles of nature therapy. The soap was a brown liquid with a meaningful lather, which covered the surface of the copper like a foaming tankard of beer. The scent was aromatic and exciting.

The Prince Regent's bed and a curtain from the little parlour were tackled at once. An alarming process of what was called 'loosening the dirt' took place in a big bath. The water turned inkpot black, while dustbin dirt hid the objects of ablution. If the ragged curtain had entered the bath a sorry mess of powdered rags, it emerged looking more than ever like seaweed which had been dragged from the bed of the ocean. The little old lady was never daunted, and appeared unmoved by this mass of weeds, red and dripping.

By the time our lives were once more disrupted by war, we had mended and re-hung twenty-eight brocade curtains, fabrics for three Queen Anne four-poster beds, and for a set of chairs. The work of restoration has gone on for thirty years, and new techniques have been developed in applying Saponaria to textiles which have been sent to Uppark for repair from Europe and America as well as Britain.

For family reasons Lady Meade was obliged to leave Uppark in 1968. During her hunt for new premises, two conditions came uppermost – there had to be a spring of pure water, without which saponaria would not function effectively, and the house had to be situated within reasonable distance of the homes of trained local craftswomen who had helped her to build up the restoration work over many years. Such a place was found in the village of Selborne, once the home of the naturalist Gilbert White, and there the herbal therapy on old and rare fabrics continued until the death of Lady Meade in 1975.

Mrs Leyel, who died in the spring of 1957, had undoubtedly left the Society of Herbalists in good hands. In recent years, since Lady Meade's death, there have been many changes, including the name. It is now the Herb Society, and seems to be geared rather more to those who make a living from herbs; the day of the gifted amateur is probably over for ever. At least the power of the herb has not been thrown overboard in the fever of present-day preoccupation with science and technology. The fact that there are still some members who will now pay five pounds a year, instead of many half-a-crown subscribers twenty years ago, shows that interest persists.

*   *   *   *

While Hilda Leyel and Mrs Grieve were collaborating in the work of compiling the latter's impressive *A Modern Herbal*, followed by the setting up of Culpeper shops, their contemporary, Eleanour Sinclair Rohde, had begun to stir up public enthusiasm for herbs by using a more literary method. She was essentially a scholar and writer, who in intervals from her desk acquired practical knowledge of herb cultivation in the garden of her home in Surrey.

The only daughter of John Rohde of the Travancore Civil Service, Eleanour was born in India in 1881. At the age of fifteen she was sent as a boarder to the famous Ladies' College at Cheltenham. There she did well, distinguishing herself particularly in English Language and Literature. Later she entered St Hilda's Hall, University of Oxford, where she read history. Degrees were not then given to women, and there is no record of her having returned to Oxford to take her award when the rule against female graduates was relaxed.

Her family, which was of Danish origin, had emigrated to England early in the eighteenth century, so her parents naturally returned 'home' to England when John Rohde retired. With Eleanour they settled at Reigate in the county of Surrey, and there she spent her life. Personal details are very scarce. She never married, and judging from snippets of information it would seem that she was of a solitary nature, inhabiting a world of her own and making few close friends.

Most of her adult years were almost wholly taken up with research and writing on the subject of early gardens and in particular herbs and herb gardening. A constant visitor to the Reading Room of the British Museum, she may without injustice be classed as a bluestocking, of gentle and unassuming nature and liked by those who came into contact with her. Her erudition was never paraded, and she made her carefully researched material live in easy prose designed to give pleasure to her readers.

Throughout her life she contributed articles to *Country Life*, *The Sphere*, *The Field*, *The Countryman*, *The Times* and the *R.H.S.*

64

Journal: work which led to her election as President of the Society of Women Journalists. *Who's Who* in 1943 gave 'writing' as her profession and 'a herb farm and cottage gardening' as her recreations.

Although she was never classed as a writer of fiction, her supposed memoirs in *Herbs and Herb Gardening*, issued by the Medici Society in 1936, apparently owes a good deal to her imagination. In it she traces her abiding interest in herbs to the influence in her childhood of a favourite great-aunt. Yet a surviving cousin told me some years ago that no such great-aunt ever existed. If 'Great-aunt Lancilla' is a fictional character, she has certainly been etched with great conviction as well as charm.

My own first recollections of sweet-leaved geraniums go back to the days when as a child I used to stay with my great-aunt Lancilla. And whenever I smell those leaves I am instantly transported to her house, and in particular to the broad, sunny passage which led to her kitchen. The sun came pouring through the sloping glass roof, and there was a whole bank of the sweet-leaved geraniums, reaching well above my head. Pinching the leaves was always a joy, for the scents were so rich and varied. And those scents now never fail to remind me of a gracious old lady who looked well to the ways of her placid, well-ordered household and was loved by everyone who served her, and every man, woman and child in the village.

When I think of scented gardens I remember hers first and foremost. . . . I can see the big bushes of pale pink China roses and smell their delicate perfume; I can see the tall old-fashioned delphiniums and the big red paeonies and clumps of borage, the sweet-williams, the madonna and tiger lilies and the well-clipped bushes of lad's love. I can see the kitchen garden, too, with its long paths and espalier fruit trees and sweet peas grown in clumps. They *were* sweet peas then, for they were deliciously scented. And big clumps of mignonette, which everyone grew in those days to mix with sweet peas and gypsophila. There were rows of clove carnations for picking, and never have I smelt any like them.

I love to think of the huge beds of lily-of-the-valley, where one could gather and gather to one's heart's content. But my chief recollection of that kitchen garden is of roses. Cabbage roses and *La France* and *Gloire de Dijon* and *Maiden's Blush*, and if one gathered armfuls it seemed to make no difference. And how well I remember the sweet, subdued scent of pot-pourri; for as well as flowers there were in every room big open bowls of the pot-pourri my great-aunt loved to have about her. In many of the bowls there were oranges stuck with cloves. Everyone loves picking these up and sniffing them, yet few people make them now-a-days.

In appearance great-aunt Lancilla was a very impressive old lady. The colour she most affected was a soft cinnamon brown one rarely sees now. Others wore bonnets; but summer and winter she wore wide-brimmed hats, almost devoid of trimming and tied under her chin with a large flat bow. Under her skirt and fastened like an apron she wore a pocket. This curious garment consisted of an array of flat, envelope-like receptacles, into which she slipped anything and everything she needed. A trowel and a small hand-fork, for instance, to say nothing of such trifles as stale bread for the ducks and corn for the pigeons. I never remember her carrying anything in her hands except flowers, fruit, or the candle lantern she took to light her way to church on winter evenings.

A catalogue of edible delights in great-aunt Lancilla's store-cupboard is designed to give as much vicarious pleasure to the greedy as are the coloured plates in Mrs Beeton's cookery-book.

Apart from home-candied rose petals, violets, carnation petals, cowslips, rosemary and borage flowers, and the damson cheeses to be found in every store-room in those days, there were triumphs of culinary art not to be had now. Candied oranges were like semi-transparent globes of gold. Before they were candied a tiny hole was made in the place where the stalk had been, and every bit of pulp was scraped out with a saltspoon. The oranges were then steeped in strong salt water pickle for a week, then soaked in fresh water for two or three days, the water being changed daily. The oranges were afterwards boiled in syrup until they cleared. In candlelight these candied oranges looked exquisite.

I remember also the bunches of red and white currants, candied whole. These were very attractive, looking as though made of glass. Rose and carnation petals were preserved by coating them on both sides with well-beaten white of egg. It was done with a little paint brush. Then the petals were spread out on very large dishes and dusted with caster sugar. My great-aunt dried these petals in the sun. When dry they were beautifully crisp, and kept so in layers of tissue paper stored in airtight boxes. Primroses done in this way look pretty, the flowers being used whole. And such syrups! Elder syrup, clove carnation syrup, mint syrup – quince juice, flavoured with mint – and saffron syrup. The cupboard also contained many homely medicines in which I took no interest.

This fascinating book had been preceded by *A Garden of Herbs* and *The Old English Herbals*. So far as I can ascertain, the author had not yet become a practical herb grower in the 1920s when these books were published. Kathleen Hunter, who took over the stock at Cranham Lodge after Eleanour Rohde's death in 1950, could not trace a precise date for the start of the Cranham nursery. The earliest catalogue I saw was dated 1932 and headed *Aromatic Plants, Bee Plants, Herbs and Uncommon Vegetables*.

During the two decades immediately before World War II she produced an amazing collection of books about gardens and gardening, and, in particular, herb gardening. Preliminary research for her comprehensive work, *The Story of the Garden*, must have absorbed much of her time and energy for a number of years. 'She spent most of her life either in her garden or looking up old records in the British Museum', as one friend put it. *The Scented Garden* (1931) contains recipes for pomanders, pot-pourri, perfumed snuffs, tobaccos and candles, toilet waters and oils. Some of the material was used again in *Herbs and Herb Gardening*, which is of greater horticultural value because it is clearly the fruit of experience gained in her own nursery.

It is impossible in a small space to do justice to the material which is packed into *The Story of the Garden* (Medici Society, 1932). It ends with gardens of the Victorian and Edwardian periods; has a chapter on the gardens of America; and takes readers through the splendours of ancient Egypt and Babylon, of Chinese and early Mexican gardens, to Druidic 'Mounts' in Britain – London with its *Llandin* or sacred eminence, the Tor at Glastonbury, St Katherine's Hill at Winchester and the Round Table Mount at Windsor – and so to the formal Tudor and Stuart pleasaunces, with their mounts or mounds derived from the holy hills of Druidic times.

She also includes interesting and little-known material about the patron saints of gardening.

Two were venerated throughout the Middle Ages – Saint Phocas and Saint Fiacre. It is pleasant to think that we can claim Saint Fiacre, for in spite of his French name he was either a Scottish or an Irish prince. Saint Phocas is the earliest patron saint of gardeners. He lived in the third century outside the city of Sinope in Pontus. His life was divided between prayer and work in his little plot.

In a time of persecution two strangers craved his hospitality. He gave them of his best, as he did all poor travellers. That night they told him they were searching for Phocas, a Christian, and had orders to slay him. The saint did not reply, but after his devotions went into the garden and dug a grave. Next morning he told the men that he was Phocas. They were overcome with horror, but he led them out and bade them fulfil their orders. They cut off his head and buried him among the flowers he had tended. Saint Phocas is represented outside the cathedral of Palermo and among mosaics in St Marks, Venice.

Saint Fiacre, who lived in the seventh century, left his home to preach to heathen Gauls near Meaux. He was welcomed by Saint Faro and lived as an anchorite in the forest, where he made a garden and dwelt unharmed by wolves and wild boars. According to one superstition, his garden was enclosed with the help of the Evil One, and this a woman reported to the Bishop. He went himself to visit the saint, and finding the tale untrue he put the curse of blindness on any woman who went near the anchorite's cell – or so it was believed. Even as late as the seventeenth century no woman went inside his chapel in the cathedral of Meaux. It is on record that Anne of Austria refused to enter it.

There is a miniature of Saint Fiacre in a Book of Hours in the Bibliotheque Nationale, showing the saint with a spade in his hand in the garden, and in the background the Cathedral of Meaux. The page has a border of flowers and leaves and butterflies. Beneath is inscribed part of the office for his day:

> *The just man will grow like a lily.*
> *And he will flourish in the sight of God.*

Saint Fiacre is also the patron saint of Paris cab-drivers, who used to hold meetings near a chapel dedicated to him. From that custom sprang the name *fiacres*, as French cabs came to be known

In her later article *The Patron Saints of Gardening*, written for *The Garden* in 1948, Eleanour Rohde added Saint Maurilius to her list. This saint spent a large part of his working life in Britain, so we may reasonably claim his patronage for British gardeners. He is depicted in an Angers tapestry of about 1460 with a halo and a violet-coloured robe, digging with a long-handled spade. The surrounding garden contains fruit trees, gooseberry bushes and flower beds. In another part of the same tapestry he is shown offering a dish of fruits to a British princess, who is seated with her husband at a table spread for a banquet. 'He is still venerated in Angers,' Miss Rohde says, 'although here we seem to have forgotten him.' She does not mention Saint Sylvanus. Some authorities describe him also as a patron saint of gardeners.

Soon after the outbreak of World War II, farms growing medicinal and other herbs became of increasing value to this country as imports were curtailed, so the growers were allotted permits to employ labour for this work. By chance I was recently re-united with an old friend of schooldays, unseen for nearly fifty years, who told me that during her war service on the land she gardened for a time at Cranham Lodge. At the same time I found an article by Eleanour Rohde about her war-time staff. The article makes an interesting companion to my friend's recollections of her.

'I don't engage my war-time staff. They engage me. I only realised this after some months. During the last two years we have asked each other at intervals "Who next will join the circus?".'

Her first amateur gardener was an extremely able woman who had travelled widely and enjoyed roughing it. She slept in one of the garden sheds and lived mostly on raw vegetables. Out of a small car she produced 'every sort of thing, including a bath, a husband, a sack of Welsh flour and goodness knows what else'.

The next employee – a racing motorist of Czech origin – was described by his wife as being able to cope with any task, from bringing a child into the world to laying out the dead. He also played the violin. Another Czech, a mere lad, used to devour wild rose hips and gave his employer a sound scolding for her waste of this most valuable food. To upgrade the staff, socially, came a 'society beauty' with a luxury caravan which became one of the local sights, attracting hordes of visitors but not the gratitude of Miss Rohde.

There followed an airman's wife with a dog as large as herself, and my old schoolfriend, described as 'a schoolteacher who never uttered an unnecessary word, but whose silences expressed whole books'. Lastly there was an old family servant, Ethel, who preferred working in the garden and explained that she now regarded her legitimate duties as a waste of time.

The silent schoolteacher wrote to me saying that when she arrived at Cranham Lodge in March 1941 Miss Rohde was ill and interviewed her in bed.

The whole place was at its lowest ebb. There was no working gardener so for the time I weeded jungles, dug up and packed plants and made myself generally useful. An extra acre of ground had been rented about half a mile away from the Lodge. It had heavy clay soil. We also cultivated the big garden of an untenanted house, a place called Hillbrow. It had sandy soil and some beautiful trees, which gave welcome shade. We had glorious weather in those war years.

I saw rather more of Miss Rohde than my fellow gardeners did, because I came and went to her house in the mornings, collecting orders and then cycling to one or other of the gardens to dig up plants, I have kept in touch with the secretary, but even she cannot add much to our scanty knowledge of our employer. At this time of her life she seemed to be the breadwinner for her family. Her old mother was still alive and a fairly large house had to be kept going. There was an elderly cousin, a charming graduate who helped with the chores. The maid Ethel could be pleasant, but took violent dislikes to people and woe betide those in her black books. Luckily she approved of me. Probably Miss Rohde was forced to be 'on the make', and to us she appeared a little stingy. I admired her excellent brain and powers of writing, but thought her rather weird and eccentric.

Kathleen Hunter, who took over the herb farm business and shifted it to Cornwall, sent me a rather different memoir. 'Eleanour Rohde had a charming presence, gentle and kind and rather "mystic". In other people it could have been termed vague, but somehow not in her. She was a very strict vegetarian, also a British Israelite. She was ill when I knew her, and obliged to give up on health grounds. I never worked at Cranham Lodge, but took the plants straight down to Cornwall.'

Miss Hunter's partner, a Scotsman, said he found Miss Rohde difficult at times – 'prickly' was the word he used of her. As she was ailing when my schoolfriend joined her staff in 1941, she had good reason to be easily upset. She certainly had friends of high repute in the world of horticulture, including Vita Sackville-West and Gertrude Jekyll, and when she died her loss was described by one of them as 'irreparable'.

The next-door neighbour, who gave the author help with letters and proof-reading during her last illness, sent me the following tribute:

She was a very remote person and a dignified one, but in spite of that

70

remoteness she had friends all over the world. Some had been made during a six-month world tour before the war, when she lectured in many countries including the United States. She gave a number of broadcast talks for the B.B.C. Her last, a contribution to the Schools Programme, was actually recorded in her sick-room.

Eleanour Sinclair Rohde died in a Reigate Nursing Home on 23rd June 1950 after a long illness, just before her sixty-ninth birthday.

Her published works number nearly a score, without counting those books in which she collaborated with other authors. *Oxford College Gardens* (1932) describes the gardens as she saw them, but also contains much historical matter. She re-peoples the walks with various notable inhabitants of earlier times. This was followed in 1934 by *Gardens of Delight* and *Shakespeare's Wild Flowers*, both full of interesting little historical asides. In the horticultural sphere she contributed several articles to *The Encyclopedia of Gardening*, and during World War II she issued some very practical books: *Vegetable Cultivation and Cookery*, *The War-time Vegetable Garden* and *Culinary and Salad Herbs*. With that fine naturalist, Eric Parker, she collaborated in *The Gardener's Week-end Book*. Her last work, reprinted after her death, was called *Uncommon Vegetables and Fruits, How to Grow and How to Cook*. On the death in June 1950 of this ex-President of the Society of Women Journalists, *The Times* printed an obituary, one-third of a column in length, in its issue for 24th June.

5

Pioneers of Herb Farming

Dorothy Hewer and Margaret Brownlow

Dorothy Hewer, who in 1926 founded the Herb Farm at Seal near Sevenoaks in Kent, gained much of her knowledge and enthusiasm from her friend Mrs Grieve, author of *A Modern Herbal*. A Londoner, educated at The North London Collegiate School, she went on to take a B.Sc. in Pure Science at Bedford College for Women, University of London. Her training as a botanist had no element of horticulture, and I cannot find any reference to early interest in gardening. To start with she took up teaching – work which she enjoyed – and only the slow, inexorable onset of deafness caused her to re-shape her career after some years in the classroom.

A big, energetic woman with a liking for country life and the freedom of being out of doors, her first idea was to make a living by cultivating and selling herb plants and products derived from herbs. Mrs Grieve gave invaluable support to this project, both expert advice and practical help with the purchase of initial stock. By the time Dorothy Hewer had bought nearly two acres of land and paid for the construction of a pleasant little white-gabled house, she found herself short of the capital required to develop a successful business.

This problem was neatly solved. With her experience of teaching, which had been an agreeable episode, she now decided to take a small group of resident pupils to study practical herb growing. The individual instruction would not tax her hearing, and the girls employed for much of the day at the routine work on the farm could supply a good proportion of the labour required for planting, harvesting and drying produce. Her scheme soon proved a success. Some of the original entrants, students who pulled their weight and stayed the full course, were in the end given a refund of tuition fees, paying only for their keep. By that time the Herb Farm had become a going concern.

Miss Hewer was a forthright personality; outspoken, sometimes blunt to the point of harshness, but essentially kind. Although students occasionally trembled under her criticism, they all felt that she had their welfare at heart. But they were made to work to the utmost limit of their capabilities. On certain days, particularly in hot weather, angry epithets such as 'slave driver' would be muttered. In later years, as often happens, the 'slaves' were able to appreciate their disciplined training. Several ex-students left to start their own herb farms, among them Madge Hooper, who is still growing and selling herb plants and herbal products at Stoke Lacy in Herefordshire, and Barbara Keen of Valeswood, Little Ness, Shropshire.

Probably Margaret Brownlow's fellow students would have considered this small, delicate girl as the least likely to succeed Dorothy Hewer as owner of the Herb Farm; but if this was the case, they were due for a surprise. Margaret, born in 1916, had been brought up in a well-to-do professional household, the only girl in the family and regarded as delicate from birth. The Brownlows occupied a handsome house in three acres of Kentish soil. They were efficiently waited upon by a staff of servants. Apart from tending her childish garden plot, Margaret had not engaged in any rough work. I do not know if, like Gertrude Jekyll, she considered herself 'armigerous' but on one occasion when I suggested slyly that she was born to be waited on, she sighed, smiled ruefully, and said, 'Well, yes, I suppose I do feel that way.'

She did well at school, matriculating early, and was earmarked by her teachers for an academic training with a good degree at the end of it. Her headmistress thought of horticulture as a job for physically powerful dunderheads, and was distressed to hear that this clever and fragile pupil contemplated it. But Margaret, for all her delicate air, had a kind of mole-like persistence which won her several battles, and in particular those against physical disability and ill-health in later years. First came her love of gardening and interest in plants. She saw no reason why she should not pursue these subjects of her own choice and quietly reiterated her determination to do so. Opposition was in the end vanquished.

Once across the first hurdle, she came up against another.

73

Swanley College for Women (now closed) was in 1933 at the height of its fame under Dr Kate Barratt. Being of excellent repute and situated in the same county, it must have seemed the ideal training school for Margaret Brownlow. Accompanied by her mother, the seventeen-year-old girl paid a preliminary visit to the college. It was not a success. Mrs Brownlow and her daughter, both reserved by nature and possessed of punctilious manners, found the physique and boisterous ways of Dr Barratt's students, and their crowded timetable, more than a little daunting. This was not the right environment for Margaret, who came away feeling dejected.

A friend then suggested the Herb Farm at Seal as likely to provide satisfactory training in a smaller, less alarming school. Dorothy Hewer had by now run her farm successfully for seven years, so the place had a well-established look. Seeing a group of happy, neatly dressed girls knee-deep in lavender, Mrs Brownlow assumed that the work would be pleasantly undemanding and just the thing for her daughter. So Margaret was immediately enrolled.

It did not take her long to discover that the old-world charm of herb-growing was based upon very strenuous work, in which no member of her small student group ever eluded the sharp eyes of its Director. Life in the hurly-burly of crowded Swanley College might in practice have given an inconspicuous student more opportunity for drawing breath than was allowed by Miss Hewer at the Herb Farm. But it was too late to turn back.

There is no doubt that even stronger pupils found the work exhausting. Some duties, such as harvesting sage throughout long, hot summer days, at the rate of twenty to thirty pounds per hour required by Miss Hewer, taxed many of them to the limit of their powers. In Margaret's own words, it induced a fierce – if transient – dislike of herb growing. But she was intelligent enough to appreciate the quality of her tutor, and somehow managed to keep up with both manual and academic work. Evenings of study when physically exhausted took every ounce of her 'stickability'.

Dorothy Hewer belonged to a medical family, which may have accounted for her great interest in medicinal herbs. In her booklet *Practical Herb Growing* (1941) she suggests that the poisonous herbs: 'Aconite, Belladonna, Henbane, Digitalis (Foxglove), Colchicum and Stramonium (Thornapple)' were best left for cultivation by big drug farms, and not introduced into smaller enterprises. The other medicinal plants, described as non-poisonous, which she did consider worth her while to cultivate were

74

'Chamomile, Hemlock, Horehound, Hyssop, Liquorice, Opium Poppy, Peppermint, Scullcap, Valerian, Wormwood and Tansy' – although many herbalists would now delete hemlock and opium poppy, which Miss Hewer describes as 'poisonous only if taken in excessive quantities'.

On the subject of fragrant and essential-oil plants she has this to say:

> Essential oils from plants grown here are usually of great excellence and command higher prices than continental oils. This is particularly the case with Lavender and Peppermint. Both these plants have for several years paid well for cultivation. It must however be remembered that it is no use growing less than half an acre of a plant which is to be distilled, and that it is very necessary to be within a few hours of a distillery in terms of lorry transport. Distillation is a highly skilled proceeding involving expensive stills, and it is not possible for a small grower to attempt it. Both Lavender and Peppermint are grown for drying as well as distilling. Rather different treatment is then neccessary in cultivation. Another plant successfully grown here to produce commercial oil is Clary Sage.

Margaret Brownlow survived the rigorous training and became a credit to her tutor. In 1934 she came first in Class I of the Junior Examination of the Royal Horticultural Society and was awarded the silver medal. The following year she passed the Society's Senior General Examination. Now pressure was again put on her to take a university degree course, and this time she agreed. A place was offered to her at Reading, where she took a B.Sc. in Horticulture in 1938. She also passed the preliminary examination for the National Diploma in Horticulture of the R.H.S.

The final could be taken only after some years of practical experience, so Margaret returned to work at Seal, taking her N.D.H. in 1943. The compulsory practical tests for both these qualifications afflicted her with nervous terror bordering on prostration. Her description of efforts made to control the violent trembling of her fingers while attempting to make a graft on some delicate stem under the critical eye of an examiner, suggested to me that many an honour has been given for lesser feats of courage and will-power.

After a short spell at the Waterperry Horticultural School near Oxford, she again returned to the Herb Farm, on this occasion as assistant to her former Principal. Soon World War II came to change most people's lives – even for those engaged in so pacific a business as herb growing; cessation of imports led to a big demand for home-produced medicinal and culinary herbs. Some used in medicine, such as aconite, colchicum and liquorice, suddenly became commercially important. The root of valerian (*Valeriana officinalis*) was in great demand. This is not the red or pink flowered centranthus (spurred valerian) commonly seen on old walls and in cottage gardens. It is a taller, stiffer and rather less attractive plant, whose stems bear corymbs of pale, flesh-coloured flowers.

The root, so powerfully attractive to cats, is repulsive to human beings and becomes even more foul smelling when dried. Old country people expressed their repugnance by naming the plant 'phu'. It was at one time grown to considerable extent in Derbyshire, where it had the status of a village industry. Although it has valuable tonic properties, it is apt to put patients off their meals, for however quickly it is swallowed the flavour of very bad drains rises up afterwards.

As well as working on the cultivation of these and many other herbs, Margaret Brownlow was given time off occasionally to gather useful plants in the wild, to satisfy the national demand. Lord Sackville gave her permission to reap the large quantity of belladonna which grew profusely in Knole Park, where she spent happy hours amid the beeches and bracken of Vita Sackville-West's beloved home.

Dorothy Hewer grasped the opportunity to fill the gap caused by dwindling imports of culinary herbs. The Herb Farm flourished, as did the Herb Farm shop which she organised in conjunction with Maud White in North Audley Street, London. Mrs White's claim to fame, as Barbara Keen of the Valeswood Herb Farm has recorded, lies in her revival of that charmingly fragrant conceit, the pomander. She also made quantities of pot-pourri, for which Dorothy Hewer provided the flowers and other herbal ingredients. The Herb Farm at Seal next obtained an outlet for its now considerable production in the business of W. H. Allder at Linslade.

Soon after the end of World War II Dorothy Hewer, the big, strong woman, was found to be suffering from incurable illness. She grew increasingly feeble and died, in her late fifties, in 1948. In this sad and difficult period Margaret Brownlow carried out the duties of secretary and virtually managed the Herb Farm, although she 'lived out' and a nurse took charge of the invalid. The combined responsibilities of management and outdoor work, together with preparation of material for her first book, brought about a breakdown in her own health, and she was forced to rest for some months.

Her comprehensive work, giving the history, cultivation and uses of all kinds of herbs, has twenty-eight colour plates of her own design. For the sake of economy, most of these were reproduced by a tricky process of superimposed stencils (one for each colour) run off on a Gestetner duplicating machine in use at that time. The story of how this was done is told in her second book, *The Delights of Herb Growing*, issued by the Herb Farm in 1965. The first edition of the herbal, *Herbs and the Fragrant Garden*, with its do-it-yourself illustrations, is now a collector's piece. It was published in 1957 by the Herb Farm. In 1963 the well-known firm of Darton, Longman and Todd brought out a new edition with Margaret's drawings reproduced by lithographic printing, and a revised impression of this book came out in 1978.

From an early age Margaret delighted in drawing and painting, encouraged by the art mistress at school. Later on, in her student years, she practised the more austere art of botanical and biological diagrams. All this was good discipline, and useful when she began to delineate the subtle differences between the many varieties of small herb plants for her book. The original issue was a brave venture on the part of the Herb Farm, which had become a Limited Company in 1935 with Margaret as a director from 1945. Her brother and another member of the family joined as co-directors in 1958. Mr W. E. Denham, described as 'a mainstay of the Herb Farm', directed its finances for thirty years.

Margaret Brownlow possessed a very sensitive nose and had acquired a discriminating knowledge of the scents produced by herb plants. These are discussed in some detail in *Herbs and the Fragrant Garden*.

In general, herbs grown on warm slopes, where the soil is light sandy to medium loam, have the best essential oil content, and therefore the strongest flavour or aroma. Our English climate produces culinary herbs of excellent flavour, and high quality Oil of Lavender as well. The constituents making up the scents and flavours of plants are a complicated blend; while the intensity of our summers at their best favours the finest constituents, the fierce heat of more southerly climes seems to cause formation of the more pungent compounds of the turpentine, camphoraceous and other groups, rather than the delicate fruity and flower scents. Most scented leaves have some of the basic compounds, such as those of the turpentine groups, giving the pleasing scent to pine needles; the eucalyptol or camphoraceous compounds, which give a distinctive 'tang' with other combinations, to Wormwood, Tansy, Sage amongst others; menthol, a characteristic of Mints, as thymol is of Thymes; and sulphur-containing compounds which give the distinctive taste to Garlic, Onion and various *umbelliferae*.

The wonderful range of leaf-aromas is obtained when these constituents are blended with the flower and fruit scents. For instance, a blend of eucalyptol, thymol and lemon scent gives Lemon Thyme, while there is a merging of lemon and rose in Lemon Verbena, and in Citrus Mint there is the lemon and menthol combination, with other ingredients.

Under violent summer heat the tendency appears to be for the delicious flower or fruit-scented constituents to diminish, leaving the pungent ingredients to have a dominating effect. Even in our occasional heat-waves we see something of the same result; some Mints, such as *Mentha cordifolia*, lose the ethereal freshness of scent and flavour and an almost acetylene scent predominates until damper weather comes. This Mint, on the other hand, is excellent in spring and autumn. It seems that if our English-raised Lemon Thymes are sent to be grown in – for instance – Spain they lose their lemon qualities and smell like common Thyme.

During the year 1964 I was engaged by the American Museum at Claverton near Bath to produce a herb exhibit and help with the making of a new herb garden, for which Miss Brownlow supplied the plants. In the little herb shop we sold sweet-bags, pomanders and the like, and as it was called an 'American Colonial' herb display, we obtained samples from the United States. When sweet-bags arrived from across the Atlantic, I was amazed by their powerful scent. Two small bags, each measuring an inch and a half square, filled my bedroom so powerfully with their aroma that I had to remove them at night. Yet I kept a pile of larger, home-made ones in my chest-of-drawers without noticing any scent until the drawer was opened.

At Claverton we feared that customers would despise the milder English scent, supposing that it would evaporate in a short time, but what actually happened was the reverse. My American bags soon ceased to give off any aroma, while the home-grown herbs exuded steadily without appreciable falling-off for over a year. No doubt the hotter climates do, as Miss Brownlow said, produce the more pungent scents in abundance, but perhaps they are less persistent than the delicate fruit and flower fragrances and flavours which develop better in our more temperate zone. I should very much like to experiment with woodruff from America, or melilot. That new-mown hay scent which is released as those plants are dried (the effect of coumarin contained in their foliage), is one of the most pleasing and evocative of all, and very lasting in spite of its delicacy, when English-grown plants are stored.

Most of the culinary and fragrant herbs now flourishing in transatlantic herb gardens were taken from Europe by early settlers; but one essential difference between European and American plantings is the inclusion, across the Atlantic, of 'dye herbs', as they are known in the States. When Margaret Brownlow was asked for plants of this description to furnish the Claverton project, she confessed that the term was new to her.

In America such species as woad, indigofera, pokeroot, and madder, which produce dyestuff but are not edible (except for young shoots of the pokeroot), were commonly grown alongside our familiar culinary and fragrant herb plants and used for dyeing the household hand-spun handwoven fabrics. In Europe dyeing was, apart from tweed-weaving in Celtic corners of the British Isles, a trade carried out by commercial growers. It is said that the Celtic word *Glas*, meaning blue-grey, in the place-name Glastonbury, is derived from the glaucous hue of the woad which used to be grown in quantity around the small Somerset town.

There are other plants which provide edible matter as well as fragrances and dyestuffs, and the classification of these for an indicator board beside the Claverton herb garden kept me occupied for weeks. Certain versatile subjects, such as tansy, turned out to have been used, at different times, for each of the four purposes – medicinal, culinary, fragrant and dyestuff. Today the powerful taste is too strong for most palates, and tansy is little used in medicine. Some handweavers still obtain good, fast bronzes and greenish yellows from the flowering tops, and the pungent foliage is dried and used as a moth-deterrent.

In all these excursions into the field of herb lore Margaret gave generously of her thirty years' experience to boost my novitiate, and many letters exploring points of detail passed between Bath and Seal. In winter-time, when specimens were unobtainable, her descriptions of scents were evocative and helpful as a means of identification. 'It smells like a mixture of caraway and floor-polish; rather like lemon and old leather suitcases; coconut and new-mown hay; bananas and coffee . . .' are some of the pointers I received from her. But in all our talk of scents, we could not remember one which had inspired fear in us as children, although the solid, sensible Gertrude Jekyll had experienced this more than once.

Writing in *Children and Gardens* of her own young days, when she was often in a garden by herself, Gertrude says:

> Among all the delicious flower smells there was, now and then, a nearly nasty one. There was one smell I always thought odious – that of the common Barberry. The smell is not really bad, but of a faint, sickly kind. Yet I remember years when it was to me so odious that it inspired me with a sort of fear; when I had forgotten that the Barberries were near and walked into the smell without expecting it, I used to run away as hard as I could in a kind of terror.
>
> Since I grew up I have only once met with a smell of a growing thing that gave me the same sort of feeling of intense repulsion. It is a spongy weed looking like pale green coral that grows in the mud in shallow water. I used to see it in a backwater of the Thames. The smell to me was horrible, and yet, curiously enough it was not a really nasty smell; it was certainly aromatic, very much like the smell of Myrrh. But though I was twenty-four I felt again that sense of fear that I remembered having in childish days about the Barberry.

When I was a girl most people around us, at the mention of 'herb' thought of those plants which were cultivated for their fragrance and essential oils. This may have been largely due to the fact that our home in Surrey was not far from Mitcham, which in years before Cobbett's 'wen' of London engulfed it, was a rural area famous for its lavender fields. Bottles of 'Mitcham Lavender Water' were still sold in chemists' shops in the first decades of this century.

At the Herb Farm, attention was always paid to the cultivation of the best lavender for sale in boxes and sweet-bags. Also the making of pot-pourri had been carried on for some forty years, interrupted only by the increased production of essential culinary and medicinal herbs in time of war. A spicy eighteenth-century recipe, a lemon-scented one called 'Lady Anne' and the 'Rose' and 'Bouquet' kinds were blended and sold. Although her assistant

Florence Craggs did much of the work in this field, Margaret Brownlow found it one of the most congenial sections of the production at Seal.

Two questions most people wish to ask about any form of commercial horticulture are 'Does it pay?' and, if the answer is yes, 'How profitable is it?' These are awkward queries to put and to answer. Very few owners of small businesses care to be cross-examined on the subject of finance, and fewer still would agree to having figures published in a book. To social historians of the future, balance sheets and wages bills would be of the greatest interest, but these pages are not the place for such disclosures. All that has emerged in regard to the work at Seal is that Dorothy Hewer made ends meet by taking pupils, and Margaret Brownlow added to the receipts of the Herb Farm by writing articles and books, by designing herb gardens for clients, and by her lectures on herbs and herb-growing.

Since the war a little extra land had been added to Dorothy Hewer's original farm, making the total area just over two acres. The post-war policy of growing more herb plants for sale to the public led to the erection of two large new greenhouses, of the Dutch-light type with metal frames and all-glass sides. Given this shelter, it became easier to find women willing to work full-time or part-time in all weathers. At the time of my last visit, in 1965, two full-time helpers, both dedicated gardeners, were capable of doing all the work involved, from secretarial duties to making pot-pourri, and during their many years of service to the Herb Farm had stood in several times for Miss Brownlow in her periods of ill-health. Mrs Doreen Dennis and Mrs Florence Craggs were with her to the end, and invaluable.

Throughout her life Margaret Brownlow had to face bouts of serious illness. One of them kept her flat on her back for ten months. Later on she was told that she would go completely blind unless both eyes were operated upon. When the bandages were at last removed, she recorded her bliss at the sight of flowers in the hospital ward. An accomplished herb-grower, she had earned the title of 'expert', yet she was not in the least 'high-hat'. Always she retained sympathy with people who brought queries to her, from the enthusiast with a tiny garden plot, the child with a few pots on the window ledge and the Londoner whose ground was overrun with cats, to an amateur wishful to learn all about herbs in twenty minutes and a little old lady wanting recipes for pot-pourri.

A quiet corner of the Chelsea Flower Show – where Margaret and her steady helpers designed each summer for over ten years some new arrangement of herb plants to please the visiting public, has been described as 'For Ever Herb Farm'. Those of us who enjoyed its old-world charm still heave a sigh of regret at its passing. Whether by accident or design, this site's near neighbour was the First-Aid tent of the St John's Ambulance Brigade. Every year Margaret Brownlow was befriended by the Commandant and his resourceful men, looked upon, she said, as 'half a casualty' owing to her lameness.

When I last visited her stand, she drew me into the haven of this tent, where we were given chairs, cups of tea, and the opportunity for a quiet talk. An odd little memory to keep fresh in the mind for many years; but somehow typical of Margaret. She required more care and attention than most people, and with her gentle manner and appealingly fragile appearance always found friends to provide for her needs. She died suddenly on February 17th 1968 in her fifty-second year, after writing me a letter saying how much she looked forward to seeing the first spring flowers.

6

Flower Gardeners (National Trust Gardens)

V. Sackville-West, Mairi Sawyer and Phyllis Reiss

The Hon. Victoria Mary Sackville-West, known as 'Vita', was born in 1892, the only child of the third Lord Sackville, and brought up at the great house of Knole in Kent. A succession of governesses provided most of her orthodox education, so she had little contact with children of her own age and class to supplement book-learning with human experience and friendly contemporary criticism. She grew up in a state of bitter disappointment at not having been born a boy and thus able to inherit the noble house, home of her family since 1586, in which her whole being was so deeply rooted. No doubt her solitary condition drove this canker inward.

Somehow she managed to combine in her young life strict formality indoors with frequent escapes to wildly unconventional activities outside, where her playmates were chiefly dogs (some trained to rabbit-coursing in the park) and other pets. We hear nothing of gardening at this stage. At the time of the Boer War a band of children from the village was imported for employment as camp followers in military games. According to Vita's own references to her youth, some of these children were treated with brutal disdain. She made a great fetish of being tough and hardy, as boyish as possible, always grubby and unkempt, and shed tears of rage because her khaki drill suit had to be made with a skirt when she demanded trousers.

Her adolescence was even more painful than most. Vita felt

herself to be a disappointment to her parents – her mother in particular – and took to writing ambitious historical novels, hidden away in one of the attics at Knole, to avoid playing the dutiful daughter among her mother's guests.

In the closing pages of her book *Knole and the Sackvilles* (Benn, 1922) she describes some gentler interludes with her grandfather, a queer and silent old man.

He knew nothing whatever about the works of art in the house. He spent hours gazing at the flowers, followed about the garden by two demoiselle cranes. He turned his back on all visitors, but sized them up after they had gone in one shrewd and sarcastic phrase. He and I, who so often shared the house alone between us, were companions in a shy and undemonstrative way.

He would put after dinner a plate of fruit for my breakfast into a drawer of his writing table labelled with my name, and this he never once failed to do. There might have been thirty people to dinner in the Great Hall, who watched, no doubt with great surprise the old man who had been so rude to his neighbours at dinner going unconcernedly round with a plate picking out the reddest cherries, the bluest grapes and the ripest peach.

I used to go down to his sitting-room in the evening to play draughts with him – and never knew whether I played to please him, or he played to please me – and sometimes, very rarely, he told me stories of when he was a small boy, and played with the rocking-horse and of the journeys by coach with his father and mother from Buckhurst to Knole or from Knole to London; and of their taking the silver with them under the seat; and of their having outriders with pistols; and of his father and mother never addressing each other, in their children's presence, as anything but 'my Lord' and 'my lady'.

I clasped my knees and stared at him when he told me these stories of an age which already seemed so remote, and his pale blue eyes gazed away into the past, and suddenly his shyness would return to him and the clock in the corner would begin to wheeze in preparation for striking the hour, and he would say that it was time for me to go to bed. Although our understanding of one another was so excellent, our rare conversations remained always on similar fantastic subjects, nor ever approached the intimate or the personal. Then he fell ill and died when he was over eighty, and became a name like the others, and his portrait took its place among the rest, with a label recording the dates of his birth and death.

Vita's escapist historical novels may have justified her later description 'leaden stuff, pretentious, pedantic, and quite uninteresting', but they were preliminaries to a highly successful career as a writer. In her book *Pepita* (1937), a vivid biography of her Spanish grandmother, she was able to write with sympathy about her own mother, although in girlhood she had been afraid of her. She felt happier in the society of her father, a quiet conscientious country gentleman, who shared her distaste for week-end parties.

His daughter afterwards pictured herself in those years with savage frankness. 'I think between the ages of thirteen and nineteen I must have been quite dreadful. I was plain, priggish, studious (oh very!), totally uninspired, unmanageable and lankily tall. Seeing that I was unpopular – and small wonder, for a saturnine prig – I wouldn't court popularity. I minded, rather, and used to cry when I went to bed after coming home from a party, but I made myself defiant about it.'

Had she been born into a less exalted family, or at a later date, Vita might have gone to Oxford or Cambridge, free to develop her mind and broaden her experience of the world, and possibly to sow her wild oats earlier rather than later. Her enduring chagrin at not being a boy encompassed, in addition to the ban on inheriting Knole, regret that she had not been given a boy's education, with training in Greek and Latin prior to entering a university. Unhappily, as a daughter of the Sackvilles in the early years of this century, she was required to shine socially rather than intellectually.

What might she have become, given a masculine education? After ten years at Eton and Balliol, would she have composed her long poem *The Land*, which won the Hawthornden Prize in 1927? Given the freedom of a young man, could her creative imagination have found outlet in such books as *The Edwardians*, *All Passion Spent*, or *Family History*? Above all, would she have developed a splendid garden such as that at Sissinghurst , for which she is now so famous? To the inheritor of Knole, the purchase of a substitute castle would never have occurred. For us there is cause for gratitude to the fate which made her a female.

For her, the parting from Knole gave such intense pain that for over thirty years, from 1928 to 1960, she refused to enter it. After the war, in 1947, that great house was perforce handed over for safe-keeping to the National Trust, when the Sackvilles could no longer maintain it. Vita wrote of this decision with anguish, considering it to be a betrayal of all the tradition of her ancestors and the home she loved with abiding passion. Three years earlier, in February 1944 Knole, which lay in the path of Nazi bombers in their last attempt to beat Britain into submission, suffered from local bomb-blast. The damage was not severe, chiefly consisting of shattered windows in house and chapel, but when the news reached her she was deeply shocked. 'I always persuade myself that I have finally torn Knole out of my heart, and then the moment anything touches it, every nerve is alive again.'

Those words are contained in corrrespondence with her lifelong companion and confidant, her husband Harold Nicolson, with whom she exchanged daily letters from the time of their engagement in 1911 until her death in 1962. Her coming out in 1910 she described as a distasteful and unsuccessful process, but the death of Edward VII saved her many festivities. It was just then that she met Harold Nicolson, son of Sir Arthur Nicolson, later Lord Carnock. 'He made everything seem fun, with his energy, vitality and buoyancy; but we didn't become particular friends,' she wrote. 'I think he looked upon me as more of a child than I really was.'

We are not given details of developments during the next twelve months, but by 1911 there was a curiously secret engagement. Not until 1913 were they married – in the chapel at Knole, of course. At twenty-one Vita was still very young, very much the caged bird of her conventional ladylike upbringing, so at first the marriage worked perfectly. 'For sheer joy of companionship, I think the years that followed were unparalleled or at least unsurpassed. I was really gentle, self-sacrificing; I was too good, if anything. We were a sort of by-word for happiness and union. Harold was like a sunny harbour to me.'

They made their first home in Constantinople, where Harold, a promising young diplomat, had a post in the British Embassy. In the summer of 1914 they returned to London, Harold to the Foreign Office. Two days after declaration of war with Germany on that grim fourth of August their first son, Ben, was born. Those winters of World War I were spent in the capital, the summers at a cottage called Long Barn which they bought at Sevenoaks in Kent, not far from the great house of Knole. Vita wrote of this time: 'There was never a cloud, never a squabble. I knew that if Harold died I should die too. It all made life very simple. In the winter of 1917 Nigel was born.'

As she watched the little boys grow, she began to write seriously. Her very first printed book, a drama on the life and death of Chatterton, had been privately produced before her marriage; but the first real publication, *Poems of West and East*, was issued by John Lane in 1917 and her first novel, *Heritage*, by Collins in 1919. *The Land* (1926), which won her the Hawthornden Prize in 1927, was written partly at Long Barn and partly in Tehran, where Harold went as Counsellor in 1925. Vita did not accompany him; her visits in Persia were limited to two short holidays; but she derived much inspiration for her gardens by observing Persian ways with plants.

In 1927 Harold Nicolson was moved to the British Embassy in Berlin. Still Vita did not accompany her husband. Her son has said of these years, 'Great as was their distress at being separated for long periods, even greater was her horror of exile and of the social role which she would be expected to play. She remained at Long Barn, writing, writing, writing. I can see her now at her sitting-room table, writing *The Land*, looking up over her spectacles as we burst in, patient with our interruption, but closing the blotter over the manuscript.'

Already his parents were going their own ways; but, although this marriage defied all accepted rules of behaviour, it lasted without the slightest lessening of deep affection until the end of their lives. In a recently published book, *Portrait of a Marriage*, Nigel has brought to light his mother's diary of her love affairs in early married life with women, in particular Violet Trefusis. Violet tried desperately to alienate Vita from Harold, but although the two young women eloped for a short time together, Harold by superhuman patience and understanding won his wife back in the end.

This poignant story could not be released until Harold Nicolson and Violet Trefusis were dead. Some friends of both families thought it had better be suppressed forever. As a picture of the wonderful endurance of love, and a tribute to Nigel's father, it is inspiring, whereas any discredit – if so it be regarded – to his mother has perhaps been taken too seriously by some critics.

Given Vita's wild, exuberant love of adventure, her early frustrations, her desire to belong to the opposite sex, it is hardly surprising that the temptation to assume a masculine role under the mesmeric influence of Violet proved overwhelming. Dressed as a wounded subaltern (known as 'Julian') she walked down Piccadilly at night, accosted by prostitutes, and even visited her old home,

Knole, without having her identity suspected. Of course she must have revelled in all this, watched and praised by the jealously adoring Violet.

When her escapades leaked out, there were some who thought all she needed was a strong, masterful husband who would drag her home and force matrimonial obligations upon her. Harold Nicolson was not that sort of man, and deep down he must have felt that his high-mettled partner could not be tamed by such means. If at times he recalled the old saying 'A woman, a dog and a walnut tree, the more you beat them the better they be', he made no attempt to put that precept into practice.

In later years he seems to have been afraid that he might have failed Vita by too ready compliance with her vagaries. In 1941 he wrote to her: 'I wonder whether you would have been happier if married to a more determined and less sensitive man. On the one hand you would have hated any sense of control or management, and other men might not have understood your desire for independence. I have always respected that, and you have often mistaken it for aloofness on my part. What bothers me is whether I have given way too much to your eccentricities. . . .'

Her reply sounds mildly surprised. 'I don't quite see what you mean by my eccentricity. I can't see that I am eccentric in the least, unless liking to live here [Sissinghurst] is eccentric, but lots of people have been recluses by nature, and not being in sympathy with the modern world, one's natural avoidance deepens. It is a form of escapism. You have always been more sweet to me than I can describe, and I *quite* certainly don't wish that I had married anybody else!'

Of her literary work her son wrote: 'She believed that she had had to struggle for recognition more than a man. When a reviewer referred to her as an "authoress" or a "poetess" she would raise her fists in the air with rage that was not diminished by our amusement. "If I'm anything," she expostulated, "I'm an *author*, a *poet*. Nobody ever talks about a "gardeness". Why on earth, then, a "poetess"?' Her strong independence came out in a number of ways: one being a dislike of the formalities of marriage, as if from that moment a woman 'belonged' to a man. She never introduced Harold as 'my husband', nor he her as 'my wife'. Once she quoted to Violet Trefusis the magnificent retort of the first Queen Elizabeth to her ministers: 'Had I been crested not cloven, my Lords, you had not treated me thus.'

After two years in Berlin, Harold Nicolson resigned his post. He seemed certain to rise to the top of his profession, but long years of separation from his wife were too high a price to pay. Although she could not face the social trivialities of a diplomatic life, Vita, too, hated the partings. After seeing Harold off to Berlin in 1929, she wrote to him of feeling 'horribly desolate and sad'. She was also depressed by trouble with her mother, now widowed, who turned against her daughter and made life miserable.

In 1930, re-united with her husband, who had accepted an offer from Lord Beaverbrook to join the London *Evening Standard*, Vita achieved popular success with her novel *The Edwardians*, which sold 20,000 copies in the first four weeks. But soon the Nicolsons' happiness was clouded by the news that builders were to develop the land surrounding their country home, Long Barn. To be hemmed in by rows of houses would destroy their peace, so they decided to hunt for new premises.

It was Vita who found Sissinghurst, a ruined sixteenth-century castle set in a wilderness of neglected land. She saw its possibilities at once. Already something of a gardener, for she had made some excellent plantings at Long Barn, she wanted the place not only for its romantic atmosphere – substitute for Knole, possibly – and for the peace and seclusion as a refuge for writing in, but from the start had visions of creating a fine garden there.

In after years she wrote of this time:

The site of Sissinghurst was not a new one. It went back to Henry the Eighth. This was an advantage in many ways. Some high Tudor walls of pink brick remained as the anatomy of the garden-to-be, and stretches of much older moat provided a black mirror of quiet water in the distance. The soil had been cultivated for at least four hundred years, and it was not bad soil to start with, being in the main what is geologically called Tunbridge Wells Sand. It consisted of a top spit of decently friable loam with a clay bottom.

The place when I first saw it on a spring day in 1930 caught instantly at my heart and imagination. I fell in love; love at first sight. I saw what might be made of it. It was Sleeping Beauty's Castle: but a castle running away into sordidness and squalor; a garden crying out for rescue. It was easy to see, even then, what a struggle we should have to redeem it.

Harold Nicolson and Ben went down from London to see the

'find', being met by Vita, Nigel and various dogs. In his diary
Harold wrote, 'We get a view of the tower as we approach. We go
round carefully in the mud. I am cold and calm but I like it.' After
surveying the derelict buildings, the family walked by the fields to
the brook and round by the woods. They came suddenly upon the
nut-walk, and from that moment decided to buy. It was April. On
6th May the Land Agent telephoned the Nicolsons after dinner.
Harold wrote: 'Vita answers the telephone. "Quite – yes, of
course." She puts down the receiver, and says, "It is ours." We
embrace warmly.'

Little did they know that at this moment was conceived one of
the loveliest gardens in England, a creation to make the name of
Sissinghurst famous all over the world, and one which would live
long after they were both dead.

Work perforce began in a singularly undramatic fashion. It took
the new owners over two years to clear the derelict ground of
accumulated rubbish, which they did with the help of an old man
and his son. At the same time builders made the tower safe and
more or less habitable. Vita spent two nights there quite alone in
October 1930, and was then joined by Harold for a week-end camp.
They used truckle beds and water drawn from a well; their only light
came from a couple of candles. By the end of the same year the
small south cottage was fit to live in, and they had dammed up the
stream and made a lake.

Initial planning of the garden, its 'bone structure', fell almost
entirely to Harold. Vita wrote in the *R.H.S. Journal* (November
1953):

> The walls were not all at right-angles to one another; the courtyard was
> not rectangular but coffin-shaped; the tower was not opposite the main
> entrance; the moat-walk, with its supporting wall, ran away on so queer
> a bias that the statue we placed on the bank behind the moat stood
> opposite both to the tower and to the seat at the upper end of the
> moat-walk. All this was disconcerting, and there were also minor
> crookednesses which somehow had to be camouflaged. I do not think
> you would notice them from ground-level now; though if you ascended
> the tower and looked down, you might still give sympathetic thought to
> the worried designer, with his immense sheets of ruled paper and his
> measuring tapes and his indiarubbers, pushing his fingers through his
> rumpled hair, trying to get the puzzle worked out.
>
> I could never have done it myself. Fortunately I had acquired,

through marriage, the ideal collaborator. Harold Nicolson should have been a garden architect. He has natural taste for symmetry, and an ingenuity for forcing focal points or long-distance views where everything seemed against him, a capacity I totally lacked. After weeks of paper struggle he would come home to discover that I had stuck some tree or shrub bang in the middle of his projected path or gateway.

We did, however, agree entirely on what was to be the main principle of the garden: a combination of long axial walks, running north and south, east and west, usually with terminal points such as a statue or an archway or a pair of sentinel poplars, and the more intimate surprise of small geometrical gardens opening off them, rather as the rooms of an enormous house would open off the arterial corridors. There should be the strictest formality of design with the maximum informality in planting. This is what we aimed at, and is, I hope, what we have achieved.

And achieve it they did, in full measure, without faltering.

By August 1934 the main work of constructing and planting their garden had been done. Harold and his younger son, Nigel, took time off for a project worthy of the silly season. They tried to build an island in the lake for use as a bird sanctuary. It was to be called 'Ithaca'. Of this Harold recorded: 'Vita is not at all pleased. She calls it a waste of time. She calls it mud-larking. She says we shall never finish it: she says it will be washed away. . . . We cease, discouraged. The outline of Ithaca straddles the bed of the lake like the Loch Ness Monster with stones in its mouth.'

A few weeks later my mother and I took for the winter an Elizabethan cottage not far from Sissinghurst, at Smallhythe. It belonged to Ellen Terry's daughter Edith Craig and adjoined the last home of the great actress, now a theatrical museum. Ours was called The Priest's House. It was inconvenient and beautiful. Water came from a garden well, and if we desired a bath it meant walking down through the orchard to wallow in a huge tub installed in the Terry farmhouse by Ellen's last husband, an American named Carew.

Edy Craig, ever kind and generous to young people, invited me to a lecture on English gardens since Roman times, delivered in Tenterden by Vita Sackville-West. It was a marvellous experience. Vita, shy yet perfectly self-possessed, explained that she would have to read her lecture because otherwise she would probably forget it. We clapped. Then came a pause, an exclamation of dismay, whispered words to the organiser. Something essential had been mislaid.

The promoters rushed hither and thither, the audience rustled and gaped, the temperature boiled over, and only the lecturer remained cool and unperturbed. She seemed immune from mundane pother, inhabiting a world of pure thought and imagination whose serenity the malice of material objects had no power to disrupt. I was entranced by her, wondering how long she could maintain her calm detachment. Probably it was no more than five minutes before the affair sorted itself out and she began her reading: but those minutes had a whiff of immortality about them.

Afterwards Edy took me up and introduced me to Vita. Hearing of my daily rides about the Kentish lanes on a stout cob, she gave me an open invitation to visit her at Sissinghurst when next I rode in that direction. A week or so later I took advantage of this, my diffidence overcome by the thoughtful Edy with a trumped-up errand to be carried out on her behalf. Thus was I privileged to see the garden in its first stage of growth. It looked very young, vulnerable; I recall especially the separate unfeathered plants of yew, forming embryo hedges, which suggested startled virgins caught emerging from a bath. If the Nicolsons on 6th May 1930 had no idea of the great work of art they would create at Sissinghurst, I had even less foreknowledge of that in 1934. It was Vita herself who caught at my attention.

Vividly I remember her standing in the garden against her rose-pink tower; both of them tall, both English, but with soft overtones of foreignness. Her words about Sissinghurst apply equally to its owner as I perceived her that day. 'It is a romantic place. . . very English, very Kentish, it yet has something foreign about it; a faint echo of something more southern. That is why figs, vines and roses look so right, so inevitable. I planted them recklessly.' She herself had a subtle underlying core of something southern; a warm Mediterranean bloom on an English peach. There was a hint of passion, extravagance, even a submerged tenth of violence far beneath the surface gentleness. Both she and her castle possessed Bacon's 'excellent beauty that hath some strangeness in the proportion'.

War brought changes to Sissinghurst, but not the complete eradication of all that the Nicolsons knew and loved there, which at first they had feared. Labour became more and more scarce, and land had to be used for food production; but somehow Vita kept the

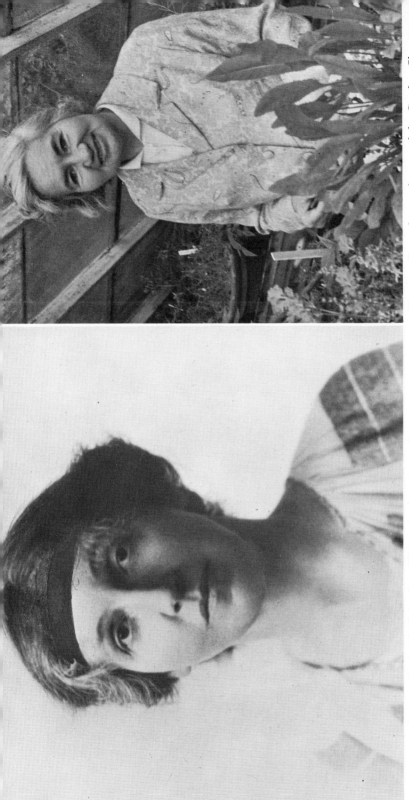

Margaret Brownlow – photograph by Gordon Clemetson.

Eleanour Sinclair Rohde, circa 1902 – photographer unknown.

Vita Sackville-West, circa *1958 – photograph by Jane Bown*
(The Observer).

Vita's Tower at Sissinghurst (Amateur Gardening).

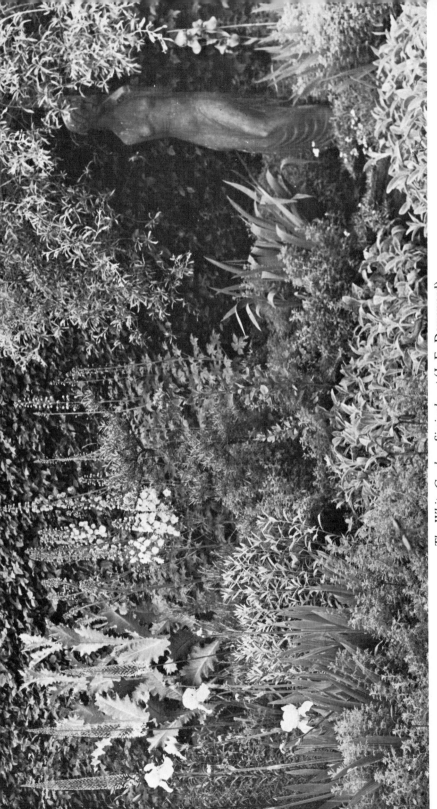

The White Garden, Sissinghurst (J. E. Downward).

garden in being, helped by Harold on week-end leaves from London. He represented West Leicester in Parliament from 1935 for ten years. She was herself physically courageous, but suffered agonies of worry about the safety of her husband amid air-raids in London and of their two sons, both of whom saw active service abroad. Vita also suffered a severe shock in 1941 with the suicide of her best friend, the distinguished writer Virginia Woolf.

Her great strength and sanity overrode these troubles. Gradually the continuity of country life took precedence over the disruption of war in her thoughts. An extract from *Country Notes in Wartime* (Hogarth, 1940) expresses this attitude.

Every evening at dusk the tramp of feet goes up my tower, passing the door as I sit working. Very slow and heavy they go, like the tramp of men-at-arms. Seventy-five steps they climb, dwindling into silence, and when I go out later I see two figures outlined against the moon behind the parapet. My solitary old tower! It must have watched many things, and whenever it rocks in a gale I reflect for my comfort that it must have rocked in many gales without coming down in the last four hundred years.

It watched three thousand French prisoners quartered here in 1760 under the guard of Edward Gibbon; it watched German prisoners in 1916. Now in 1940 it acts as a look-out post for the Home Guard, with their tin helmets and their rifles slung across their backs. The baker's boy and the blacksmith's son are carrying on the tradition.

It watches also the seasonal processes which must be familiar to it, since it is forty years older than Thomas Tusser's publication, *Five Hundred Points of Good Husbandry*; the calm processes which have never yet been interrupted. We are still making hay and shearing sheep. My tower was already standing when Queen Elizabeth said in a temper, 'I will not have my sheep marked with a strange brand, nor suffer them to follow the pipe of a strange shepherd.' She would have said the same today.

She who had gift of phrase and mettle far removed from meiosis, would, I think, have approved the baker's boy and the blacksmith's son watching the English meadows from the top of a tower already half a century old when the Invincible Armada sailed against England. She would have felt a virago pride in seeing this tower standing English, perennial, rustic and alone.

All through those war years, Vita Sackville-West wrote steadily.

Grand Canyon, *The Eagle and the Dove* – a study of two saints, Teresa of Avila and Teresa of Lisieux – and a long poem, *The Garden*, were produced during the conflict. She gave valuable service as a county representative for the Women's Land Army. These activities were combined with the struggle to maintain her garden. With only one man (unfit for war service) and a land girl to help her, she carried out a great deal of rough, tough work herself. No doubt heavy digging and lifting caused the back trouble from which she suffered pain.

The end of the war in Europe is quietly described in Harold Nicolson's diary for May 1945. On 7th May he wrote: 'At three comes the news that . . . Germany was obliged to surrender unconditionally. Ben and I dash to tell Vita who is in the courtyard. The three of us climb the turret stairs, tie the flag to the ropes and hoist it on the soft south-west breeze. It looks very proud and gay after five years of confinement.' Next day in London he records: 'Looking down Fleet Street one saw the best sight of all – the dome of St Paul's rather dim-lit, and then above it a concentration of searchlights upon the huge golden cross.'

In 1946 Vita's second long poem, *The Garden*, won the Heinemann Prize, which cheered what for the Nicolsons, as for so many people in Britain, must have seemed a tired period of anti-climax. The Government fell, and in the subsequent election Harold failed to retain his seat. Winston Churchill took defeat with humour. Someone said to him, 'At least, sir, while you held the reins you managed to win the race!' 'Yes,' said Churchill, 'I won the race and now they have warned me off the turf.'

Now it was once more possible for Vita to write and to garden without the undertow of constant anxiety for the safety of her country and of those she loved. All three men returned safely. A phrase often used in her letters, 'Another quiet day at Sissinghurst', which before the war raised laughter in the family, had ceased to be a joke. Gradually the garden regained its pre-war glory, and in 1947 began the series of *In Your Garden* articles for the *The Observer*, which continued each Sunday until 1961 and made V. S.-W. the best-loved journalist in Britain. She had reached the age of fifty-five when this new career opened for her, and in 1948 came the crowning distinction of being appointed a Companion of Honour.

Five years later we met again, this time in the far north-west of Scotland where I lived at Inverewe with Mairi Sawyer and worked in her famous gardens. Mrs Sawyer's sudden death, a few months after she had handed over the gardens to the National Trust for Scotland, left me feeling stunned. With reluctance I agreed not to run away, but to stay and deal with visitors until a permanent custodian could be found.

One wet September morning in that doleful autumn of 1953, I opened the door to find Sir Harold and Lady Nicolson (as they had now become) waiting for admission to the gardens. Although they were both outwardly older, directly Vita spoke it was obvious that in spirit she had not aged at all. Ignoring the wind and rain, she looked at everything with terrific enthusiasm, not forgetting such trifles as a common little lobelia, self-sown beside the drive, which she praised for the particularly fine quality of its blue flowers, derived from our acid peaty soil. Her warmth and integrity were unforgettable.

In 1958 my publishers sent her a copy of *Oasis of the North*, in which I recorded her Inverewe visit. The acknowledgment in her own handwriting is still treasured.

It was most kind of your publishers to send me a copy of your delightful book on Inverewe. It did take me back to that day when we came and bothered you, and you so charmingly accompanied us in the garden, and gave me some seed of *Myosotidium nobile*, and picked a Watsonia for me. How well I understand your love of that beautiful country. I often think of the lovely, wild, lonely road along Little Loch Broom – and I also remember climbing up Gruinard (is that right?) Head and seeing the Shiant Islands far out in a glittering sea, which thrilled me because they belong to my son, and I had never seen them before.

You must surely miss it all very much.

Anyway, thank you very much indeed for giving me a great deal of pleasure.

Yours very sincerely,
V. Sackville-West

P.S. Of course Harold belongs in a way to that part of Scotland, because his ancestors came from Skye.

To my intense regret I did not manage to revisit Sissinghurst during her lifetime. In June 1962 Vita Sackville-West died, leaving a chasm in the lives of many, even of those who knew her only through her garden and gardening articles. At the foot of the tower stair is a memorial tablet, finely lettered by Reynolds Stone:

HERE LIVED V. SACKVILLE-WEST WHO MADE THIS GARDEN.
BORN AT KNOLE 9TH MARCH 1892. DIED AT SISSINGHURST
2ND JUNE 1962.

In 1966, one year before Sissinghurst went the way of Knole in becoming a property of the National Trust, I began to collect material for a book about women gardeners.

Inspired by Vita's garden from the outset, I made my way to Sissinghurst once more. Mr Nigel Nicolson, although welcoming, sounded sceptical about my ability to understand his mother. 'She was a very complex character. I will show you a corridor lined with bound volumes of family letters and diaries. It would take you years to study them properly.'

Nigel Nicolson is a publisher and a writer, immersed in the printed page. It would not occur to his specialist mind that someone who had been for years equally immersed in plants and gardens might be able to apprehend the thoughts of a creative gardener through the language visible all around us as we sat at the luncheon table – her garden.

Not that any one person could aspire to complete understanding of the gardener. Nigel himself did not, for he has written: 'Our relationship was one of reaching out with finger-tips to grasp what can only be grasped with the whole hand. Almost my last memory of her is when I arrived at Sissinghurst one summer evening in 1962 and she tried to rise from her chair to greet me (me, her son!), only to fall back in exhaustion. Two days later she died.'

This unfailing, instinctive courtesy might, I think, have been deduced from the treatment she accorded also to her land and her plants. Except for some over-vigorous shrub roses, which she afterwards regretted having placed too close for comfort, their needs were carefully regarded and met. Although she described her planting scheme as being 'profusion, even extravagance and exuberance, within the confines of the utmost linear severity', there is evidence of meticulous taste and complete avoidance of the flamboyance-trap into which lesser gardeners fall. The home of Vita Sackville-West is part cottage, part castle, and her garden skilfully reflects both aspects in a balanced whole.

Reading of some financial worries in 1932, a time when the Nicolsons were maintaining a London address as well as Long Barn and the as yet uninhabited Sissinghurst, I was puzzled by an entry in the list of employees. Among the six indoor helpers and three gardeners there was a lady's maid. Knowing that his mother hated buying clothes and habitually wore breeches and gaiters in winter with linen slacks in summer, and boasted of owning no evening dresses (one was found after her death; it dated from 1927), I asked her son what a lady's maid found to do. He thought for a few moments and then replied that his mother was a very fastidious woman and changed her underwear every day of her life.

After this I was set free to wander in the garden alone, and what was more, to enter the tower room, V. Sackville-West's sanctum where most of her writing was done. From the beginning she had chosen this for her own, a retreat from which she could see without being seen. It remained hers for the next thirty-two years. Few people were ever admitted. Her sons used to go only to the foot of the staircase to shout that a meal was ready, or that she was wanted on the telephone. The walls and hangings grew old and faded; the occupant would not have anything changed. It seemed to me that she herself was still invisibly preserved and present.

With some hesitation I opened a folder marked 'Vita's Garden Notes'. In it was an assortment of nurserymen's catalogues, letters from friends, odd scraps of paper and an exercise book full of lists, queries, critical assessments of plants, and other gardening matters. It was queer to find entries for the very autumn (1934) when I as a young woman rode over from Smallhythe and met Vita for the second time.

In brown ink, now faded, she had inscribed names of plants admired at shows; queries about their suitability to Sissinghurst soil; much down-to-earth sense, next to lines of poetry. 'Move *Iris sibirica* by the lake to a place where it will not be eaten off by cows. *Two swans are on the lake. They speak the very essence of my love. Pure, plumed, majestical.* Among plants ticked off as ordered, we find 'One Mermaid for the Boys' bathroom. Moat wall, north side. *Rosa paulii* to hang down over west corner. Ordered from Murrell, who says it will make a 15ft waterfall of blossom. Large white flowers'.

It was a woman, Hilda Murrell, granddaughter of the founder, who rebuilt Murrell's Nurseries after the war and developed the Shrub Rose and Old Rose sections which particularly interested Vita. Others who corresponded with her about these favourites included Nancy Lindsay of Sutton Courtenay, daughter of that well-known gardener Mrs Norah Lindsay, who was said to have raised the first 'Blue Poppy' (*Meconopsis baileyi*) seen in England, and Mrs Ruby Fleischmann of Moreton-in-Marsh.

The latter wrote of a pink rose, *Souvenir d'un ami*, collected by her mother in County Mayo. She sent cuttings for Sissinghurst, saying that she would like Vita to add an 'e' to 'd'un', making it *Souvenir d'une ami*. Nancy Lindsay asked if Vita knew the Elizabethan gilliflower rose. 'I may have the only plant in England. It is dwarf, 1½ to 2 feet, with bottle-green foliage. The very double (2½ inch or more) flowers of ruby crimson are best described as exactly like the painted Tudor roses, sepals and all. It is amusing to recall the arguments as to how stylized the painted Tudor roses were – they weren't, they were exact copies of my little rose.'

Small vases and jugs still contained a few roses – Stanwell Perpetual, the 'Victorian Valentine Rose', of which Vita wrote with great affection in her *Observer* article for 19th October 1952. It is included in the second volume of reprints, *In Your Garden Again* (Michael Joseph, 1953). She hated 'arrangements' and always had little bunches stuck in water as a child might do the flowers. There were books on shelves, on tables, on her desk, along with personal treasures, photographs of Harold and of Virginia Woolf. Everything appeared to have been handled recently.

When I reached the top of the tower and stepped onto the leads, the entire plan of the garden laid out below looked as clear-cut as Sir Christopher Wren's plan of St Paul's Cathedral, which I had recently studied. The 'rondel' of yew hedge below me echoed the circle of the Whispering Gallery on his drawing. Yet when I came down and explored the garden itself, it turned into an obscure series of secret chambers.

The tower lawn, the rose garden, the white garden, the cottage garden, the herb garden, the lime walk and the nuttery opened out of each other strangely, with quirks of design not seen from above. I was kept guessing, with an idea that at some moment I might enter one of these green compartments and find no way out. The classical logic of the design has been overlaid by something deep, secret and infinitely beguiling.

At the weekend I came back once more to Sissinghurst, walking from the village early on a fine Sunday morning. The main road was awash with coast-bound motorists. One of their victims, a tiny wren, lay dead but still warm in the gutter. Yet within minutes of my turning off on the country lane which led to the castle, all was peaceful. That spectacle of modern progress, left behind so recently, seemed as remote as last week's nightmare.

Soon Vita's tower came into view between clumps of trees, its twin pepperpot turrets sharp against the blue of the Kent hills beyond. The sun gained power; a few late spires of betony in the hedge bottom glowed rosier where the morning rays touched them. The castle clock struck ten, discreetly in a low voice as though mindful of the Sabbath.

Not a soul stirred in lane or buildings. It was still the Sleeping Beauty's castle seen by the would-be purchaser on that momentous first visit in 1930. I put my half-crown in a box left trustfully at the gate for early callers, and walked beneath the entrance arch along a flagged path to the tower. Floating on the soft westerly breeze there came rich scents of good earth, well-fed foliage and a late flush of roses. The twin weathervanes creaked gently, and on the southern face of the tower sixteen white pigeons snoozed and crooned.

Knowing that this place would soon become a property of the National Trust, I rejoiced that it was to be preserved and felt that in the competent hands of Pamela Schwerdt and Sybille Kreutzberger (the Waterperry-trained gardeners described by Vita as her 'treasures'), the original character and well-being would be prolonged. And yet . . . when the spirit which created a garden is taken away, there is bound to be gradual dilution of its essence. I shall always be grateful for the opportunity of following the progress of Sissinghurst from inception to maturity, in the hands of that great and imaginative gardener, Vita Sackville-West.

*   *   *   *

In the 1860s the widowed Lady Mary Mackenzie of Gairloch in Wester Ross bought the lands of Kernsary and Inverewe, where her son Osgood (born in 1842) started his now famous gardens. His half-brother Francis, the sixth baronet and thirteenth Laird of Gairloch, had inherited the title and his father's estate, lands which had never been bought or sold. They were acquired in the fifteenth century from the Clan MacLeod – by means not of silver but of cold steel.

In 1862 the Inverewe Peninsula, called in Gaelic *Am Ploc Ard* – 'the High Lump' – was a singularly unfruitful place, a windswept ridge of Torridon Red Sandstone with a layer of black peat on top. It grew nothing but heather, crowberry, and a couple of stunted willow bushes. Here young Osgood began his ambitious scheme by planting hundreds of trees for shelter-belts – pine, larch, beech, birch and oak. For five years they seemed to make no progress, but Osgood said they were 'growing down instead of up'. They were, and their roots helped them to stand against gales off the Minch, coming straight from the Atlantic with no land protection apart from the long, low island of Lewis on the horizon.

Meantime Lady Mary supervised the building of a turreted mansion halfway down the slope overlooking Loch Ewe and the village of Poolewe. This Victorian house is no longer there. It was destroyed by fire in 1914, and for over thirty years the gate lodge, enlarged to hold the family, did duty as their home. After a time the ruins of the original Inverewe House were clothed in climbing plants and became known as 'The Burnt House Garden'.

Osgood Mackenzie's garden lasted much longer. The astonishing young man must have been well endowed with patience, for he had to wait about fifteen years before his shelter grew sufficiently dense for trial plantings of more tender subjects. He then cleared small spaces and enclosed them within six-foot deer fences. Tender trees and shrubs, such as Eucalyptus and Tree Fern, never before grown in this northern part of Britain, seemed to adapt very well. Of course Osgood knew that the warm Gulf Stream came close inshore, and that if the salt spray and wind could be kept off these plants from milder climates, they had a fair chance of survival.

On an old beach along the edge of Loch Ewe (a sea-loch) he made a walled garden, with a terrace cut from the rock above it. By 1878, after Osgood had married and become the father of a girl, his garden was taking shape and was full of promise. People even came north from Kew Gardens to see how plants which were kept under glass in the southern winter thrived outdoors at Inverewe, agapanthus, the South African so-called 'Blue Lily', was one.

By the time Osgood's only child, Mairi, reached her early teens the marriage of her parents had come to grief. A separation was arranged and Mairi had to make the agonising choice between her mother and her father. How much her loved Inverewe came into the decision nobody knows, but Osgood Mackenzie and Inverewe won the day. Father and daughter formed a loyal and devoted partnership which was not weakened when Mairi in 1907 married Robert Hanbury, a cousin. Her grandmother had come from the Hanbury family, which belonged to Essex and was well-known for its gardening talents.

The young Hanburys settled at Inverewe, where before very long they experienced the great sadness of seeing both their children die in infancy. Forty years afterwards I heard people in and around the village of Poolewe telling the dreadful story. It was believed that some crofters who had been living in a tumbledown croft on the Inverewe peninsula, when re-housed to make way for the new mansion and garden, had laid a curse on the Mackenzies to ensure the end of their line. Despite medical evidence that both children fell victims to common disease, the horrific legend lingers on, and will probably survive to chill the spines of generations yet to come.

Although Mairi had not become embittered by the disruption of her parents' marriage and the loss of her children, her natural shyness and reserve may well have been deepened by these shocks, so that in later years she grew more and more absorbed in the care of Inverewe, giving to her gardens the selfless devotion which other women bestow on their families. Her attitude was that of a creative artist to her work. Creative, and an artist with plants, she certainly was – in so quiet and subtle a way that it escaped the notice of many of her relations and friends. Nothing was more irksome, to those who appreciated her rare talent, than to observe traces of patronage, usually masculine, which hinted at a dutiful daughter doing the best she could to carry on after the death of a parent who was the real genius of Inverewe.

The truth is that not only had she inherited a large share of the traditional gardening ability of the Gairloch Mackenzies and the Hanburys, but she had worked closely with Osgood for about thirty years and developed into an observant and highly skilled plants-woman, meriting the highest praise as a designer and maker of gardens in her own right. When asked to write an article for the *R.H.S. Journal* about Inverewe, and later a guide to the garden for the National Trust for Scotland, she exclaimed that writing about it was a waste of time, for plants died or were transferred to new sites, and new ones replaced them constantly. She was arranging, rearranging and planning vistas all the while, and to her mind the living gardens were too fluid to be suitable material for a book.

Between them, father and daughter managed Iverewe for ninety years, a long span which may be roughly divided into three: the first thirty years when Osgood was making his garden, a middle period of partnership with his daughter (who planted her first rhododendron at the age of ten), and finally the years between his

101

death in 1924 and hers in 1953, during which Mairi supervised the gardens alone. She was widowed in 1933 and two years later became Mrs Ronald Sawyer; although both her husbands helped to run the estate, neither of them knew much about gardening.

More than once I was told the story of an amusing incident soon after Mairi's second marriage. Ronald decided to lend a hand with the making of a rockery, with two of the Gaelic-speaking employees to fetch and carry the big stones. Obediently they placed these according to his instructions. It was Mairi who overheard and understood their remarks, one being 'It will look hideous, of course, but he is English and I suppose we must do as he says'. Ronald Sawyer, who did not 'have the Gaelic' went on giving orders quite happily, ignorant of the criticisms.

The unwieldy Victorian mansion built by Lady Mary Mackenzie had a short life, being destroyed by fire in 1914. It was not replaced until long after World War I had ended. Mairi had always wished to rebuild on the original site, so following her second marriage she set to work, designing the present white house of Inverewe with memories of the Dutch South African homesteads which she had admired during stays in that country. A great deal of stone from the ruins was used to construct the existing rockery on slopes between the lawn and the shore below.

The new house managed to fit into the Highland background successfully, and combined up-to-date comforts with an established air. It is the only modern dwelling known to me which developed instantly into a real home, somehow mellowed from the start. It was peaceful, warm, welcoming and always fragrant with the scent of resinous wood fires. For the last sixteen years of Mairi Sawyer's life, it became famous for the traditional Highland hospitality dispensed under its roof, most of the delicious food being prepared by her own hands. Some visitors thought she must possess a 'double', to account for the load of work that her way of life involved, all carried through without fuss or sense of strain.

Unless the journey to Loch Ewe is made by sea, visitors must pass through wide expanses of rugged mountain landscape, treeless except for the occasional deep glen and remnants of the ancient Caledonian Forest along the shores of Loch Maree. Although so wild, it is not savage or forbidding country. Few of the hills have jagged pinnacles, and their boulder-strewn flanks are clothed in bracken and heather, the rocks themselves clad with lichens of warm colour. Rainfall is heavy, but soon drains off in the peaty soil,

102

allowing the gardener to work free from plastering mud.

Inverewe when I first knew it after World War II, was not so much a garden as a way of life. To reach this remote Highland fastness on the coast of Wester Ross, a traveller in the mid-twentieth century made a longer journey than seven hundred miles of road and rail could provide. Coming fresh from the hubbub of city life in southern England, the new arrival took a trip backwards in time – a journey, it seemed, to the very beginning of the world.

It was truly an oasis: not of cool shade in a hot and dusty desert, but of sheltered havens and pictures related to human stature, after the vast natural tapestries outside the gates. Here Mairi Sawyer toiled alongside her Gaelic-speaking men six days a week in all weathers, switching with ease from their tongue to mine as I worked with her. Beginning as an 'extra' during vacations from my job in England, I became 'permanent' and resident for the last year of her life. Little did either of us think that the permanence was to be so short.

We developed that great depth of mutual confidence and understanding which exists independently of the spoken word between minds in tune, and spent happy days together almost in silence. We both loved the natural background-music of wind and water, of seagulls, wading birds, and the comfortable crooning of eider ducks. All this, and the fluting of woodland birds within the garden policies, came to us unspoilt by the sound of internal combustion engines on sea, land or in the air. Planes were rare and, in those days when the road from Achnasheen was of single-track width for thirty-nine miles, road traffic consisted almost entirely of local residents and the daily bus, which carried mail as well as passengers. The sight of a strange vehicle would cause us to speculate on its origin and errand. As for boats, the few we saw were powered by oars or sails, silently.

For my first six months as a resident I was allotted a small cottage outside the gates, semi-detached, the other half being occupied by one of the gardeners, his wife and two daughters, the elder of whom was house-maid at Inverewe. Not until the hand-over of the gardens to the National Trust for Scotland was I moved to the gate lodge which had been the Mackenzie home for so many years. In spite of drawbacks – including a lean-to kitchen with a roof so leaky that in really bad weather I had to cook in gum-boots – I grew very much attached to my cottage by the burn. It was backed by a wooded brae where I could observe pine marten and wild cat, while collecting dry whins and branches for my fire. Rain dripping into the porridge pot seemed a small price to pay for such delights.

Picture a fine, calm morning in early summer, with small waves on Loch Ewe coming ashore in tiny splashes, meeting and greeting the bubbling fresh water at the outfall of the burn. The night-fishing herons are all gone, the mail bus has just passed round the loch shore, and I am the only living creature in the landscape. A thread of blue smoke rises from the kitchen chimney of the Big House, so somebody must be alive up there. In truth, Mairi Sawyer has been about for hours, having breakfasted and prepared lunch before the stated time at which she could be ready to set my novice hands to a task.

Walking along the drive, with tall gum trees, scimitar-leaved and fragrant, leaning forward on my right hand, I can see below the retaining wall on my left two of the gardeners busy in the vegetable garden, that fertile strip made from an old sea-beach by Osgood Mackenzie nearly a hundred years ago. What labour had gone into the enterprise! The men who first dug the ground had each a boy or girl at his side, ready to gather up and remove the stones, which were replaced by good soil carried up in osier baskets from the bed of the loch, and with material from old turf dykes elsewhere on the estate. Above the beach level a terrace had been carved out of the rock and a great wall built to support the driveway. Here, facing south, fan-trained fruits were interspersed with ornamental 'Bottle-brush' and 'Parrot's-bill' shrubs far from their homelands in the Antipodes, while neat rows of green vegetables had trimmings of the red *Schizostylis coccinea*, the 'Kaffir Lily' of South Africa, also pink varieties.

Although Osgood and his daughter had travelled widely in search of plants for the garden, they were proudly and essentially Highland in their sympathies and outlook. This precluded the making of a self-consciously artificial plant-show in their magnificent native setting. Amid the shelter-belts, a selection of rarer, exotic subjects had been skilfully introduced in a way which allowed them to take their places as naturally as possible in the scene. The connoisseur's pleasure in collecting and raising unusual specimens, which can so easily damage the general design of a garden, was here firmly subordinated to the effect of the whole. Good manners in caring for the soil and the environment have seldom been better demonstrated.

Even the huge Himalayan lilies with stems like bamboos were

104

induced to look at home here, together with camellias, magnolias, hydrangeas and rhododendrons in great variety. There are usually some of these to be found in bloom from November through to July, and the growths of many natural species provide a study in themselves; stems of various colours and leaves with golden and silver linings, which come in all shapes and sizes. People who have seen only the showy hybrids, 'Pink Pearl' and such, may well think, as did Vita Sackville-West, that rhododendrons are not worth bothering with. It all depends what you mean by rhododendron.

At the western end of the walled garden, near the gate, I visit on my way to the house a clump of the spectacular Chatham Island forget-me-not. With its shiny rhubarb-like leaves and trusses of brilliant blue flowers, each blossom the size of a shilling (now called five pence), this plant was one of the spectacular attractions of Inverewe, and Mairi Sawyer liked to tell the story of her flourishing aliens. Although the friend who gave her the two original seedlings had brought them over from New Zealand, little was known of their native habitat in the off-shore island; for a time they looked homesick, just clinging to life and no more.

One day *The Times* printed an article written by a sailor who had recently explored the Chatham Islands. He had been amazed to find on the shore plants with large rhubarb leaves and trusses of gentian-blue flowers, flourishing among rotting carcases of sharks and bundles of tide-cast seaweed. Mairi realised that this plant must be none other than *Myosotidium hortensia* (originally thought to be *M. nobile*) and quickly put a mulch of seaweed near her own starved little plants. There were no dead sharks lying around Loch Ewe, but when the tide ebbed she collected pailfuls of herring fry to make a rich top-dressing.

Almost immediately the plants shot up and grew lustily. When the first wonderful blooms appeared next season, she felt very glad indeed that she had read the article. Before long the plants seeded themselves naturally, and in a year or two many groups were planted out in the woodland gardens. Thanks to *The Times*, Chatham Island forget-me-not has been a popular feature of Inverewe ever since.

My enjoyable morning walk to work in the gardens comes to an end at a summerhouse near the front door of the 'Big House', as it is known locally. Mairi Sawyer, busily tidying away the mess made when she and the young housemaid packed hampers of flowering shrub and foliage for the mail bus to take, tells me that one of the best Edinburgh hotels often telephones Inverewe to ask for special material when some important occasion demands the finest creations of the flower-arranger.

There are usually surplus branches of flowering shrubs, rhododendron in bud and eucalyptus foliage, and many of these benefit from skilled thinning; '*but*', says Mairi, 'I will not let anyone else cut them'. (In the wrong hands irreparable damage can be done in a short time.) Although she has been at work for over an hour, following an early breakfast, there is no pause. I am accompanied to a tangled piece of woodland, which we weed and clear together for the rest of the morning.

The necessary tools are transported in a light wooden handcart with high sides, which runs on pram wheels. Being narrow it slips neatly along winding paths and does no damage to overhanging branches. I can never picture Mairi Sawyer in her gardens without this green-painted truck alongside her. She must have pushed it for hundreds of miles over the years.

During my previous holiday visits, she had taught me to distinguish between seedlings of the 'good' rhododendrons – offspring of the huge variety of natural species from such distant places as China, Burma, and Tibet, all of which she cherished, and the 'bad' or wild indigenous *Rhododendron ponticum* which usurped every inch of open soil and throttled more valuable young plants unless uprooted at an early stage. Mairi really hated this shrub, not only for its invasiveness but because she thought the habit unattractive and the massed dark-green foliage dull. She constantly expressed regret that her father had used the 'ponties' for shelter belts amid his trees, believing as she did that the more attractive Griselinias and Escallonias would have served the purpose equally well, encroached less, and produced seedlings of some worth instead of unwanted surplus material.

Her species rhododendrons gave us unfailing pleasure. Their elegant growths were kept carefully balanced by skilled pruning – often very hard pruning, too – and given room for each to develop and display its character separately, never crushed into a solid mass. 'I *hate* masses of plants, masses of flowers, those awful herbaceous borders which the English call "glorious masses of colour"!' Mairi would exclaim. If at some point congestion threatened, a shrub was taken out and moved to another site. Often I saw a large rhododendron apparently propelling itself towards me along a winding path between trees. The barrow, the gardener pushing it, and Mairi herself behind him were all obscured by this 'Birnam Wood' stage-effect. Most of those transplants were highly successful.

This morning, while I stoop diligently to my tasks, Mairi Sawyer suddenly stops working and stands perfectly still looking at the scene. 'Isn't it *lovely!*' she says, with a quick flash of her blue eyes, willing me to take time off to share her enjoyment. Away at the eastern end of the loch a saddle-peaked Ben, called in Gaelic *Beinn Airidh Charr* ('hill of the summer sheiling'), turns dark blue as a stray cloud puts shadow across it. 'I have watched it change for sixty years, and this morning it looks different again.'

So many busy gardeners seem incapable of standing back to admire the effect. For them, work has become a fetish, time too precious and short to be 'wasted', and so they appear to gain little reward for all their toil. Mairi Sawyer, in spite of her enormous responsibilities, retained her zest and capacity for enjoyment to the end. At this time she had fifty acres of cultivated garden and only (as she put it) 'two and a half gardeners besides myself', when I came on the scene.

In this connection, some old friends of Inverewe have been amused by high-flying journalism in a Sunday colour supplement and more recently in a reputable London daily paper. Two different contributors, describing Highland holidays, have mentioned the 'two-thousand-acre gardens of Inverewe'. As my letter of correction was not published, many readers must have been left with a picture of gardens of gigantic size. The fact is that the whole estate amounts to some two thousand acres, mostly moor and hill, and of this area the peninsula on which Osgood Mackenzie created his gardens occupies only a fortieth part. Even so, it is a large garden by any standards, and more than enough for its last owner to care for.

The worst of dispensing hospitality is that guests usually ask you back, and in my capacity of general assistant to Mairi Sawyer I was sometimes saddled with the task of inventing good excuses, for latterly she preferred not to accept invitations. 'I like my own house and garden best,' she would cry, 'so why must I bother to go out?' Sometimes she added in a meaningful voice that she liked plants better than people. The twinkle in her eyes made it clear that she had not intended me to make myself scarce. She always seemed pleased to have me around, and for my part I felt content to stay with her for the next ten or fifteen years, as seemed likely, for Mairi Sawyer in her seventies got through the work of two people, while her mind and heart appeared ageless and her gaiety never failed.

Then, out of calm skies, dropped a thunderbolt. That an eye operation on so fit a person could lead to a swift, fatal attack of pneumonia may not astonish the medical profession, but to the patient's lay friends it was unbelievable. Even the nursing-home in Edinburgh sent reassuring messages, predicting a quick recovery with the aid of antibiotics. Perhaps the patient felt life slipping away. She sent urgent appeals for an ambulance to fetch her home; but the doctors forbade this journey. Given hindsight, we who survived her wished that she could have been allowed to die at her beloved Inverewe.

Death came cruelly soon for those who mourned her going; but for her this sudden end in the full flush of activity may not have been unkind. A slower fading out, with gradual decay of faculties, all the frustrations of old age, and inability to care for her gardens, would have been very hard for her to bear. Also she felt deeply the handing over of Inverewe to the National Trust for Scotland, which took place a few months before her death. Although she put a brave face on it, the irrevocable moment had shaken her far more than had been expected while the long negotiations were in progress.

I was with her on that spring morning in 1953 when a parcel of Trust notices arrived for the gates of Inverewe. Nothing much was said, but her pain could be felt. Her efforts to find niches where the placards would not show seemed infinitely sad. Symbols of Trust ownership aimed body-blows at her which she could not parry except by avoiding the sight of them. This did not in any way involve disrespect to the Trust. The finality of handing over cherished gardens, for one whose whole life has been devoted to them, is bound to be distressing.

Mairi Sawyer was like a stream that runs underground for most of its course, a deep and reticent person. Her garden, too, had reticence and understatement. Its wonders were not immediately obvious. Its beauties lay in wait for those who took trouble to discover the secrets. There were few main, open walks, and she dearly loved the narrow, winding peaty paths which suddenly revealed surprises of tree or shrub in flower, of clematis climbing forty feet up a larch, or of loch and hill vista. In her day the gardens were open to the public (in aid of a District Nurses' Fund) but little was done to attract visitors. No advertising, no gimmicks or showy display. With the change of ownership all this began to alter, although at a very slow pace in her lifetime. I was often assured that

108

Mairi Sawyer at Inverewe, circa 1950.

Chusan Palm and Tree Fern, Inverewe – photograph by R. Adam (D. C. Thomson).

Inverewe and Loch Ewe – photograph by Robert Adam (National Trust for Scotland).

The Small Pool and Tintinhull House (Amateur Gardening).

The Memorial Garden, Tintinhull (The Field).

the Inverewe gardens were to be kept always 'as they are now'.

After her death, as a result of full-time opening seven days a week combined with publicity and the improvement of access roads, visitors flocked to see the gardens. From 2,000 a year the numbers rose to 60,000 within a decade, and now seem stabilised at around 100,000 annually. To cater for this influx of people, car parks have been constructed, a restaurant built beside the loch, walks widened and surfaced to stand the traffic of so many feet. Nobody who knew it as a privately owned property could pretend that it has remained as the owner left it; but whether the visitor regrets or approves such changes, all must be grateful to the National Trust for Scotland for maintaining the place and its splendid collection of plants with such care.

In this great garden there is no opportunity of grasping the layout from some vantage-point, such as the tower at Sissinghurst. Even if there were a high structure, Inverewe's fifty acres are too extensive and thickly wooded to be seen at a glance – eight times the area of Vita Sackville-West's garden. Despite a plan, printed ever since 1950 and currently used in the Trust's *Guide to Inverewe*, a certain number of visitors have always contrived to lose themselves. It was not uncommon in my day for worried organisers of parties or drivers of coaches to ring at the lodge door and inquire how missing members of a party could be located.

Asked how much time should be allowed for a visit to her garden, Mairi Sawyer used to reply, 'An hour for ordinary visitors, a day for keen gardeners, a week for botanists.' I would say at least three hours for everyone, and better still a whole day with rest and refreshment in the restaurant half way through. Just as the most worthwhile people seldom reveal themselves at a brief meeting, so a garden like Inverewe repays quiet, unhurried attention.

The place still holds plenty of thrilling surprises in store for those who trouble to look for them, but one will never come again. Very many people have written to me over the twenty years since my book, *Oasis of the North*, came out, saying that their most vivid memory of Inverewe is of meeting Mairi Sawyer herself at work in the gardens. She was always genuinely welcoming, gently patient with the questioning of novices, and often bestowed seedlings of some particularly admired plant upon a delighted stranger.

She enjoyed fun and loved to share it. On one occasion, when a group of serious gardeners mistook me for the owner, I felt sorely tempted to invent long Latin plant names (of which I was then largely ignorant), in order to parry their questions. Recalling Edward Lear's *Manypeeplia upsidedownia*, I felt it might not be beyond me to think of others. Always ready for a joke, Mairi exclaimed regretfully, 'Why didn't you!' She then told me of a wet evening when an elderly man strode up to her as she bent down to remove some weeds. In her tattered old macintosh, and a faded felt hat pulled over her ears, she was not looking impressive.

'Are you the Head Gardener, or just one of the under ones?' he asked in a loud voice. 'Just one of the under ones,' she murmured, sticking out her underlip dejectedly and stooping again to her task.

She was a great gardener, a great lady (but not starchy), and a very down-to-earth human being who never lost touch with her fellows.

*   *   *   *

The charm of Tintinhull, so often described as typically English, derives from a combination of a modest Somerset manor house with its setting, a series of small, carefully proportioned gardens. They are planned somewhat in the manner of those at Hidcote, but the effect of Tintinhull is at once gentler and more austere than that of the earlier twentieth-century prototype. Perhaps the climate of Somerset, so much less exposed than the Cotswolds, has had something to do with the gentleness, together with the fact that the garden was to a large extent made by a woman; also, the classical bent of Phyllis Reiss may account for the measure of austerity.

The house of Tintinhull, dating mainly from about 1600, has the later addition of a quietly handsome façade built of dressed Ham stone from nearby quarries. The beautifully proportioned windows, four pilasters – the central pair supporting a pediment – and fine doorway flanked by Tuscan columns, demonstrate how the Renaissance permeated England at the beginning of the eighteenth century. The façade is raised above a half-basement, with a flight of stone steps up to the entrance door.

There is no record of a garden until the distinguished botanist Dr S. J. M. Price came here in 1900 and laid out the initial design of formal enclosures. Only the solid stone paving of the central path leading from the west front to the fountain garden is believed to be contemporary with the façade of 1700, together with the walling of a small enclosure against the house, known as Eagle Court because stone eagles on pillars guard it. Probably the great Cedar of

110

Lebanon on the lawn is of similar date. This variety of Cedar was introduced into England in 1676.

The basic character of the place must have been established when Phyllis Reiss and her husband came to Tintinhull from the Cotswold house of Dowdeswell, Andoversford, in 1933; but Mrs Reiss herself developed the garden into an unusually attractive and balanced design, a synthesised whole of sufficient merit to make it worthy of permanent care by the National Trust. Sylvia Crowe in *Garden Design* (Country Life, 1958), still the best book on the subject, says that among gardens of this size divided into 'rooms' there can be few better examples. Although Tintinhull is larger than today's average garden (about one acre excluding kitchen garden), the same principles are applicable to smaller areas.

'The relationship of closed and open spaces, which runs through all the classic gardens, can still be translated on the smallest site. Because one should be dominant over the other, grass walks and borders should not divide the space equally between them. Because there should be clarity of design, the open spaces of lawn should not be cut up or dotted with planting.'

The word 'classic' may give us a clue to the mind of Phyllis Reiss. Although it is essentially English, the garden she left was created from carefully controlled line and mass without any element of go-as-you-please. When asked about this, Sylvia Crowe seemed unwilling to discuss the education and background of her late friend, referring me instead to Margery Fish for an assessment. Although the highly articulate Mrs Fish often visited her neighbour, she had difficulty in describing Phyllis Reiss, who was given to extreme reticence about herself. Plants and gardens were the subjects they talked about, not people, and least of all themselves.

In this connection it is noticeable that the grey-green slate tablet near the wrought-iron entrance gates omits the usual date of birth. The inscription reads: THESE GATES HAVE BEEN CREATED IN MEMORY OF PHYLLIS REISS BY HER MANY FRIENDS 1933-1961. (1933 was, of course, the date of her arrival at Tintinhull.) Another plaque records the gift of this property to the National Trust in 1954.

Mr Graham Thomas, whose sympathetic expertise had done so much to conserve the original character of many Trust gardens, wrote of Phyllis Reiss in *The Gardener's Chronicle* for February 1962. Having visited her in August 1961 only a few weeks before she died, his article is in the nature of an obituary. Although it gives a vivid account of their last meeting, biographical details are conspicuously absent. His subject eluded 'That frost of fact by which our wisdom gives/Correctly stated death to all that lives'.

At the time of my first visit, in 1965, a relative of the late owner, Miss Katharine Bevan, lived in the house and watched energetically over it and the garden. I was given generous leave to explore the place on a day when the public was not admitted, and talked with George Mapletoft, gardener at Tintinhull for over forty years. From these people who knew and worked with her I obtained no details, beyond the remark that Mrs Reiss hated publicity. Her *garden* was there to be enjoyed and written about as much as the visitor pleased.

Apparently she had left no garden diaries or notebooks of value to future custodians and those interested in garden history. (Nothing to suffer the fate which befell Mairi Sawyer's records. Over several months of long winter evenings I had helped her to sort, file and label a mass of valuable material dating back to the inception of Inverewe gardens, all of which was bundled out and burned soon after her death, when certain furniture had to be sent away to legatees. A body such as the Garden History Society might well look into these matters and persuade every owner to maintain diaries and notes in safety, with legal instructions for their ultimate disposal.)

Being left from the start to read the mind and heart of Phyllis Reiss through her garden, I deliberately choose now my earliest notes, made in 1965 when it was still virtually her own creation, summing up all the experiment and conclusions of nearly thirty years' work at Tintinhull. Her artistic, fastidious and sensitive nature are at once plain to the observer. She must, I divine, have been a lover of all the arts, for there is a flow of musical rhythms to be felt in her garden, and a poetic quality, as well as the ability to paint pictures with living plants. Also, I think she had a deep appreciation of architecture, being conscious all the time of her house as a vital element in the whole composition. I have an idea that she had travelled much, with a love of Greece and Italy – a guess later confirmed.

Public admission to the garden is necessarily made from a courtyard to the east of the house, which has big gates opening to the street. Tucked away in a corner near the house entrance there is a door in the wall through which one enters the north garden. This open grassy space is dominated by the immense old Cedar of

112

Lebanon, with a small successor growing up beneath its layers of shade. These are at the far side away from the building. On the opposite boundary, close to the house wall, several yews – smaller, darker and shaggier that the clean-limbed cedar – form a sort of bosky colonnade. A neighbouring magnolia contrasts well with the rich depth of the evergreens.

Although this asymmetrical part of the design is in keeping with the older, humbler, less formal style of the north elevation, I prefer to have my first view of the garden by means of the house-door opening to steps down from the later, classical west façade. Here one descends to the great terrace, and so to the paved walk between small domes of box, grown with two-thirds of their circular skirts on the lawn, the rest overlapping the path. From the terrace, this path leads the eye down between the box bushes through the Eagle Court and the next 'room', with its apse-shaped lawn and beds of azaleas, to the pond and fountain garden at the far end.

A fine group of helmet-shaped *Quercus ilex* trees in the south-west angle of the middle compartment echo in their own style the dark mass of the huge cedar which towers up at the north-east corner of the land. This vista, this walk and those fairly small 'rooms' are the core of Tintinhull. They could, if need be, serve of themselves to make a self-contained and satisfying garden for the house. But there is more to come. As your eye roams through them from the west front there are indications that a small outlet in the north boundary wall will lead elsewhere. After the walk through Eagle Court and the central court between clipped boxes, another vista on your right opens up a different world.

This section is a modern design, made from the old tennis court after the war in memory of a nephew, Michael Lucas, who was killed during a Malta convoy action. A long rectangular pool, large enough for human swimmers but occupied by goldfish, stretches for nearly the whole length. It has a paved surround, parallel strips of lawn on each side, and a stone loggia, flat-roofed and adorned with classical columns, at the northern end. So open, bright and gay it looked, with clear water reflecting blue sky, that I felt it had a Mediterranean character and named it 'Arcadia'.

It must be a cheerful place to stroll or sit in, even during winter months. In spring there are bulbs and flowering cherries; in summer, with roses flanking the loggia, vases filled with geranium and agapanthus, great mixed borders along the side boundaries, added to the reflections in water, it is livelier still. The plantings I

113

saw had marked contrast between east and west borders. One was a rich feast of warm colour, with reds, flame and pink enhanced by coppery foliage, the other a pastel mosaic formed of pale yellow roses and other flowers in delicate mauves and pale pinks. White appeared here and there, and silver artemisia showed up brilliantly against the dark yew hedge. The profusion of colours and scents produced what Sylvia Crowe calls an *'enveloping sense of the joy of creation'*. A splendid way to keep alive the memory of a young man who died serving his country.

In addition to the recurrent background of yew and the binding effect of stone walls and paving, these gardens have been given unity by the use of a few plants all through the design. *Senecio greyii*, bergenias, *Anemone japonica* – always white – and white everlasting pea are repeated again and again. Thinking about the value of repetition, I observe how the neat little columnar Irish junipers at the southern entrance to 'Arcadia' echo the classical columns of the loggia at the opposite end of the pool. A narrow slit opening in the hedge to the west allows a glimpse of the kitchen garden, where massed blooms grown for cutting between fruit trees suggest a peasant market outside some patrician demesne.

By taking a path through this blaze of bright colour and then re-entering the series of 'rooms' through another gap in the hedge, I gain the maximum contrast with the little pond court, whose white and silver scheme of planting comes upon the visitor like a cold shower after a hot bath. This court is the third and final section of the chain of small compartments leading from the west front of the house. Compared with the light open space of 'Arcadia' it is a cosy little parlour. Even the central lily pond is a miniature whose thin fountain jet has the appearance of a parlour game, the lily leaves reminding one of a tea-set on a tray. The surrounding silver plants and delicate white flowers are the lace curtains of our 'Jane Austen' room, and at the centre of the western wall there is a seat.

From this we get one of the best vistas in the whole garden, looking eastwards past the ilex trees, up the long, paved walk between neat box domes, and below the aloof eagles with their stone wings heraldically displayed, to the lovely west front of the house. The versatile Ham stone has an extraordinarily varied blend of colours in this façade. It shades from palest waxy-candle at the top through old parchment shades and Devonshire cream, honey and toast to rich amber, bronze, and dull maroon like claret spilt down the south corner.

The pattern of paving in the seventeenth-century path is a bold and simple one of narrow rectangular shapes placed end-to-end to form side borders, enclosing large squares with smaller squares set diamond-wise inside them. Although there are very few man-made curves in the whole garden, these few are used in exactly the right places. Stone copings of the old brick walls between pillars in Eagle Court form graceful concave supplements to the convex pediment above the entrance door of the house, and a shallow flight of curved steps leading from the yew colonnade in the north garden to 'Arcadia' provides an ampler, built-in echo of the movable earthenware vases which are the only artefacts not composed of straight lines in that rectangular conception.

To quote again from Sylvia Crowe, 'Although Tintinhull is a country garden, it is almost wholly in-looking and owes little to the surrounding country'. Perhaps Phyllis Reiss herself could be described in similar terms. Again I approached Margery Fish. Had her late friend and neighbour been inward-looking? 'Well, yes, perhaps she was.' And had she classical tastes? 'I remember at one time Phyllis said she wanted to put a row of pedestals with busts on them along the yew hedge. I said I wouldn't care for that. She replied that it would cost far too much, but I think this would have been done, had she possessed the means. Yes, she was a bust-y sort of person.' After a pause, Margery added, 'Phyllis had an unusual habit, for a practical gardener. She was always looking for a place to sit and contemplate things, in her own or other people's gardens.'

'Above all,' said my friend, 'Phyllis gardened like a man. She was quite ruthless about plants, throwing out anything that did not conform to her ideas. She never allowed sentimental feeling for individual plants to interfere with her overall scheme.' Here was the root of that austerity – that classical restraint and control so noticeable in her creation.

In the published account of his last visit, Mr Graham Thomas, who had often looked round the Tintinhull garden in company with its owner, says, 'This time there were no discussions on future plantings. no programme of work passing through her mind.' She said to him, 'I am sorry about all this upset for you; it will make such a lot of work for everyone. But I am so thankful that I have been privileged to live and work here all these years, and my only regret is that I must leave my garden. But I know it is in good hands. I am glad I thought of putting in that little cedar. I feel it is part of me.' In these few but revealing words she may be said to have written her

115

own obituary. In the young cedar, planted in 1961 where it could some day replace the aged giant, Phyllis Reiss left her own special memorial.

Many years earlier she had contributed to a radio programme, *In My Garden*. 'My garden is, I think and hope, a happy one. The birds have become so tame that in winter-time they share scraps on the lawn with my cocker spaniels, and the cat has kittens in an old yew tree cheek by jowl with a starling feeding its young and a tit nesting in a box bush a couple of feet away. All seem quite undisturbed by each other and by an old owl who has lived in the top of the tree for years – so I really do think it is a friendly garden.' And so it always will be.

7

Flower Gardeners Elsewhere

*Margery Fish and her Friends;
Elsie Matley Moore; the Countess of
Haddington; Flower, Lady Furness;
Cecily Mure; Enid Money; Betty Prentice*

I first met Mrs Fish briefly in the garden of her Somerset home, East Lambrook Manor, in 1964, when she showed me her embryo plant nursery and what she called her 'own' garden, where hired hands were usually forbidden to work. I was also shown her sixteenth-century house, a rambling L-shaped place built of golden stone from the Hamdon Hills, whose sharpest knoll, *Mons acutus*, gave its name to the great house of Montacute near by.

Two years later, in 1966, Margery Fish was persuaded to address a garden conference at Girton College, Cambridge, organised by the Women's Farm and Garden Association, which I was temporarily running as a part-timer at the London office. Old English cottage garden plants was her subject, and she kept a large audience enthralled by her enthusiasm and expert knowledge. In addition to her horticultural talent, Margery proved to be a thoroughly professional speaker. She was clearly audible to members seated in back rows and kept strictly to her brief without wandering down side-tracks or wasting a word. Excellent slides were shown – portraits of many old favourites which had nearly died out until she rescued and propagated them.

The curious herbaceous plant known as Bleeding Heart was one of the examples, a subject now back again in most commercial catalogues, thanks to her work. It is not generally known that a century ago this was a favourite pot-plant, often seen on cottage window-sills. Another old plant which Margery found and propagated – astrantia or 'Hattie's Pincushion' – is like a scabious. The usual colour is a greenish-white, and Margery grew also a soft pink variety. It would not do to begin cataloguing her finds here. Three of her books, although out of print at the time of writing, are obtainable from the Margery Fish Nursery. East Lambrook Manor, South Petherton, Somerset. Reprints in paperback of three more are issued by Faber and Faber. These contain comprehensive lists of the plants she grew.

Companioned by a neighbour who had a wide knowledge of such plants, Mrs Clive of Brympton d'Evercy, Margery Fish (from 1937 to 1952) learned on the spot, with the ideal mentor. Together they collected specimens from friends, from derelict gardens, and from the hands of elderly village people who were pleased to have their pot plants and mixed borders singled out for admiration. Many of the subjects the two women rescued were propagated and given to botanical gardens for safe-keeping. As the demand grew, Margery began to form her nursery business. Having gleaned this much from the meeting at Girton, I was glad to accept an invitation to revisit East Lambrook.

The earlier impression of a forthright, no-nonsense personality did not change when opportunity came to know her better, unhampered by official duties. Margery Fish made a striking contrast to the three 'private persons' of Sissinghurst, Inverewe and Tintinhull. Since her untimely death I have come across articles which give an impression of a shy, private, withdrawn character desirous of seclusion among plants. Of course she had her secret self – who hasn't? – but although she felt supremely happy alone in her garden, I found her outgoing, sociable and most generous of heart and hand. East Lambrook Manor fronts the village street, and much of its garden is visible from the drive gates. To one friend who remarked on this, saying she wondered why Mrs Fish had not chosen to live and work in greater privacy, Margery replied with great vigour that she loved being in the village and would hate to be separated from it.

Her first book, *We Made a Garden* (1956) makes it clear that she took no interest in gardening during her early years. She worked, and for the most part lived, in London. When staying with sisters in Essex, she had left them to do the outside chores while she went off to play golf. In response to my probing Margery admitted that both her parents were accomplished gardeners from whom she might have learned a lot, but as a child she resented being used as on-the-spot labour, with no say in what should be sown or planted, and no experimental plot in her name. 'You can't really be keen on gardening until you have one of your own. Doing as you are told in other people's gardens is a bore,' she said.

She was born in August 1892 at Stamford Hill in North London, and educated at the Friends' School, Saffron Walden. Margery described her schooling as plain and sensible without any frills. She did not pretend to have enjoyed it very much. As a strongly individual personality, the strict discipline probably irked her. Nevertheless her honest, upright and extremely conscientious character developed to the full among the Quakers at Saffron Walden. I forget which well-known gardener spoke of her afterwards as a 'splendid person'; but all who knew her agreed whole-heartedly.

After her marriage to Walter Fish, who retired from the editorial chair of *The Daily Mail* in 1929, the couple began to think about leaving London for the country. As Mrs Fish had spent most of her working life in Fleet Street, this was a big change for both of them. It may be that Walter Fish had access to the temperature chart of Europe and foresaw that such a fever must end in war, when London would not be a healthy place to live in. The search for a rural home took a long time. In September 1937 they first saw the Manor, empty and derelict, the roof patched with corrugated iron. Walter stopped at the door and refused to go further. 'It smells of dry rot,' he said; 'I won't have it at any price.'

After two more months of fruitless searching they drove along the Yeovil road on a different errand, and seeing the signpost which said 'E. Lambrook 1 mile' they decided to have another look at the old house. Perhaps at bottom Margery had an intuitive certainty that this was destined to be their home. If so, she wisely kept quiet about it, for her husband was very much the dominant male who had to be responsible for decisions. This time they saw the frontage cleared of weeds and the tiled roof restored, while a fresh smell of paint smothered that of decay. Walter Fish allowed himself to enter. That step led to purchase of the house, outbuildings, garden and orchard, at the time amounting to about two acres of land.

Nearly thirty years had gone by when I arrived to stay in 1966, on a fine day in late summer, with a warm welcome from Margery

Fish at the gate. I was taken through the garden door into the heart of her quiet home, a placid structure which creates an unforgettable impression by its very freedom from any desire to impress. Evening sunlight filtered through the mullioned casements, and I detected the lingering fragrance of wood smoke, although there was no fire on the vast canopied hearth, only a mattress of ash several inches thick. 'That has often been a funeral pyre for dangerous weeds,' said Margery, 'and provides a convenient source of potash or charcoal when supplies are wanted.'

Above and around us timbers of pale pinkish-brown, coloured and striated like the gills of a field mushroom, were exposed in ceiling and walls. They leaned in ancient attitudes so lazy that it seemed the house formed a prop for them, not they for walls and roof. Most of them had been there since the original thatched dwelling was constructed in 1470, so they had good excuse for feeling a little weary. The elm stair, with its shallow risers and wide treads, rose as though it had sprung naturally from the flagged floor without the aid of men and tools, although in fact restored by craftsmen of the 1930s.

There was no sharp division between house and garden. Wistaria and roses wandered round mullions and peered into rooms, while sprays of lace-cap hydrangea looked out from jugs on the sills. Bowls of dried acanthus, teasel, artichoke, physalis and eucalyptus were in the ground floor rooms, and when night came I was given a posy of white jasmine to take upstairs to bed, 'to sweeten', as the old herbals put it. I saw at once that Margery Fish was a herb lover. 'Smelly herbs', she called these plants. She had sympathy with my belief that every garden should be provided with some of them, to give scent from foliage continuously, which plants having scent only when in flower cannot do. Rosemary, rue, curry plant and *Choisya ternata* (Mexican orange) were some of the perennial scented herbs I noticed at first glance. The choisya, of course, has scented foliage as well as blossom.

When I awoke in the morning, another warm sunny day at the start of September, different scents came through the open casement near my pillow; scents from farm and garden, sharply fresh, mingled in a pastoral pot-pourri, while sounds of garden robin and cackling farmyard hen made a cheerful introduction to the heavy lowing of some cows who presently pattered down the road outside our gate on the way to pasture from their milking-shed. This is essentially a village house, rather large to be called a cottage, but it was a cottage garden that Margery Fish wanted from the start. In *We Made a Garden* (Collingridge, 1956), she gives a full account of the way they went about it.

'One of the things we tried to do was to make the garden as much as part of the house as possible. The big door in the hall, where we always sat, opens directly into the garden. The hall is paved with flagstones and we paved the garden outside, which is on the same level. It was difficult to tell where one ended and the other began.' The construction of a drive, lawn and paths was essentially the province of Walter Fish, who had very definite ideas about them. The drive must be large, wide enough to take twelve parked cars outside the old malthouse building used as a garage. He was sociable and there was not room in the street for cars of guests. His lawn had to be of the largest size that the level ground from the drive to the back of the house could accommodate.

His wife was in agreement about this. 'We knew that the bigger the lawn the more spacious would be our garden. A wide stretch of uninterrupted grass gives a feeling of space and restfulness. Why, oh why will people cut up their lawns and fill them with horrid little beds? I can sympathise with the desire to grow more flowers, but one long bed holds just as many plants as a series of tiny ones, and avoids the spottiness of small beds dotted about the lawn.'

Until drive and lawn were finished Margery had to work as a labourer. When they were done she was allowed to amuse herself with the making of a flower garden to the west of the house. This piece of ground lay above the level of lawn and drive and sloped up to a small orchard. A slope either way is better than a garden all on dead level with the house, but ground sloping away from buildings is easier to manage than an upward tilt, which may easily become top-heavy. She set to work terracing this. Each terrace had a support-wall in which to grow rock-plants, with wide paths to give spaciousness.

I didn't realise at the time that I was setting myself the hardest task any gardener could have. I was trying to make a series of borders, each of which must look well from four angles and also combine with the borders in front and behind. There were three terraces on the left, and three on the right; but on that side I had to dovetail in a fourth bed, triangular, to fill up the space. We all know the saying about fools. I had never done any gardening before we went to Somerset, and had certainly never thought about garden design. My only desire was to get

121

the project under way before Walter complicated matters with too much criticism and advice.

We had a very early fall of snow that year, and I can remember walking out the plan in the snow. Walter was a fair-weather gardener, busy with indoor jobs while weather was bad, so he left me to my own devices. When he discovered the foundations of raised beds with paths running between them he wanted to know what all those 'canyons' were for. Later he referred to the terraced garden as 'the floral quarry'.

But Margery persevered, and her terraces became a charming feature of the garden. The winding path leading to the orchard at the end nearly came to grief when Walter insisted on bordering it with poles for climbing roses, which made an awkward top-heavy effect seen from the house down below.

A clever friend solved the problem by persuading Mr Fish that small, clipped cypresses would be more in keeping with this Elizabethan concept. The offending poles were taken away, and a posse of grey-green *Chamaecyparis lawsoniana fletcheri* installed, later to be known as 'Margery's pudding trees'. She never ceased to rejoice in them. 'The amazing difference these little trees made to my garden brought home to me how important it is to include some evergreen trees or shrubs in any scheme. A formal garden calls for formal plantings of clipped shrubs. On each side of steps leading to a higher garden a pair of Irish yews give accent and meaning; a low spreading evergreen clothes an awkward corner; and if it is not practicable to train climbers up a house, tall conifers planted near will be silhouetted against bare walls. Most rock gardens are improved by judicious use of slow-growing conifers, and in borders something solid and substantial helps the landscape when there are no flowers.'

By the time all the existing land had been laid out and planted, Margery wanted to use part of a ditch – the boundary between their orchard and the next one – as a water garden. Walter then bought the whole ditch and a strip of orchard beyond it. Helped by her sister, the new owner cleared an accumulation of weeds from the ground. 'Clearing bindweed is far more exciting than golf or fishing. Tracing this tenacious creeping Judas of a weed to its source and getting it out without leaving any small broken pieces behind requires skill and patience. The reward is a barrow-load of obscene twisting white roots and the joy of burning them'. (She was too polite to use the north-country name of Devil's Guts.)

˙The water garden did not turn out as expected. No sooner had they widened the bottom and placed flat stones on it to make pools and waterfalls than the water vanished, and has not been seen again. Possibly someone else dug a well or made deeper drainage in the vicinity to remove the supply. Margery took it calmly. 'The absence of water makes it easier to work in the ditch, and I spend a lot of time there. The bank facing east is now made into a series of pockets with lumps of Ham stone, and here I grow my primroses and rare polyanthus. Half the opposite side is given up to alpine strawberries, and in the other part I have scooped out clay to make a peat garden. I planted Asiatic primulas in what had been the bed of our river. It seemed a pity to waste a position so admirably suited to them, so I dug out the heavy clay and filled the channel with leaf-mould, sand and compost. Here the Bartleys, the Postfords, the Millars and their foreign relations enjoy life with their feet in damp earth and their heads in the sun.'

It will be seen that Margery Fish wasted no time trying to adapt hard outdoor work to the 'delicate hands and feet of woman' as Jane Loudon had done. If Phyllis Reiss gardened like a man in her ruthless attitude to plants which failed to suit her scheme, Margery, who was big and strong, dealt with the hard stuff of garden toil in a manner few men could outdo. With some eighteen years of experience, she published her first book, which was fairly soon followed by others. After the death in 1947 of Walter Fish, the rescue and propagation of old, fast-disappearing favourites which used to grace many a cottage garden became her great mission in life. Her *Cottage Garden Flowers* (Collingridge, 1961), now reprinted by Faber, contains a mass of information on the subject.

In it many of the old vernacular names are given. It is a valuable work of reference and a testimony to the sharp-eyed country folk who in past centuries tended and named them. What could be better than 'The King in Splendour' for great, stiff rosy-purple spikes of woundwort (*Stachys* or *Betonica grandiflora*) or, at the other end of the scale, 'Wee Folks' Stockings' for the invasive *Corydalis lutea*? Some are less polished: 'Old Bloody Warrior' for the double red wallflower, and 'Bloody Butcher' for the blue and pink flowers of lungwort, named in days when every butcher wore a blue-and-white striped apron, usually streaked with red stains, like the common lungwort.

Of the stonecrop she wrote: 'There will nearly always be a yellow stonecrop (*Sedum acre*) covering flat surfaces of old walls,

123

that little sedum that goes by the name of "Wall Pepper" because its leaves have a peppery taste.' She does not quote the name I heard years ago from the wife of a rather bibulous old ploughman in South Devon. The roof of their cottage was covered in a mat of this yellow plant, which I had not seen in quantity before. In answer to my question she said: 'Why, midear, us do call it *Welcome-home-husband-though-never-so-drunk.*'

In the autumn of 1966 I stayed for a fortnight in a cottage near the manor, helping Margery Fish in her garden by day and writing a book at nightfall, and in the early morning. She, on the other hand, wrote far into the small hours and got up late. I went cautiously about touching her cherished plants. Given a skimmia to prune, I pricked my thumb on a tiny but vicious bramble at its heart. Knowing how her ground-cover plants grew into shrubs and up walls, it occurred to me that this plant might not be the intruder I had thought. At my query Margery stalked over, looked down on my stooping form and said, '*that* is a common bramble'. 'So I imagined – but in *your* garden it might be a rare specimen from Outer Mongolia.' Margery Fish was not amused.

Presently I found some wizened little plantains in between the paving stones of a path I had offered to weed. Rubbishy-looking objects, but I dared to seek instruction again. 'Oh, no, don't touch those, they are seedlings of my green rose plantains, used in knot gardens in Tudor times.' 'It just shows that one can't be too careful in your garden,' I said. This time she laughed. From that moment we were friends, and I think she trusted me. Much of it was nerve-racking, for her treasures were both thick on the surface and quite often in layers, one above the other, and only she herself could do the Pelman game of remembering what lay out of sight below. One rainy day I sorted out a soggy bed full of varieties of mint, replanting suitable pieces in some sort of order. I became wet and muddy from head to foot. When I left, Margery presented me with her latest book, which delighted me; but she seemed unaware of the reason for my broad grin. The title was *Carefree Gardening*. It is still a treasured possession.

I heard a lot about the friend now dead, whose knowledge and enthusiasm for plants influenced the writer so much in her greenhorn days before there had been any thought of published books about gardening. Mrs Clive of Brympton d'Evercy used to arrange expeditions to notable gardens in the West Country. Margery drove, and Mrs Clive furnished valuable introductions. No plant could escape the eyes of these hawks. Many treasures were given them, to cherish and propagate in their own gardens. The gardens of Brympton d'Evercy were crammed with rare subjects, for Mrs Clive had travelled widely, as far afield as Japan, and as was the custom of Edwardian lady-botanists, she brought numerous finds home in her sponge-bag.

One of her favourite stories concerned an unfortunate visitor who, knowing absolutely nothing about the plants in this renowned garden, felt she must make some sort of appreciative remark. Unable to name anything, she managed to murmur, 'You do grow marvellous *dandelions!*' to the immense pleasure of her hostess. One plant which had spread all over the East Lambrook garden, the old herb *Saponaria officinalis* (Soapwort) was coveted by Mrs Clive, but in spite of her skill and knowledge, it would not settle at Brympton. Many times Margery gave her baskets of roots, thankful to get rid of her surplus, but it obstinately died out. Amateurs may derive comfort from the fact that plants are no respecters of persons.

When we took time off, Margery drove me around to local gardens, and I asked if we might see Brympton. She shook her head, saying that since Mrs Clive died in 1952 the place had gone to seed so badly that she could not bear to visit it. The great house had been let to a school. Together we visited Tintinhull, and instead of Brympton I was shown the splendours of Barrington Court. This imposing place, with marvellous lawns, a huge iris garden, rose garden and lily garden made a great impression, and Margery said ruefully that hers would look messy by contrast. I said that I felt slightly uneasy when I saw a great garden so immaculately kept, wondering if the growths were quite real. We came home to the gates at East Lambrook, and as I opened them for her to drive through I exclaimed 'Your garden has the better *smell!*' All those herbs in a walled space produced a rich pot-pourri fragrance on a hot afternoon, giving us joy.

After many years I learned from the National Gardens Scheme booklet for 1979 that Brymptom d'Evercy had been restored and opened to the public. Mrs Clive's grandson, Charles Clive-Ponsonby-Fane, who inherited the property, has since 1975 been refurbishing it and developing several enterprises. With his wife and small daughters he lives in the great house – now vacated by the school – and it is once more a real family home. Judy Bushby, who became Mrs Clive-Ponsonby-Fane in December 1974, is a real down-to-earth gardener, by whose efforts the immense task of clearing the old garden is gradually being carried out. It was found impossible to reinstate the design as it stood in Mrs Clive's day. That sort of gardening, described in modern terms as labour-intensive, has of necessity almost died out. But the green-fingered and tireless Judy is planning and planting her own scheme to suit the site and present conditions. A large section, formerly occupied by herbaceous borders, is now being developed as a vineyard.

The story of Brympton d'Evercy is told in an illustrated booklet obtainable at the house, whose seven state rooms are open to the public. This estate has been in the ownership of three different families since records began in the thirteenth century, the last of whom, the Fanes, came here in 1731. Sir Spencer Ponsonby, who assumed the name on inheritance in the 1870s was Private Secretary to Lord Palmerston. While serving as Treasurer to the M.C.C. he laid the foundation stone of the pavilion at Lords. (He was a co-founder of I Zingari and the Old Stagers at Canterbury, so his name is probably remembered more in sporting circles than anywhere else.)

His granddaughter Violet, born in 1875, married Edward, son of General Edward Clive. She is described by her grandson as an 'eccentric in the grand manner'. She played hockey for England, rowed for the Leander Club and became a master carpenter and landscape gardener. The gardens at Brympton used to contain plants brought back by her from many parts of the world. This remarkable Edwardian lady was highly intelligent and extremely practical. She worked hard in her gardens, dressed so casually as to be mistaken frequently for one of her own employees. She was one of those gifted amateurs often bred in England before the 'career woman' appeared on the scene. The garden to which she devoted so much skill was a private one, shared with a few friends and never publicised.

Mrs Clive, who died in 1952, was a realist. She knew that the abundant labour of her young days would not be available to owners of such a property in the second half of the twentieth century, and so would easily have accepted and approved of the labour-saving ideas being put into practice by her grandson's wife. Unfortunately very few of the plants in her garden survived the years of neglect suffered at Brympton after her death. We may rejoice that the help and encouragement which she gave to the up-and-coming gardener Margery Fish resulted in perpetuation of many treasures at Lambrook, and that the latter by her books, lectures and plant nursery enabled a wide section of the gardening public to share them.

Charles Clive-Ponsonby-Fane wrote to me about what he calls 'a family tale that Mrs Fish gained her enthusiasm at Brympton and went on to become a great authority in her own right'. I can testify to the accuracy of this and to the way in which Margery herself often acknowledged her debt to Mrs Clive, in conversations with me. She would, I feel sure, have liked this tribute to Violet Clive of Brympton d'Evercy.

Other skilful gardeners to whom she expressed gratitude were Mrs Norah Lindsay of Sutton Courtenay and her daughter Nancy. A number of interesting plants came to Lambrook from their garden. Mrs Lindsay is credited with having raised the first 'Blue Poppy' to flower in Britain, early this century. Neither the Lindsays, nor Mrs Clive (or indeed Margery Fish herself,) dreamed in the far-off days of their initial meetings that she would become so famous for her development of ground-cover, foliage and cottage-garden plants that makers of new gardens are now overheard saying that in this or that border they must have 'Fish Plants'. Her best-selling books spread her ideas far and wide. In addition to those already mentioned, she published *Gardening in the Shade*, *A Flower for Every Day*, *An All-the Year Garden* and *Ground Cover Plants*. She also contributed regularly to *Amateur Gardening*, *The Field* and other papers.

Margery was always an extremely hard worker. When, sometime in 1967, her doctor advised her to take life more easily because of a heart condition, she refused to alter her ways. To me she confided the secret of this diagnosis, adding that her life would not be worth living if she had to curtail her gardening. 'I prefer to go on until I drop, and would really like to drop down dead in my garden,' she said. As it happened, after about two years she suffered a sharp attack while at work, which proved fatal in a short time. Those of us who are also gardeners could ask for no better end.

I attended her memorial service on a lovely summer day in 1969 in the old church of Kingsbury Episcopi where she had worshipped regularly. The large congregation included people distinguished in the world of horticulture, many of whom had travelled down from London. The service ended with her favourite hymn, *All Things Bright and Beautiful*. For such a solemn occasion it may not be a conventional choice; but it seemed exactly right for Margery Fish.

Her house and garden, left to her nephew Henry Boyd-Carpenter, are now being cared for by his parents. Margery's sister, Nina Boyd-Carpenter, has described their strenuous efforts to keep the place going in spite of financial and other difficulties. The house is open to the public on Thursday afternoons from March through October, and the garden every day. More than 6,000 people came in 1978, which proves the value of keeping this garden alive. Many of the plants whose use Margery Fish advocated, still to be seen growing in her garden, may be purchased from the nursery, including the stunning silver wormwood which she raised (Lambrook Silver), her improved form of *Santolina incana* (Lambrook variety) and the single magenta dianthus (Lambrook Beauty).

In 1975 the Boyd-Carpenters set up a Margery Fish Trust which it is hoped will ensure survival for her house and garden after their own time. Those who have obtained untold help and pleasure from the work of Margery Fish must number many thousands of gardeners. I wish we could form a society, called Friends of Lambrook or some such title, with the aim of assisting – by means of voluntary labour and a small annual subscription – to keep her work and her memory green.

*   *   *   *

From rich Somerset countryside to the heart of a cathedral city in the West Midlands is a big step, and yet Miss Matley Moore and her brother have made in this enclosure a delightful small garden, almost monastic in character and rivalling rural Lambrook in its peacefulness. The Greyfriars is a splendid example of a fifteenth-century town house, half-timbered with that lavish amount of oak which, in 1480, had not been restricted by law. It is but a few minutes' walk from the cathedral, and fronts the only street of that period in Worcester where intrusive property developers have so far left intact groups of buildings which saw (and in one case sheltered) Charles the Second after that disastrous battle.

The Greyfriars is thought to have been built by Franciscans as a hospice for travellers. Although the friars who were responsible for this place may have left behind an aura of old-world quiet, the garden is entirely modern, created about twenty years ago from a heap of rubble, residue of demolished cottages. The Moores, members of an old Cheshire family, have spent most of their lives in

Worcester, where zeal for conserving local treasures has been matched by their antiquarian knowledge and skill of the highest order. Twentieth-century inhabitants permitted the Greyfriars to fall into such decay that a demolition order had been placed on the premises when this pair managed to step in and save it. At first the property was vested in the Worcester Archaeological Society, but the National Trust has now taken charge.

It is unusual for those deeply interested in the work of past ages to turn their energies to the making of a garden. The Moores have proved themselves to be designers and plant-lovers also, and without training in garden craft have produced in about a quarter of an acre a perfect complement to their ancient house. They were not young people – approaching what is called retirement age – but when hired labour had carried out the hardest tasks of levelling and laying the main paving, they set to work and did a lot more themselves, together with all the planting.

When the great oaken gates are open, people may step in and walk beneath the gallery linking the two wings of the building at first-floor level, as far as wrought-iron gates which lead to a wide terrace. It is possible from this point to look through to much of the sanctuary of the garden. On the far side of the terrace there is a low wall with widely spaced brick pillars supporting wooden beams, used as a pergola for roses. The house walls also support roses, and the fragrant viburnum has grown as high as bedroom window sills. The garden is encircled with high walls of mellow brick, all clothed in lush growths of rose, clematis, fig and vine.

The terrace inside the entrance gates has been laid with a mixture of concrete slabs, cheaper than stone paving, used in a clever design of rectangles separated by lines of blue midland brick and cobblestones. By placing the bricks lengthwise across the width of the terrace the designer has contrived to lead the eye forward and so into the garden picture. In the central opening of the pergola a semi-circular flight of shallow steps goes down to the lawn. This is nearly twenty feet shorter than a standard tennis court, but by a cunning device, known to earlier generations as 'false perspective', the full court width by the steps is narrowed to twenty-nine feet, (seven feet less) at the far end. This gives an illusion of greater length than really exists.

At the bottom of the grass Miss Matley Moore herself built a massive raised bed, circular in form and constructed of rough-hewn stone from the old city wall. It is about fifteen feet in diameter and, when in spring it is full of bulbs in bloom it makes a splendid focal point, with the additional asset of visibility from the gallery at higher level. Later in the season, hypericums form a great golden pool here. For background it has a mixed plantation of trees and shrubs – pear, quince, birch, sumach, broom and syringa, giving a bosky shade to the far end of the garden and preventing the sense of constriction which a clear view of all three walls might produce.

The northern boundary wall, facing south, accommodates some of the more tender subjects. It is buttressed by brick pillars, wider at the bottom and sloping upwards, some of them edged with a kind of gold braid made from clipped golden privet, to diversify the large amount of brick. These buttresses are of value as windshields; for the high surrounding walls seem to funnel wind, to the detriment of the less stalwart climbers. A paved walk of generous width runs along this side of the garden, edged by a procession of large terra cotta vases. At the west end, near the house, a semicircular surround of finely carved Ligurian marble (originally a window) houses a niche with a little water jet to play soothingly into its basin.

A recent addition to this terrace, a garden room, has been constructed in brick, with four pilasters on the front, these given a sort of rusticated decoration by means of bands of tiles standing proud of the surface. The frontage is topped with four stone finials of Jacobean type, the whole making a harmonious and interesting centre to the walk. It has windows and doors of nearly the full height, with a fanlight above the doors. I was happy to see how the original lunette patterns of cobble set in the paving have now found an echo in the fanlight. Anyone who wants to make a modern garden that will harmonise with ancient walls and house could learn much from this elegant quarter-acre in the city of Worcester.

During earlier visits I had tried in vain to equate the 'otherness' of this place with some comparison lurking in a dark recess of my mind. Now, seeing the garden room for the first time, that thought rose to the surface. The Greyfriars, house and garden, is like a tapestry – one of those medieval hangings in which stylised men and women, houses and castles, animals, birds, trees and flowers figure in flat but animated shapes. Such tapestries were produced before the weavers learned how to counterfeit three-dimensional perspective and even the brushwork of painters on canvas.

Passing through the doors, I was amazed to find what I at first mistook for a tapestry of the sixteenth or seventeenth century hung on the opposite wall. Looking at it closely, I saw that this hanging had been painted, not woven, and Miss Moore acknowledged it to be her own work, actually 1976 in date. Like Gertrude Jekyll, she had received an art-school training; but unlike Gertrude she had continued to paint and design as a professional artist for some sixty years. Her expertise includes heraldic art; lettering (a formal hand is kept up for everyday use); the stencilling of enormous curtains of Venetian design for the house; and now the painted wall hanging, a subject on which she gives lectures. Hangings of the sixteenth and seventeenth centuries, many Flemish in origin, have been traced to eight different houses in England, with a different type at Hardwick Hall. For this versatile artist the garden has been just one more creative activity among many.

Her painted cloth measures about twelve feet by six feet, coarse linen so handled that the grain is not lost in thick paint, but exposed in texture – a technique which fosters the initial impression of woven tapestry. The theme is of a house, garden room, gazebo and surrounding land, in style a kind of fairy-tale England, with Persian trees and mountain background. Strictly English is a very clean pig out to grass. The artist told me that this large work could not be put on a canvas stretcher, nor had she a table large enough to spread it on, so it had to be carried out in sections. 'I did not see it as a whole until it was hung,' she said. One of her letters to me mentions 'My ill-behaved plants', so it may be that for moments when the garden is not altogether to her liking she has now provided the ideal one indoors. At no other garden in Britain can the real and the ideal be seen together. The hanging alone would justify a journey to Worcester. The Greyfriars is open to the public on certain days in summer.

*　　*　　*　　*

Two ladies who for many years have cared with great success for gardens at their husbands' Scottish estates – Lady Furness and Lady Haddington – would no doubt seem suitably titled, to Italian acquaintances of ours who shrank from addressing the Mistress of Inverewe as plain 'Mrs Sawyer'. To their way of thinking, the owner had to be at least a Contessa.

Flower, Lady Furness, widow of Sir Christopher Furness of Tunstall Grange (and late of Netherbyres) has gardening in her blood. With a father who developed her interest in roses from an early age, she was well equipped to care for the roses at

131

Netherbyres, which have provided her (among other things) with the task of pruning over three hundred bushes each year.

The handsomely wooded estate of Netherbyres, situated close to the fishing port of Eyemouth on the Berwickshire coast, has been a place of some importance in the locality since the sixteenth century at least. It was then shown in records as belonging to the Crow family. An eighteenth-century heir, William Crow, became very well known for his mechanical and mathematical knowledge, which were used to build a pier at Eyemouth harbour and later to construct the unique oval-walled garden. Since 1928 this has been in the possession of the Furness family.

William died in 1750, so that attractive bield must date from the first half of the eighteenth century. The wall, with an exterior of local stone, is faced with Dutch bricks. These were brought by sea from Holland direct to Eyemouth, there being a busy trade out of the little port to the Low Countries. Wool and linen were the chief exports from Scotland. At first one half of the oval walling was lower than the other, allowing a view of the garden within from certain windows of the house. At a later date, when that part of the wall was raised, bricks of slightly different type were used in the facing.

The walled enclosure made by William Crow measures about 200 yards by 100 yards. When I first saw it, a fine stand of trees to the east provided shelter from winds off the sea. These have since been removed for road widening, but new plantings have been made to fill the gap. Inside the wall, fruit trees trained against the brick lining obtain the maximum warmth and light, the elliptical construction being designed to facilitate early and full ripening.

Part of this oval garden is laid out in formal shapes of clipped box, so beloved by garden designers from Tudor to Victorian times (when labour was plentiful) and now so often found hard to maintain in good shape. At the great garden of Tyninghame, some miles farther north on the coast of East Lothian, there is a splendid walk arched over by espaliered apple trees. It is some 120 yards long and nearly ninety years old. The path through this living tunnel is bordered on both sides with clipped box, 240 yards of it to be trimmed each year. The Earl and Countess of Haddington have had some anxiety about keeping this cut, when available staff is stretched to the limit.

To a tentative suggestion that the box might be removed, a near neighbour at Dunbar whose horticultural stature cannot be questioned, Sir George Taylor V.M.H. (formerly Director at Kew)

Margery Fish – photograph by Arthur S. Mould.

East Lambrook Manor, well integrated into its village.

Margery's 'Pudding-trees'.

The Garden House, Greyfriars, 1979 – photograph by Stephen Mitchell.

Inset: Site of the Greyfriars Garden, Worcester, 1959 – photograph by Horniblow.

Tyninghame, the Rose Garden – photograph by R. Eudall.

Tyninghame, the Apple Walk – photograph by R. Eudall.

Oval Walled Garden, Netherbyres – photograph by Sidney J. Clarke.

Flower, Lady Furness, at Netherbyres, 1979.

*Plant 'embroideries' in Kensington, made by Cecily Mure – photograph
by Harry Smith.*

Enid Money in her 'embroidery' garden, Quenington, 1965 –
photograph by Peter Reason.

The Berwickshire Mill-House garden of Betty Prentice – photograph by Sidney J. Clarke.

gave his opinion that to remove the box would spoil the famous apple walk. The joy and pride of ownership of great gardens is today commonly tempered with snags of this kind. There should be a volunteer corps of garden conservers to help out in summer. At Netherbyres, where the box is a variety of unusually neat and close texture, a biennial clipping is found to be adequate.

Frustrated in her schoolgirl ambition to become a trained horticulturist, then considered unsuitable for a girl in her position, the future Lady Furness managed to learn the A.B.C. of gardening at home from her grandparents' head gardener. Later, when the aftermath of war brought upkeep difficulties for her widowed mother, the grown-up daughter was able for a time to take over supervision of the family garden.

Nobody then guessed to what extent owners of large houses and gardens were to find themselves denuded of employees in the second half of the twentieth century. So changed are circumstances that early involvement in the really hard toil of gardening is now seen as better preparation for the lady of a great house than her parents could possibly have predicted.

Lady Furness and her son, Lieutenant-Colonel Simon Furness, operate in partnership, spending long hours at work in the garden. In addition to the roses and shrubs, herbaceous borders and knot garden inside the walled oval, there is a separate herb garden outside at the edge of a sweep of grass, which has always been in her sole charge. Simon, taking a close look at the charm of his mother's herbs as plants (irrespective of their practical uses in kitchen, stillroom or pot-pourri), has made plantings of them inside the compartments of the knot garden. Instead of the former masses of floral colour given in summertime by bedding plants, he has substituted in one place the plum-coloured red sage, in another the bright golden marjoram; and next to that 'Jackman's Blue' rue, which, although battered by the very severe winter of 1978-9, will give a fine contrast when it recovers. Another perennial herb that could be used with effect is the silver curry plant, *Helichrysum siculum*, which stands the northern winter well and is even brighter in foliage than the commoner *H. angustifolium*. Margery Fish, who advocated the first, grew it at Lambrook, where her nursery is still supplying plants.

The employment of these foliage plants in place of a brilliant annual floral display is, to some extent, a reversion to the earlier permanent pattern of knot gardens – which, in Tudor times, were laid out in coloured stones, powdered brick, shell, sand, gravel and earths of varying hues.

At Tyninghame, Lady Haddington has designed plantings in several sections of that enormous garden with conspicuous success. She has also had much to do with the delightful gardens at Mellerstain, home of the Earl's heir, Lord Binning. My favourite at Tyninghame is the 'Secret Garden' made on what was once a tennis court near the house. It is delicately designed, mainly on a theme of 'old' roses with clematis and lilac. It was created in 1965 as an enclosure where she herself could carry out the maintenance work.

This enclosure has an unmistakably French flavour, and knowing that its designer belonged to a Montreal family, I assumed that this was a French-Canadian garden, Then I found an article in the *R.H.S. Journal* for 1971, in which Lady Haddington mentions that her secret garden owed inspiration to an old French garden book found in the library at Tyninghame in Scotland. It is strange how nationality is able to sing out immediately to a stranger entering the gates for the first time.

Buildings within gardens are subjects of perennial interest and discussion. In Worcester Elsie Matley Moore has built a modern garden house with character perfectly suited to the old Greyfriars hospice. Most of us regret that the usual greenhouse – whether of timber or aluminium, rectangular, hexagonal or any other shape – is seldom a visual asset to a garden. At Netherbyres there is a large Victorian greenhouse which actually enhances the eighteenth-century walled oval; while in Lady Haddington's French garden an elegant statue of Summer, brought from Vicenza, stands beneath a charming little arbour of wooden trellis-work, made by the estate carpenter, Mr Cockburn. At one side of Lady Furness's herb garden, the white clapboard summerhouse, built by joiners at the Furness shipyard when shipbuilding was in the doldrums after World War I, looks so 'right' that I wish every herb garden might have a copy.

Both these ladies have appeared on B.B.C. radio garden programmes, and Lady Haddington has contributed not only to the *R.H.S. Journal*, but to a recent book, with the slightly misleading title of *The Englishwoman's Garden* – 'from Cornwall to Aberdeen'. Lady Furness is District Organiser for the East Berwickshire area of Scotland's Gardens Scheme. She travels with coach parties efficiently run by that scheme each year to visit gardens in various parts of Scotland.

The gardens of Tyninghame are open to the public on weekday afternoons, May to September; Netherbyres on certain days, shown in the booklet *Scotland's Gardens*, which is obtainable from Scotland's Gardens Scheme, 26 Castle Terrace, Edinburgh.

*   *   *   *

In three contrasted settings I have studied gardens which clearly reflected their designers' skills in a very different craft – embroidery. In the 1960s Mrs Cecily Mure decided to change her small plot in Kensington, London, from an inherited miscellany of bulbs, herbaceous plants and annual beddings, followed by winter blankness, to a creation resembling a permanent tapestry hanging outside the house, woven from perennial plants.

How well she succeded in this aim was expressed by that writer of long experience, Fred Whitsey, when he described her achievements as 'miracle gardening'. It was started by fundamental down-to-earth replacement of exhausted soil. The ground, consisting of separate plots sited behind and in front of the dwelling, was not easy to deal with. Having no rear entrance to it, the owner had to transport discarded soil, in sacks, through the house, and cart in fresh material by the same route. The plan provided for a good deal of paving, so that stone had also to be carried through the rooms.

Cecily Mure realised that the kind of intensive cultivation needed to maintain her all-the-year London garden in good heart would involve continual replenishment of humus, to be done by means of peat, spent hops, and composted farm manure, all delivered in polythene sacks. An initial hazard, the funnelling of wind between tall buildings, which creates draughts inimical to many plants, was dealt with by raising walls and fences – after careful consultation with neighbours. Well designed trellis-work, specially made of wood free from creosote, was preserved with a quiet-toned mixture of two standard shades of solignum, to provide an unobtrusive screen and support for climbers. Here, then, was the embroiderer's canvas.

To clothe the vertical boundaries, a system was invented in which flowering shrubs, such as forsythia and chaenomeles, were pruned hard and trained flat against the fencing, to prevent growths from thrusting forward over narrow beds beneath. Such treatment of course means the sacrifice of some blossom; but by growing

135

clematis entwined in the shrubby growths (forty varieties of clematis in all), that loss was more than compensated. The early flowering shrubs were hosts to late-flowering clematis, and vice-versa, to prolong the display.

Tough shrubs were used here and there to shelter the weaker ones – laurustinus, which survives anywhere, was allowed to lean over the brilliant but tender *Senecio leucostachys*. Mrs Mure also made use of material gathered on expeditions into the country, such as fir and broom twigs and bracken, to protect vulnerable plants in winter. This cover has to be applied at the right time, neither too soon nor too late, and its removal requires similar care. These decisions need both horticultural knowledge and prescience in regard to the vagaries of the British climate. The very small garden has the advantage of being within instant reach and visible from door and window, so that nothing is forgotten or left to wait for attention.

Cecily Mure shared with another embroiderer-gardener a taste for hellebores and hebes (hitherto known as veronicas). She had to keep the hebes small and shapely by constant pinching out of shoots, while hellebores were rationed and used as focal points. A splendid *H. corsicus* (or *H. argutifolius*) acquired, in this small picture, the importance of a specimen tree elsewhere.

In her larger Cotswold garden, Enid Money had many more of them and gave the hebes freer rein, together with hostas and bergenias, but they were used skilfully to bind the design firmly into a whole. This country garden, created in the 1950s, had been a mere jungle of wild orchard and nettlebeds surrounding an almost derelict cottage. Enid restored and enlarged the building to make a spacious and charming house, managing to retain the cottage character and to plant a new and unusual garden without trace of pretentiousness.

Although this garden – just over an acre of Cotswold hillside – differed so greatly as regards size and location from Cecily Mure's tiny plots in London, both gardens became plant embroideries in which skill with the needle extended to outdoor canvases; the precision of the needlewoman and subtle blending of colours were equally obvious in the two creations.

Away went Enid's sparrow-haunted ivies and virginia creepers, together with squalid remains of hen-runs half buried in nettle and dock. Most male gardeners would have axed all the old orchard trees as well; but she had them carefully cleansed of lichen, ivy and dead wood. Only then, after long consideration, was the decision taken to remove one or two, while those capable of fruiting were encouraged and the rest pruned into well-shaped tapestry frames for climbers. The delightful floss-silk tassels of *Clematis tangutica* and the gold-variegated foliage of a jasmine with pink flowers (*J. stephanense*) looked their best when late afternoon sun shone through the tracery.

There being no running water on this slope, a lack particularly felt by me as Enid's guest and assistant, we made a floral stream in a winding gully with snowdrops, realistic enough when seen from distant casements. At the end of a mown grass walk through the renovated orchard, the original pigsty of local stone had its walls raised to suit the human frame. When re-floored and given a handsome new roof of Cotswold tiles (called 'slats'), this housed a teak bench-seat, ideal for garden strollers caught in sudden rain. The smell of pig vanished without trace.

In a small courtyard beside the cottage, where *Hydrangea petiolaris* clothed a stable wall with foam-flowers and russet stems, Enid made a centrepiece straight out of some seventeenth-century garden tapestry. A small circular pool housed one pink water-lily, and over it stood a wrought-iron wellhead, blacksmith fashioned, with hanging bucket complete. To one side in a huge stone sink out of the original kitchen grew magnificent auratum lilies. They scented the whole place, perfume drifting indoors and out to the village street, stopping passers-by to marvel at it.

In Kensington, Cecily Mure also used an iron centrepiece in a manner both effective and practical. She disguised the essential cover plate of her coal-hole with a handsome and portable iron incinerator, bought in a junkyard. Lined with zinc, holes being cut to allow plants to trail down outside, it became a delicate piece of filigree work when pale ivy (Glacier), tiny white campanulas and silver thymes emerged in cascades. Another ingenious cover-up consisted of soil padded up between peat blocks as a surround to a man-hole. *Cotoneaster dammeri* and *C. horizontalis* were planted in the soil, their shoots trained like herringbone stitchery across the iron plate, to be pushed aside when access was required.

When staying with Enid Money and helping her with heavier work in the garden, I watched on many occasions while she wheeled small conifers, viburnums, mahonias, gold-splashed elaeagnus and pyramids of box to and fro, thinking out how best to place them, just as in the evenings she could be seen laying skeins on her

137

petit-point canvas before selecting the precise thread to work with. Unlike many amateur gardeners, she was always mindful of ultimate size, as well as habit and colour of each plant. Certain conifers were deliberately planted too close, where shelter was badly needed, with the intention of cutting some out later. The pair of fastigiate Irish yews placed on either side of steps leading to the orchard walk would, she said, need drastic work with secateurs and what she called 'darning with wire' to keep their figures slim: the 'exclamation marks' essential to her design.

The only annuals sown in this garden, love-in-a-mist and flax, both fine-textured like silk, contrasted well with small shrubby companions, various thymes, dwarf lavenders, artemisias, marjorams, also silver-splashed applemint and nepeta. In addition to the usual blue flax there were always clumps of a clear cherry-red variety, and here and there the old-fashioned 'pot' marigold sowed itself and was given house-room. The only dahlia used, a fairly low cactus-type of soft peach colour, gave a background of firm foliage and blended well with the rest. At the time I did not fully appreciate how Enid got her restful effects by very restricted choice of plants. Once she felt pleased with that choice, she would usually keep to it year by year, which again made the visitor feel the peace of continuity – something altogether different from dullness.

Enid Money's garden proved to be very popular with visitors, many of whom came regularly when it was open under the National Gardens Scheme. They liked to see how the new design and plantings progressed, and to borrow ideas for their own gardens. Most people also took an interest in the embroidery on which Enid spent much time when the weather or short evenings prevented outdoor work. The french windows standing open always on fine days, many visitors were made free of the drawingroom, there to find examples of petit-point and other work done by Enid and some of her skilful forebears. It was an unexpected bonus for their admission fee, as many said.

In the 1960s embroidery was stepped up, and to some extent farmed out among volunteers in the village. The project of covering some eighty kneeling stools for the Norman church of St Swithin took Quenington by storm. I was pressed into service as a designer, on a theme of small animals, birds and flowers of the countryside. I managed to get in a few seabirds, pointing out that nowhere in Britain were we far from the ocean. Enid worked the motifs in petit-point (sometimes mixed with gros-point, done by splitting the threads of her canvas), and then the rather less experienced 'hands' filled in backgrounds and borders. Since her death in 1972 I have not revisited the garden; but the embroidered kneelers are still giving pleasure to worshippers and singing, in their own way, the praises of the Creator of all things great and small. Cecily Mure's garden has also been bereaved. I have not seen it since she died in 1970. Gardens are the most fragile of all handiwork.

The third embroiderer, still happily gardening at Cockburn Mill in Berwickshire, uses a much broader technique than the others, perhaps more akin to the modern-style collage of fabric associated with stitchery. The old water mill which dominates the site – a garden house of the most imposing appearance – had just ceased to function as a corn-grinder when Betty Prentice and her husband took the mill house and its surrounding land in 1945. Three generations of the Hastie family had run the milling business, and the idea of some day restoring the mill must have lingered in the minds of the new owners for a long time.

To begin with, the property was used for a holiday home, an escape from the family's town house in Berwick-upon-Tweed, fifteen miles to the east. It provided a playground for the five children and at first little gardening was done. During a fierce storm in 1948 the river Whiteadder flooded the old mill to a depth of six feet and washed against the mill house, bringing debris of every kind down from the hills. When at last the flood subsided, it was found that the Whiteadder had changed its course, leaving the water wheels high and dry without a mill lade to work them.

Years later the Prentices came to live at the mill house permanently, and then the garden began to take its present form. Betty Prentice, the moving spirit, began her gardening in childhood when, as a new pupil at the Convent in Mayfield, she was given a small plot and allowed to sow her name in mustard and cress. How many little girls began gardening with those same seeds! Whether grown on real soil or on wet flannel indoors, the thrill was similar, and at any age one still feels excitement when the little brown seeds wake up and sprout. Soon Betty Prentice graduated to helping in the big garden of the convent, and in time became known to the nuns as their chief garden assistant. At that stage sweet peas were her favourites.

A Roman Catholic, her taste in plants is also catholic. It is hard to imagine her expressing dislike of even the humblest plant. Nevertheless she has her favourites still, mostly 'old' roses and their more modern counterparts, hybrid 'shrub' roses, all of which she grows lavishly. In July 1979 the pink 'Marguerite Hilling' put on a spectacular display, the finest I have seen in any garden. Profusion of bloom is the first impression made by this garden in summer – profusion and warmth – for it occupies a sheltered nook within the bounds of the encircling stream. It is reached by a roughly surfaced, narrow drive, leading from one of Berwickshire's many winding roads: altogether a secret place. The soft rippling of the Whiteadder, the cooing of doves, sounds of lambs, nanny-goats and kids, all blend into a pastoral concerto to enhance the colour and fragrance of the garden, which has slipped into the country scene without any hard dividing lines.

Paving beside the house, a wide area for sitting out, has been imaginatively designed. An old grindstone used as a step near the entrance fits into a semi-circular step built behind it, echoed by an elegantly curved stone bench and several large pots of Mediterranean style. Between the stones, thymes and other bee-haunted plants stitch the paving together with rich insertions of colour.

Beyond the lawn are mixed borders, a number of 'old' roses here testifying to the warmth and shelter they enjoy, notably *Roseraie de l'Hay*. At the back of a wall there is a surprise packet, a maze of small trees, narrow paths winding between lilacs and other shrubs, roses, tall herbaceous geraniums, *Euphorbia griffithii* guarding one entrance, low-growing herbs, *Viola cornuta*, some rock treasures and all shapes and sizes of plants, including a superb single paeony of that clear red which used to be called cerise.

At one side a large greenhouse and conservatory attached to what were once stables (now a residence) is crammed with pelargoniums and the zonal type known as geraniums, many of unusual varieties and subtle shades of colour. There is also a bush of myrtle, which has been in existence ever since the year 1777, when it was rooted from a sprig taken from the bouquet of a famous local beauty, Miss Lucy Johnstone, given to her at a ball held in her honour.

The river embraces the whole of this demesne in its generous curves. The further bank, a precipitous green rampart, gives valuable protection from cold winds. This is a garden which needs even more than most to be seen and felt. It is like something from a dream, at once sharp and clear and yet impossible to photograph and very difficult to depict in words. When I have left it, I am never quite certain that it will be there next time I traverse the drive.

By some unusual combination of circumstances – one being the skill and foresight of the owner – a similar effect to that which Tintinhull had on Dame Sylvia Crowe has been achieved here in the Scottish Borders. Although removed by hundreds of miles from what is generally regarded as the more favoured county of Somerset, it can best be summed up in Dame Sylvia's words as giving out 'an enveloping sense of the joy of creation'.

Overlooking it stands the splendid mill, built three hundred years ago of the warm, pink-toned, local stone seen all over Berwickshire, and now carefully restored by Betty Prentice, much of it having been done by her own hands. She resembles Gertrude Jekyll in the breadth of her interests and capabilities, from joinery and masonry through gardening to fine embroidery. All the original beams, wheels and grinding-stones, with wooden cog-wheels and shafts, are to be seen now within the three-storey bield under a stout roof. Only the mill lade which worked this machinery for so long is still missing. With rising costs and fuel scarcity, it may be that water-power will once again be sought after for grinding corn. Perhaps a new channel will be dug, and the Whiteadder put to work again.

In the fall of the year, when summer's flush of blossom has gone – and flowers in Scotland, 'where the climate seems to produce more brilliant flower colour than in the south', as Russell Page has written, leave a correspondingly greater coldness behind – it might be supposed that the garden of Cockburn Mill would relapse into a grey northern twilight. This is not so, for as the interior growth dies down an outer skin or layer of coloured foliage comes fully into view. It is provided by young specimens of Persian ironwood (*Parrotia persica*), varieties of sorbus and malus, the so-called 'Fossil Tree' or 'Dawn Redwood', with the glowing barks of *Acer griseum*, *Prunus serrula* and *Betula jacquemontii*. Planted along the perimeter of this sheltered garden, they hang on to their leaves longer than most trees in Berwickshire, providing a welcome, unexpected echo of all the past summer's richness.

8

Training Schools and Professional Gardeners

Study of the preceding chapters shows that, with the exception of certain herb-growers, none of the women gardeners so far named attended courses in horticulture, although Jane Loudon received some practical instruction at home from her husband.

Gertrude Jekyll qualified as an artist and craftswoman; Vita Sackville-West devoted her creative energy to writing until well on in life; Margery Fish spent her professional years in a London newspaper office, and Mairi Sawyer – in occasional bursts of candour – described herself as having had almost no education at all!

This is not in any way a disparagement of horticultural schools and colleges or the knowledge they impart. It merely confirms that in the field of gardening, as in other arts, Britain has had a gift for raising talented amateurs who 'do their own thing' independently with immense dedication and ultimate success, unworried by academic rules and standards. But it must be remembered that all the makers of fine gardens have had behind them the work of plant hunters, of skilled nurserymen, of qualified botanists at Kew and other Botanic Gardens, and in some cases of full-time assistants trained at horticultural colleges.

In 1895 the Director of Kew, Sir William Thistleton-Dyer, tried the experiment of employing female gardeners. Their dress occasioned much discussion. The girls were instructed to wear clothing 'similar to that of the ordinary gardeners'. They adopted thick brown bloomers and woollen stockings, tailored jackets and peaked caps. The Director ordered them to wear long macintoshes on the way to work, so disguising the bloomers. Londoners soon

142

found that they were visible at work inside the gardens, and this was recorded in a daily newspaper:

> They gardened in bloomers, the newspapers said,
> So to Kew without waiting all Londoners sped;
> From the tops of the buses they had a fine view
> Of the ladies in bloomers who gardened at Kew.

At the close of the nineteenth century, the idea of horticultural training for women was a novelty. When women were admitted to Swanley College in 1900, Miss Wilkins became the first woman Principal. In 1902 this college started to take only women students, among them a gifted girl of seventeen, Kate Barratt, who in due course became Swanley's Principal, retiring (as Dr Kate Barratt, C.B.E.) after twenty-three years in the post. She died, aged ninety-two, in 1977, having kept up her skill with plants until the end of her life. In place of Swanley there is now a mixed-sex institution, Wye College near Ashford, Kent.

Another Horticultural College for Women, Studley in Warwickshire (founded in 1910), had as its last extremely able Principal Miss Elizabeth Hess, N.D.H., who served from 1956 to 1969, when the College was closed down. Before World War II Miss Hess held the post of Lecturer in Horticulture at Swanley. Both she and Dr Barratt were keenly interested in the Women's Farm and Garden Association, founded at the turn of the century to further the education and employment of women in agriculture and horticulture. Viscountess Wolseley's School for Lady Gardeners at Glynde opened at the same time.

At that period most henwives and dairymaids were members of the farmer's own family. The employment bureau set up by the W.F.G.A. was an innovation, and to many employers the idea of engaging a woman as gardener seemed almost shocking. Now that women are accepted in most careers, and young people prefer mixed-sex education, the Association has to some extent shrunk, but it still exists to supply a ready source of comprehensive information to young women interested in training for some aspect of work on the land.

It is affiliated to the Associated Countrywomen of the World, the National Council of Women, the Royal Horticultural Society, the Royal Agricultural Society, the Council for the Protection of Rural England and the National Advisory Centre on Careers for

Women. Rising costs have forced the W.F.G.A. to relinquish its offices at Courtauld House in London. The present secretary runs affairs from Lilac Cottage at Birch Green, Colchester.

Following the example given by Viscountess Wolseley with her private 'School for Lady Gardeners' which opened at Glynde in Sussex at the close of the Victorian era, other women interested in horticulture set up small training schools elsewhere. From the Fruit and Flower Farm School of Miss Hughes-Jones at Thatcham near Reading came an apt pupil who developed into one of Britain's most distinguished twentieth-century gardeners. Miss Beatrix Havergal, V.M.H., whose hard-working life, consistently down-to-earth, earned admiration and respect from all who knew her, must be given just due in these pages.

Beatrix began her career as single-handed gardener to a young couple who busied themselves in building a new home near Newbury in Berkshire while she turned the surrounding wilderness into a garden. An older woman, who often walked her dogs along the lane and stopped to pass the time of day with young Beatrix, turned out to be Miss Olive Willis, Headmistress of a boarding-school for girls, Downe House – an establishment still going strong today.

Miss Willis needed a gardener, and Miss Willis wanted Beatrix Havergal. What Miss Willis wanted she usually got. When the new garden had been laid out and planted, Beatrix became Head Gardener at Downe House School. She was only twenty-three, and now had several men under her supervision. We do not hear anything about their reactions, but this must have been a novel situation for male gardeners at that time. With tennis courts and playing fields to be laid out for what was a new school, there seemed plenty of scope for gaining wide experience. No doubt Beatrix benefited to the full from this, but she was not content to work permanently at someone else's school. She soon became set on the idea of founding one of her own, a school of horticulture for women.

A youthful housekeeper trained in Domestic Science (as it was then called) liked the idea too, so in 1929 Beatrix Havergal and her friend Avice Saunders broke away from Downe House and set to work as partners in a joint venture. Luckily for them, Olive Willis was large-hearted enough to approve of the project, and forgave Beatrix for appropriating her excellent housekeeper. She offered the pair practical help as well as her blessing.

144

The young partners acquired a six-roomed cottage at Pusey near Faringdon, and rented a two-acre walled garden attached to Pusey House. The gardener originally engaged by the outgoing tenant agreed to stay on. This indispensable man, Fred Whitting, remained with the school for the rest of his working life. Beatrix and Avice must have been good people to work for. As they were in dire need of cash – their total assets amounted to under £250 – they set up a stall in Swindon market and began selling plants, cut flowers and vegetables. It was an anxious time, waiting for pupils to appear.

The father of the first, a Swiss, caused a flutter by telephoning for details of their 'Training College for Women'. Although informed that as yet the new establishment was not worthy of that title, he came down from London to see the place and entrusted Annalise to the young women for three months. She in fact stayed for two years. By the time she left, the school had grown considerably, and when it was well on its feet, Beatrix had managed to take her National Diploma in Horticulture.

Because the little Pusey School held in it the seeds of the later and larger Waterperry, the plan is worth describing. Pupils were taught the theory and practice of gardening. Outdoors they worked with the professional employee, Fred Whitting, to produce vegetables and fruit of good standard for the market stall, together with cut flowers. The Principal and her partner, Avice, whose main duties were those of Warden-Housekeeper, also gardened along-side the students. In this way, theory and practice were closely integrated in a production unit selling directly to the public, while each pupil's character and capabilities were studied at close quarters by those in charge.

Years later, Beatrix Havergal spoke to me of similar conditions at Waterperry. 'This gives students excellent training in commercial practice. They take a turn at every task, including selling, and so the market garden is an asset educationally as well as financially. But it must be understood that it does not run on student labour. Such a scheme would be impracticable.'

In 1932, when Pusey had been outgrown, the school was moved to an old forty-roomed manor house owned by Magdalen College, Oxford, whose governing body agreed to let the property for educational purposes at a sliding-scale rent. This rose to an economic figure at the end of five years, when the school had had time to develop its full complement. The partners planned to take twenty-five students with six or seven resident staff and part-time

145

visiting lecturers. With a twenty-one year lease signed, the Waterperry Horticultural School was well and truly launched.

For seven years it developed peacefully. Then came World War II. A small number of full-time trainees were kept, together with batches of volunteers for the Women's Land Army. After a time it was arranged for an Army exercise to blow up trees, which made some twenty-five acres of parkland available for food production. It was a case of all hands to the pumps to keep Britain fed. The school emerged into the post-war period with thirty-eight acres under cultivation, divided up into eleven acres of orchard and soft fruit, about the same area of vegetables and a similar amount laid out in lawns, herbaceous borders and shrubs. The rest was to contain rock gardens, an alpine and other nurseries and a series of demonstration plots.

Behind the house a fine range of glass, both commercial and garden-type structures, completed the lay-out, with old stables adapted for storage of apples and packing of crops for sale at the school's own shop in Oxford. But the residents were not concerned solely with material matters. Beside the house stands the tiny parish church, a building of Saxon origin with an Early English chancel, Jacobean woodwork and some little windows of thirteenth-century glass. There I met that old friend of the school, Fred Whitting. 'Who plays the organ? Why, Miss Havergal does. If it weren't for her, there might not be any more Sunday services here. She used to read prayers every morning; but young people don't want that any more. They don't know what they are missing.'

Beatrix Havergal, whose musical talent emerged in her school-days, had to forgo dreams of a career on the concert platform when her father's illness and straitened family circumstances put a stop to advanced tuition. Such a career could not be financed by government grants when she was young. Organ and cello were played as recreation when time permitted, and she kept up her singing by joining the London Bach Choir. There she met Ellen Willmott, another musical horticulturist, who expressed acid criticism of women as professional gardeners, but approved of Beatrix Havergal. Old and impoverished by 1933, Miss Willmott was obliged to relinquish her great garden at Warley in Essex. She signified her fondness for Beatrix by giving a number of treasured plants to Waterperry, including a fine ailanthus ('Tree of Heaven') which was successfully moved at a fairly advanced age.

An individualist herself, Miss Willmott probably appreciated

146

the unique position of Waterperry as an educational centre of deservedly good repute which had been developed entirely by private enterprise without any state aid. It had a high ratio of twenty full-time employees, many of whom combined practical work with instruction, to twenty-five students. But for the keenly practical nature of its commercial operations, it could not have remained solvent for nearly forty years. Unfortunately the rapid rise in costs during the late 1960s, coupled with the official habit of directing applicants for grants to County Institutes for Horticulture, ultimately brought this splendid school to an end, in spite of all the strenuous efforts made by its Principal and her associates and friends to keep it alive. Beatrix Havergal outlived her school by a decade. She died in April 1980.

Now that Britain has its first woman Prime Minister, and one who favours the encouragement of private enterprise, it is all the more regrettable that Beatrix Havergal could not maintain her brave venture into the era of Margaret Thatcher, who probably saw those magnificent Waterperry strawberries on show at Chelsea at some stage during her life in London. The sight and smell of that delectable exhibit will be remembered by all who visited the stand.

In 1966, when presenting Beatrix Havergal with its highest award, the Victoria Medal of Honour, the President of the Royal Horticultural Society had this to say:

The strawberries were even better than usual this year. You could smell them from beyond the roses! How often have we overheard such remarks! We have feasted our eyes and our noses, and some lucky ones among us our mouths, upon the fruits which Miss Havergal and her young ladies produce each year. Her College of Horticulture at Waterperry in Oxfordshire, to which we are sending our Emmie Clough Scholar, is rightly renowned. Miss Havergal is invaluable on our committees, especially those dealing with examinations and education. Horticulture, Miss Havergal, owes you a great debt, only superficially repaid by this Victoria Medal of Honour.

By that time Waterperry had been awarded a total of eleven Gold Medals and nine Hogg Memorial Medals for its strawberries; one Gold and three other medals for apples; and Valerie Finnis with her alpine plants had taken seven Floral Medals and six Banksian Medals.

Valerie Finnis, who also received the Victoria Medal of Honour,

147

deserves a chapter to herself. She became an international authority on alpine plants, as well as a first-class horticultural photographer. In a letter to me Beatrix Havergal asked for emphasis to be put on the team-work and vital leadership of Valerie, of Joan Stokes and others who between them built up the reputation of Waterperry.

Valerie Finnis, now Lady David Scott, continues to cherish a remarkable collection of alpine and other plants at the Dower House adjoining the Duke of Buccleuch's ancestral home (one of them) at Boughton near Kettering, where a two-acre garden gives delight to its owners and to visitors privileged to see this 'home for plants', as it is described. Valerie in November 1978 gave a stimulating talk on Radio Three, afterwards printed in *The Listener*. Always a humorist, she says of the several plants named after her: 'I am a very nasty rose, a dreary little saxifrage, and I'm also going to be an orchid. I don't like being an orchid, really.'

The story of her former colleague, Joan Stokes, is as remarkable as that of the Scots girl afflicted with deafness (see pages 154-156). When Joan, as a small and severely handicapped teenager, applied for entry to Waterperry, Miss Havergal from her superior height looked down and wondered how she could tactfully refuse to accept so crippled a girl. But Joan showed such tenacity of purpose that the astonished Principal felt obliged to give her a trial. Here Joan was able to take advantage of the more elastic nature of Waterperry as compared with larger and more impersonal government-financed training schools, which might have refused her entry.

It was a lucky choice for her, and even more to the advantage of the school, for she became not only a prize pupil, but later one of the most loyal and valued members of the staff. She built up a fine glass-house section and was responsible for that remarkable display of strawberries at Chelsea each year. She was awarded the R.H.S. Associateship of Honour in 1969.

At this presentation the President, Lord Aberconway, said: 'For twenty years you have been responsible for the production, and the difficult matter of timing, of the strawberries shown at Chelsea. Never during that time has a strawberry unworthy of the name of *Royal Sovereign* found its way to Chelsea – unless perhaps you have inserted such a one at the back to make its fellows blush scarlet with horror at the right moment.'

Although far from being a feminine organisation, the Royal Horticultural Society must be mentioned as one of the greatest and most popular educators in Britain, horticulturally speaking. Those of us who are familiar with the grounds of Chelsea Hospital during the days of the famous Flower Show often wonder if women outnumber men on the R.H.S. roll of members (they are customarily known as *Fellows*); but the discreet official reply to inquiries firmly states that membership is assessed by subscriptions paid, with no separation of the sexes.

One thing is certain. The Council of the R.H.S. was, from its inception in 1809 (the date of the Society's Royal Charter), composed entirely of men until Mrs Frances Perry, M.B.E., made history by her election to the council in 1969. She was awarded the V.M.H. in 1971. With a long experience of nursery gardening and lecturing, she has of recent years gained a large and widespread audience of amateur gardeners for her broadcasts on radio and television. She is now the wife of Roy Hay, and after relinquishing the Presidency of the Women's Farm and Garden Association in 1976 was reported to have been invited, together with her husband, to set up a botanical garden in Iran. Oil revenues could scarcely be put to better use.

Delving into W.F.G.A. archives at Courtauld House, some years ago, I found notes on the beginning (1914) of the Women's Land Service Corps, sponsored by what was then called the Women's Farm and Garden Union, whose moving spirit, Louisa Jebb, was the first woman to read for an agricultural degree at Cambridge. Not until 1917 was the full-time Land Service Corps taken over by the Government and renamed the Women's Land Army. So the credit for originating this valuable scheme belongs by right to the precursor of the Women's Farm and Garden Association.

The aim of the newly created Land Service Corps, as formulated at the time, is worth quoting as a 'period piece'. 'To create a favourable opinion as to the value of women's work in agriculture, by supplying a body of workers capable of making a good impression and thereby breaking down the prejudices of those of the farming community who are opposed to the employment of women.' By 1917 this object had been achieved. The Annual Report speaks of women as being 'firmly established on the land as milkers, carters, ploughwomen, etc., with wages for skilled workers increased from twenty-two shillings to twenty-five shillings or even thirty-two shillings a week'.

After the Government took over the full-time force, renamed

the Women's Land Army, the W.F.G.U. continued to run its Land Service Corps to recruit and place part-time labour for harvesting crops. These women and girls were employed mainly in haymaking, threshing, fruit-picking and flax-pulling. With Germany then in possession of the chief Continental flax-growing areas, Britain needed to produce some 2,000 tons for aeroplane wing fabric and textiles required for Army tents and equipment.

Flax grows to a height of about eighteen inches and has a small tap root. The plants were pulled up by hand and laid evenly on the ground with stems parallel, to be bound into sheaves and stooked for drying. As no machinery existed for dealing with this work, farmers were reluctant to grow it, knowing harvest labour to be scarce. The Women's Land Service came to the rescue and found, in 1917-18, 4,000 volunteers for this work alone. About 3,000 acres were harvested in the summer of 1918, which brought the Corps a letter of commendation from the government. At the end of World War I the W.L.S.C. and W.F.G.U. were combined and re-named the Women's Farm and Garden Association, which was incorporated under the Companies Act in 1929.

Among the many distinguished names on its roll, those of Sylvia Crowe and her partner have an honoured place. In the W.F.G.A.'s commemorative Jubilee booklet, Sylvia Crowe and Brenda Colvin described their work.

> If you are a landscape architect you have dates for surveys booked up months ahead to suit your clients, but when you get there it is usually raining. You may have come hundreds of miles to do the job, so do it you must. You work for weeks in the office, while your muscles get soft. Then you suddenly have to spend days trudging steep fells estimating how many saplings were eaten by sheep while snow lay deeper than the fences. Work ranges from the design of window boxes to the planning of school grounds in a county. Every job is different and the one thing we never suffer from is boredom. Candidates for our profession require a sound knowledge of such diverse subjects as drains, hydrangeas, gravel pits, roof gardens, slag heaps, herbs and bulldozers.

Sylvia Crowe has published a number of books, including the authoritative *Garden Design* (Country Life, 1958). At an earlier date one of the very first women to take up landscape architecture, Madeline Agar (also a member of the W.F.G.U.), wrote down her ideas under the title *Garden Design in Theory and Practice*.

Following up the careers of horticultural students who have been engaged in some form of garden work would provide material for a whole book. My personal contacts include Rene Clayton, born a member of the redoubtable clan Douglass, who married Hollis Clayton in 1946 and settled down in England to raise a family of four children, 'two of each'. After training at Swanley College, where she gained a B.Sc. in Horticulture, Rene served during World War II as Organiser of School Gardening to the Northumberland Education Committee. Her mother had been a Mackenzie and her father's father, Sir James Douglass, designed many lighthouses and was knighted for his work on the Eddystone.

In the 1960s Rene and Hollis acquired a small Georgian house, built in 1790 in the centre of the Kentish village of Hollingbourne. The pasture land at the rear, after long preparation and hard toil, was turned into Rene's container-plant nursery. At the time the idea of selling plants rooted in take-away containers or pots was fairly novel. It came originally from Australia, being introduced into England by Messrs Bygrave of St Albans. Having studied the technique at that firm's premises and obtained helpful advice, the Claytons began their enterprise. Hollis had run a garden contractor's business for some years, and his wife had raised plants as a sideline for use in his schemes, but now at the age of forty-six she was eager to expand that hobby into a full-scale business.

Rene began with canny regard for keeping initial outlay to a minimum. 'We called ourselves The Hollingbourne Scroungers,' she said. 'First we had rubble and hardcore tipped on our land free of charge by a local builder, to make standing for pots. Then we got leave to take sand from a near-by quarry, fetching it ourselves. Neighbours with boilers provided quantities of ash, boxes and cartons were collected from shops, waste vegetables for compost came from a greengrocer, and the sweep offered soot. A rabbit farm let us have manure and the local hospital supplied a lot of gallon-size tins, our first containers for shrubs.'

Rene already had a collection of herbaceous plants and shrubs brought from their former home, and she bought 2,000 rose stock cuttings from Swanley College for budding in the summer. With the help of her family and some student labour she potted up hundreds of plants for sale in the first year, 1964.

By easy stages she turned the whole field into a walk-round garden, where customers were free to wander at will and see plants in a natural setting before deciding which to buy. There were herbaceous borders, shrub borders and a rose garden, with a rockery placed near the sale ground. A large display of bedding plants near the road made a colourful show to lure the public inside.

Rene's container-plant nursery has expanded during the years and is now the established, flourishing success it deserves to be. In a life of perpetual activity she has found time to assist Dr Shewell Cooper with the judging of a competition for London gardens; to keep up her playing of the double-bass and take part in many musical events locally; to train a number of students during the year each candidate has to work in a horticultural business before acceptance at a Diploma Course; and of course to care superbly for her own family, which always comes first with her.

Further east in the same county of Kent, Carola Cochrane at Brabourne near Ashford developed her two-acre market garden after World War II, following a short course in horticulture at the Hertfordshire Institute of Agriculture and some months' experience as a labourer in the well-known gardens of F. A. Secrett, O.B.E. By very hard work and dearly bought knowledge she made a great success of her garden adjoining the lovely old seventeenth-century Court Lodge farmhouse. Flowers and vegetables were sent by rail or van to Covent Garden market, a proportion went to shops in the locality, and much produce was sold at the gate to motorists.

Although few small businesses care to discuss their profit and loss accounts, Carola Cochrane showed no hesitation about publishing hers, in her book *Two Acres Unlimited*, issued in 1954 by Crosby Lockwood. Capital expenditure on Dutch lights, frames, greenhouses, fencing etc. amounted to just under £3,000 for the first five years, up to March 1950, after which little more outlay was required. For anyone starting today, that figure would be multiplied by ten – possibly more – but the profits would not necessarily rise by the same percentage. Labour costs are now well in advance of market prices, employees of quality grow more scarce every year, and few growers encourage younger people to take up the business.

At Brabourne the profits from two acres, approximately £860 for the first two years, rose to £2,000 in the fifth year and nearly £3,000 in the eighth, 1953. The range of produce which this land supplied is prodigious: lettuces, carrots, French beans, radishes, leeks, spring onions, peas, beetroot, sweet corn, tomatoes and cucumbers, and various herbs for cooking; and as cut flowers, chrysanthemums, gladioli, Dutch irises, freesias, tulips, plus a number of pot plants and boxes of bedding plants in the season, have all been cultivated for sale. Miss Cochrane, who describes her staff as 'about one per acre', does the work of two or three people herself.

In 1979 she wrote rather sadly, 'Expenses have risen so sharply that it seems impossible to recoup them through higher prices, there being a limit to what the buyers will pay.' The invaluable foreman has had to retire owing to ill-health after thirty-years' service, so Carola struggles on with one full-time man and various part-time helpers. Owners of small concerns, although the food they produce is of immense value to the country, are given little encouragement to continue. It is strange that the production of plants for pleasure gardens, and pot-plants for the home or office, seems to be more profitable than growing fresh food for these thickly-populated islands. We appear to prefer importing much of what we eat, unless war causes a sudden shift of policy.

Carola Cochrane is reticent about herself, a fairly common characteristic of women in horticulture. It seems to be a case of 'if you want to know me, look at my garden'. She is no longer young, and has to undergo medical treatment for anaemia, including blood transfusions. Owing to the difficulty and expense of finding and paying suitable labour, she works harder than before. 'Weeds are apt to overwhelm us at times. We cannot get round to cope with outdoor work in addition to fourteen glass-houses. I often wish I wore blinkers! Still, I carry on for the very simple reason that I love my job and cannot conceive of life without it.'

*   *   *   *

So far, little has been said about women working for owners of flower gardens and commercial enterprises. Pam Schwerdt and Sybille Kreutzberger, employed by Vita Sackville-West at Sissinghurst, were both trained at Beatrix Havergal's Waterperry Horticultural School. Pam and Sybille were both awarded the Associateship of Honour by the Royal Horticultural Society in 1981. They proved to be invincibly reticent and modest about themselves, but seemed glad to revive happy memories of their late employer.

Lady Nicolson was not in the least domesticated. Once, when an old friend had been invited here to luncheon during the regular cook's

153

holidays, disaster threatened the meal because a stand-in failed to turn up. We offered to help prepare food, but Lady Nicolson said we must not be given the trouble. One of those 'Nice little chickens, ready-cooked at the shop' would do if heated up with plenty of butter and herbs.

We saw her take a large bunch of mixed herbs into the kitchen. After a while she came out to us in the garden, inquiring anxiously why the shelves of the electric cooker did not glow when turned on. We assured her that this was not usual. Afterwards we asked about the meal. Lady Nicolson uttered just one word – *'Repulsive!'*

In her last years Lady Nicolson seldom left Sissinghurst, even for one night. When she had to go up to London she would come home by the last train rather than spend a night in town. When seriously ill with pneumonia in 1961, she had us in, turn about, to see her in bed and to discuss the jobs we were busy with in the garden. She wore striped winceyette pyjamas which were proudly described as being 'real Woolworth'. They were glorified by the most lovely necklaces of rubies and other precious stones. Everything had to be true and real with her, nothing faked or glossed over.

Never had anyone more truly merited the title *Companion of Honour.*

One of the most remarkable professional women I know is a native of that traditional home of fine gardeners, Scotland. Madge Elder, born in Portobello, spent most of her childhood at a family farm on the southern edge of the Lammermuirs, and for the first decade of this century she attended the village school at Gordon in Berwickshire. Madge was only nine years old when her father died. Soon afterwards a serious illness left her completely deaf. Fortunately, on the headmaster's advice, she was not sent away to a special school, but given individual attention by this good friend, who believed that the child would adapt more easily to her handicap if kept at home in familiar surroundings.

As aural learning was now denied her, she developed an insatiable thirst for literature, helped by a master who provided everything from Shakespeare to Sir Walter Scott and Dickens. All went well until the family farm had to be vacated. The widowed Mrs Elder then took the children to Edinburgh, a bitter blow to the deaf girl who had so much loved outdoor life in the country.

In 1910 a new school of gardening for women was set up on the edge of the city, providing Madge with a congenial niche where she could again see hills and live close to the soil. The two Principals, both Swanley-trained, found her an apt and hard-working student, giving her every assistance, so that she emerged in 1912 fully trained and equipped to earn her own living. It had not been easy. Evening classes at the Edinburgh School of Agriculture, with examinations to follow, were tricky for a deaf pupil who had never before sat an examination of any kind. In the end she came out on top, with a chemistry prize and a first-class certificate.

After all this effort, the graduate from Edinburgh's novel school for women gardeners had a tough time persuading the outside world to accept her as a qualified professional worker. Eventually Madge and a friend managed to set themselves up in business as 'Landscape and professional gardeners'. Up to a point this venture succeeded, but the outbreak of war in 1914 provided the young women with greater opportunities.

When it was over Madge wrote, 'It seemed best to use our knowledge and training to replace head gardeners who had been called up. This was not very exciting war work, but we felt we were doing our bit, by augmenting food crops and holding posts open for the men who came back.'

Madge's most important job – at the Duke of Buccleuch's seat near Selkirk, Bowhill – began awkwardly. The great house had been lent to the Red Cross as a convalescent home for war wounded, and the matron felt dubious about putting a woman in charge of the grounds and gardeners – a deaf woman at that. But Madge produced so fine an array of certificates and references that all resistance crumbled. Madge spent the rest of the war and its aftermath producing the maximum amount of vegetables and fruit from the Duke's land, including what had formerly been the flower garden. (That great singer Isobel Baillie in childhood stayed at a cottage on the same estate, and sometimes revisited her early home. She was born in Hawick.)

With the coming of peace, having much varied experience behind them, Madge and her friend opened a plant nursery in the Border town of Melrose, combining the sale of plants with freelance gardening. This work took Madge into many of the old Border gardens. Those at Faldonside, Chiefswood and Yair were all associated with her favourite writer, Sir Walter Scott. Alison Rutherford's Fairnilee, where Madge achieved some fame by constructing a fine rock garden, had been the place where Alison (the future Mrs Cockburn) wrote her version of *The Flowers of the*

Forest, traditionally sung at the close of the Selkirk Common Riding celebrations in June each year.

Small wonder that the book-loving Madge Elder made a second reputation with her pen. Her books about the Scottish Borders, *Ballad Country* and *Tell the Towers Thereof*, are in constant demand at libraries and deserve to be reprinted. Her retirement has not been an idle one, for she has contributed many articles to Scots papers and magazines and has composed talks (mostly read for her) at the request of local groups. Her retreat at Ancrum, bordered by a small wood and surrounded by fields, provided her with a host of birds and small creatures for company.

Deafness is a lonely handicap, and has effects on the sufferer which seem strange to those who can hear. Calling unexpectedly on Madge one afternoon, I failed to make her answer the door bell. Fearing to startle her if I were to walk round the house peering in at the windows, I dropped a note in the letter-box instead. This brought a sad reply. Madge had been at home and would have been very glad to see me. 'I have long since *grown used to being startled*,' she wrote. 'next time, stamp your feet in the porch and I shall feel the vibrations through the floor boards.' Her home was called The Bield, an old Scots word meaning shelter. Since my last visit Madge has removed to a less isolated house in the small town of Lauder in Berwickshire.

Florence Craggs and Doreen Dennis, who served Margaret Brownlow at the Herb Farm at Seal so faithfully and well, are the only full-time employed women on my list to have had no training in horticultural school or college. Margaret gave them all they required.

Doreen grew up with a love of gardening which she derived from her father (a policeman) and grandfather, a farmer who possessed a charming Old-World flower garden. Although a real country-woman, she had to begin her working life in the county offices at Maidstone. Many years later, when her adolescent daughter, who put in some spare time at Seal, told her of an opening for an experienced office worker at the Herb Farm, Doreen was glad to take it. After assisting with the preparation of Margaret Brownlow's now famous work, *Herbs and the Fragrant Garden*, she became an all-round helper outdoors, as well as doing duties as secretary to the Herb Farm, responsible for wages, book-keeping and the paperwork accompanying plant orders. In this capacity, she served full-time for sixteen years, from 1953 until 1969, when the

Herb Farm was wound up, and the goodwill sold to Bunyards after the death of Margaret Brownlow.

She used to spend half the day outside with Florence, propagating and potting up little plants and preparing orders for despatch by post. In the busy seasons they used to pack between thirty and forty parcels every day. When these had been loaded into the van, Doreen drove them away to Seal Post Office for dispatch by the afternoon post to every corner of the United Kingdom and beyond. She also had the responsible job of seeking orders in London for the Herb Farm pot-pourri and boxes of dried herbs in decorative packages, of which the Medici Society was a good customer in the weeks before Christmas. On top of all this, Doreen used to plan the Herb Farm exhibit which many of us remember as a delightful corner of the Chelsea Flower Show each year in May.

Florence Craggs also joined the Herb Farm from an indoor occupation, serving it for some eleven years. Margaret Brownlow used to call her the expert pot-pourri blender, and when visiting Seal I thought the shed where this work was done the most fragrant place in the world, and Mrs Craggs the most exquisitely scented person. This work was carried out to recipes which Margaret made her promise to keep secret. Between them, the two employees kept the business going during Margaret's long absences in hospital. They even 'stood in' for her on the radio and at lecture engagements. Both must deeply regret that it was not found possible to let them continue running the Herb Farm into the 1970s. Up to that time, profits on herbs and herb plants were very modest indeed. Then came a sudden upsurge of popular interest in the subject of herbs, paperback books appeared on the bookstalls, and in recent years less experienced people have flocked into the business to reap harvests laid down by the hard work of earlier pioneers.

Florence, who was invited in 1969 to start the Herb Garden at the Old Rectory, Ightham, not far from Sevenoaks, continued to work there for ten years. The usual working hours – 9 a.m. to 4.30 p.m. with an hour for lunch, – latterly proving rather much for her, taken in conjunction with a large garden at home, she was reduced to doing a part-time week. She found customers increasingly interested in the medicinal uses of herbs, a reaction from the synthetic drugs so freely prescribed by orthodox medical practitioners. Students display curiosity about the properties of plants as dye-stuffs for handspun wool and other weaving material, an aspect not as yet much developed by herb nurseries.

One disadvantage which did not plague the old Herb Farm at Seal is the marked deterioration of postal services in Britain. From time to time complaints are received from customers whose plants arrive in poor shape after spending up to a fortnight in transit. No amount of careful packing can prevent damage to plants, which suffer from such inordinate delay, and there is nothing the supplier can do to expedite delivery, although it is now customary for a date of despatch to be clearly marked on parcels, so that recipients with a grievance may see where the blame lies.

Although she still made up pot-pourri and sachets to the original Herb Farm recipes, Florence kept strictly to the promise she gave Margaret Brownlow and would not divulge the secrets to her employer. Faithfulness to every small detail of plant care being essential for good gardening, it is of interest to notice that this woman gardener displays the same characteristics in all her concerns.

Like everyone else, she worried about some of the less skilled labour which had to be entrusted with certain tasks. Watering is the most difficult art to teach, and over-watering can soon cause havoc among small propagated herb plants. Either you have an instinct for giving plants what they need, or you have not. Florence believes that good gardeners are born, not made; but unfortunately they do not come with 'Green Finger' labels attached. When labour is scarce, it is not practicable to discard hands of the wrong hue.

If gardening schools for women, establishments large and small, turned out to be a temporary expedient suited to the interim period – little more than half a century – between the upsurge of demand for a variety of feminine careers and the developement of some sex equality legislation and mixed-sex training colleges, an enterprise of ballooning educational value to the public seems assured of a very much longer life. The Soil Association, whose principles in the beginning were often derided as 'muck and mystery', finds itself in this last quarter of the twentieth century very much the champion of developing conservation and ecology movements, while tens of thousands of amateur gardeners now regard the compost heap as a vital part of their equipment. Even the most conservative farmers and agricultural institutions have conceded that there is 'something in' organic methods of cultivation.

What is the Soil Association? The central concern is applied ecology, and ecology in the broadest sense is as complex as it is fascinating. It represents, as Lady Eve Balfour has made clear in writings and speeches, a whole philosophy of living, and that means living in harmony not only with our own species but with all others, including the micro-organisms found in what she has called *the living soil*. Interest – that which is between – is primarily a matter of relationships, which are the material of ecology. Those interests with which The Soil Association is chiefly concerned occur between soil, plant, animal and man. Our own well-being is directly dependent on the fecundity and healthy vigour of the first three in association, to which we must contribute by wise management.

In 1952 the Editor of the Soil Association's *Journal* wrote:

> . . . while human fertility, powerfully reinforced by medical science, is expanding world populations by at least twenty-four millions every year, the fertility of the soil on which the human race depends is declining. Each year billions of tons of topsoil are washed or blown away. This grievous loss is but symptomatic (erosion being merely the end-phase of soil exhaustion or disorganisation) of a soil degeneration that is now well-nigh world-wide.
>
> This process, there is reason to believe, also manifests itself in reduced vigour of plants and their increasing susceptibility to pests and disease, and so in turn affects the well-being of animals and man consuming those plants. There is a mass of circumstantial evidence and an urgent need for systematic investigation. Yet The Soil Association is the only body which has, so far, even initiated such an inquiry.

How did it all begin? Lady Eve Balfour, in collaboration with the late Alice Debenham, lit the flame – very small at first – by her experimental project at Haughley in Suffolk. This gradually became known to widening circles through the issue of a pamphlet, and in due course a book developed from that, called *The Living Soil*, published by Faber in 1943 and lately revised and re-issued as *Living Soil and the Haughley Experiment*.

In the Association's *Journal* for July 1952 Lady Eve described the beginnings.

> It is difficult to say exactly when the first seed was sown, but I shall begin the story in the late nineteen-thirties, the period in which the result of some of the great pioneering work was made known. Some years earlier Sir Robert McCarrison had described in the Cantor Lectures (afterwards issued as *Nutrition and Health*, Faber 1944) the

159

results of his own research work in nutrition – work that is still second to none in importance, for it provided conclusive proof that the most important single factor in promoting good health is the right kind of food. These lectures received little publicity until they were written up in popular form by Dr J. T. Wrench in his book *The Wheel of Health* (1938).

Dr Wrench focused attention on the link between McCarrison's work on human nutrition and Howard's work on plant and animal nutrition. It also gave an account of certain human communities which all possessed a full measure of sound health, the only common factor between them being a diet of indigenous natural whole food grown from naturally treated soil, or culled from the sea.

Lady Eve, born in 1898, is a niece of Lord (A. J.) Balfour and a daughter of the second Earl. At the age of twelve she made up her mind to become a farmer, an unswerving desire which caused her parents to put her name down for Reading University College, where she became a student in 1915. Two years later she gained an Honours Diploma in Agriculture. After that, a stint as farm student was followed by a job training the Women's Land Army of World War I.

After the war she began to farm on her own account in Suffolk, where for fifteen years her outlook and practice were conventional and in accordance with her training. A major change in her attitude to the land came when she read Lord Lymington's book *Famine in England*. In her opinion the author seemed to have a bee in his bonnet, but 'a bee with an interesting buzz which I must find out more about'.

She now read everything with a bearing on the subject, and met Sir Albert Howard, then engaged in writing his *Agricultural Testament*. This account of his own research showed that even if food was of the right kind for health, it could fail to produce health unless it came from healthy soil – that is, soil packed with humus and life. Visitations of pests and diseases were an indication of unbalanced soil and conditions, leading to unbalanced nutrition of plants and unbalanced diet of animals.

Through contact with Sir Albert and his friends Dr Wrench and Dr Picton, Lady Eve increased her understanding of the soil, and began to experiment with practical tests of the things she had learnt. She made compost, and applied it to her own garden and to certain fields. Then she began to eat compost-grown food, and her own

160

health showed marked improvement. Diligent study of all available material showed that nowhere had a long-term, comparative and controlled experiment been undertaken to test the theories advanced by Howard and others, although there were any number of indications to support those theories. Lady Eve became impressed with the urgent need for establishing some such test, and felt inspired to embark on the project herself.

At this time (1939) she was the owner-occupier of New Bells Farm at Haughley in Suffolk, and farmed also the adjacent Walnut Tree property as the tenant of Alice Debenham. The latter in youth had been one of the first women to study medicine in England, but was forced by ill-health to give up that career. Ordered to live out of doors, she had practised farming for many years. To her keen mind, with a practical knowledge of agriculture added to some basic medical training, Lady Eve's new project made immediate appeal. From the outset she provided generous assistance by forming the Haughley Research Trust, to which she gave her own Walnut Tree Manor House and farm land.

The year 1939 also saw publication of two more important books, *The Rape of the Earth* by Jacks and Whyte (Faber) and the *Medical Testament* of the Chester Committee, for which Lady Eve's friend Dr L. J. Picton was largely responsible. At this time the journal *Forestry* issued remarkable papers by Dr Rayner. All of these were germane to the experimental work being planned at Haughley. Dr Rayner's work on mycorrhizal association was undertaken in connection with tree nutrition, but threw valuable light on the role of micro-organisms in normal healthy plant growth. Later on, after World War II, the importance of 'good' bacteria throughout the whole nutrition cycle was revealed by the discovery of the dependence of animals and human beings on the normal micro-flora of the digestive tract.

Up to that time most people vaguely regarded bacteria as harmful organisms associated with disease and death. When the ideas of Lady Eve became known, the suggestion that 'good' bacteria in the soil must be given the right conditions in which to multiply was novel and startling. In her book *The Living Soil*, which developed from the pamphlet issued in 1941, she had this to say:

> Soil is a substance teeming with life. If that life is killed, the soil quite literally dies. It is the living organisms in the soil, and the products resulting from their activities, that differentiate soil from subsoil.

161

Subsoil is derived from the surface of the rock which forms the earth's crust. It is classified as a mineral and measured in terms of inorganic chemistry. The mistake has been to extend that conception to topsoil, for by the time subsoil becomes soil it is no longer wholly inorganic. Soil is a mixture of disintegrating mineral rock and humus, with its population of micro-organisms. The two are intermingled, and growth and reproduction cannot long be maintained under natural conditions in the absence of humus. Besides growth-promoting substances which it contains, humus gives soil its texture, its stability and much of its water-retaining capacity. A product of the decomposition of animals and vegetable residues brought about through the agency of micro-organisms, humus is far from dead in the sense of having returned to the inorganic world. It is still organic matter, in the transition stage between one form of life and another.

Gradually a band of collaborators was built up. One, Maye E. Bruce, wrote a splendidly practical little book, *Commonsense Compost Making by the Quick Returns Method* (Faber, 1946), which has been reprinted many times. A year earlier, massive correspondence engendered by Lady Eve's own book led to a public meeting in London at which the Soil Association had its beginning, although it was not registered until the end of 1946. By that time it had developed into something more than the clearing house for information which had been in the founder's mind. The many clauses of its constitution may be condensed into three sentences: 'To bring together all those working for a fuller understanding of the vital relationships between soil, plant, animal and man; to initiate and co-ordinate research in this field; to collect and distribute the knowledge gained, so as to create a body of informed public opinion.

'From the start', to quote Lady Eve, 'the Association was conceived as inclusive rather than exclusive, and positive rather than negative. It came to stand among its growing membership for nothing less than an attitude to Life itself. This attitude is usually described as the ecological approach or the philosophy of wholeness – the logical outcome of a positive approach, just as fragmentation is the logical outcome of a negative approach. Our ignorance about Life is at present profound. Those who believe in wholeness know that we can increase our knowledge only by admitting ignorance, cultivating humility, enlarging our field of vision through learning to see ecologically, by respecting life – not wantonly destroying it.'

At their two small Suffolk farms (New Bells, 156 acres and Walnut Tree, 60 acres) Eve Balfour and Alice Debenham began their experiment in integration. It was a lone pioneering leap in the dark which may one day rank with the work of other visionaries, from Galileo to Pasteur and Einstein, who have widened the frontiers of knowledge for the human race. They began the practical work by dividing their 216 acres into three units, each to be run as a self-contained farm. The land is flat, subdivided by hedges and ditches into small fields averaging six to seven acres each. The soil is a nearly uniform clay-loam overlying a glacial formation of clay and flint, with pockets of sand, which in turn overlies chalk. The uniformity of these characteristics throughout both properties made them ideally suitable for the research project.

Excluding land occupied by buildings, the acreage was divided into two stockbearing units of some 75 acres each, the one wholly organic, the other given a proportion of artificial fertilisers. The third unit, 32 acres, carried no livestock. It was in fact a large organic garden. Each section was established with seed, and two with foundation animals, of common origin. After this the units bred their own requirements of seed and stock.

It takes ten years on a stock-bearing section to span a full crop rotation. From 1939 to 1947, with disruption caused by World War II, it was possible only to lay the foundations. By 1948 the project was in danger of shipwreck on financial rocks. The newly formed Soil Association then took over responsibility for the Haughley Farm Experiment and for the next five years held lengthy discussions about the enormous difficulty of evolving procedures acceptable to scientists – as meeting their research requirements – and viable by the standards of farming practice. The full story has been given in *The Haughley Experiment*, now brought up-to-date and re-issued together with *The Living Soil* (Faber, 1978).

The experiment and its findings are too complex to be detailed here. A brilliant survey of her work and ideas up to 1977 was given by Lady Eve at a meeting in Switzerland of the International Federation of Organic Agricultural Movements, a paper reprinted in the Soil Association's *Journal* for June 1978. One thing is certain; nobody can afford to ignore this research, and tributes have been paid to it by various universities, by the Nature Conservancy and other bodies of importance.

To continue her personal story, Lady Eve relinquished her post as farm manager at Haughley in 1948 to become Organising Secretary of The Soil Association. In its *Journal* for July 1952 she wrote:

> . . . from the start the farming venture was under-capitalised. The build-up of the establishment of separate herds of livestock was therefore slow. Nevertheless, we hung on and the work progressed. The Association's affairs, as distinct from the Haughley Experiment, also prospered. By 1951 we had a membership of just over three thousand from forty-two countries. We exhibit regularly at agricultural shows. The name of the Association has become known and respected.
>
> Looking ahead, an immense field of work lies open to us. There must be closer personal contact, through interchange and travel, between members overseas and headquarters here in Britain. We must have representatives travelling and seeing personally what others are doing, and searching out – not only in the practical field, but in research establishments also – the many parts of the ecological jigsaw puzzle we are trying to piece together.

She herself put this into practice in a series of fact-finding and lecture tours which took her to the United States in 1951 and 1953, to Australia and New Zealand in 1958-9. From February to April 1953 Lady Eve and her friend Miss Carnley covered thirty-one states (9,600 miles) in a self-drive station-wagon. To save expense the lecture programme had been closely knit, but Lady Eve kept all her appointments and spoke dead on time everywhere. Lectures were given on two nights out of three, and throughout the marathon both women kept fit. That alone was a good advertisement for wholefood.

Lady Eve did as much learning as lecturing. Writing of water supply, she said:

> . . . it may come as rainfall or snow, from underground reserves or from irrigation. Water supply of a given area depends fundamentally on afforestation on the watersheds and conservation lower down, but even in this basic matter techniques must be governed by circumstances and should not be confused with principle. In England it is axiomatic that conifers are poor water regulators and that the hardwood trees produce the sponge-like forest humus which allows absorption of water, so that it may seep into underground reservoirs and not run off the surface to cause erosion or floods. I did not realise that this had become almost a

Valerie Finnis at Waterperry with her alpines – photograph by Nicholas Meyjes.

Beatrix Havergal with Waterperry students, 1964 – photograph by Nicholas Meyjes.

Carola Cochrane in one of her greenhouses, 1979.

Octavia Hill – portrait by J. S. Sargent (National Portrait Gallery).

Lady Eve Balfour and Miss K. Carnley, 1950 – photograph by Sir George Trevelyan.

Modern town garden by Sylvia Crowe (Cement & Concrete Association).

Nov. 2.
1958

V. Sackville-West,
Sissinghurst Castle, Kent.

Dear Miss Macdonald
    It was really most kind of you to
ask your publishers to send me a copy of
your delightful book on Inverewe.
It did take me back to that day when
we came and bothered you, and you so
charmingly accompanied us in the garden,
and even gave me some seed of
myosotidium nobile, and picked a
watsonia for me. How well I understand
your love of that beautiful country. I often
think of the lovely, wild, lonely road
along Little Loch Broome — and I also
remember climbing up Greinord (is that right?)
Head and seeing the Shiant islands
far out in a glittering sea, which
thrilled me because they belong to my

Facsimile of letter from V. Sackville-West to the author.

son, and I had never seen them before.

You must surely miss it all very much.

Anyway, thank you very much indeed for having given me a great deal of pleasure.

Yours very sincerely
V. Sackville-West.

———

Of course Harold belongs in a way to that part of Scotland, because his ancestors came from Skye.

Rene Clayton with students in her garden centre.

Betty Sherriff at Ascreavie – photographer unknown.

Lady gardeners at Kew, circa *1895* (Royal Botanic Gardens, Kew).

principle in my mind until I discovered that in sections of America's eastern seaboard the reverse is true.

The reason for the difference is that in those parts the main winter precipitation is in the form of snow. The broad leaves of deciduous trees remain like flat shingles under the snow, and when it melts the water rushes off them into the valley below. Conifers, on the other hand, being evergreen, hold much of the snow in their branches, and when the thaw comes water drips and seeps through the more porous pine needles and so goes down instead of running off.

In the United States she was struck by the fact that in all the organic farms and gardens they visited no form of pesticide was in use, or needed. That was far more impressive in America than elsewhere, because poison spraying had become so nearly universal that the average cultivator could not believe that any crop could survive without what was called 'protection'.

Back home at Haughley, no chemical sprays whatever were used on the organic farm. Insects were not a problem, and weeds were not eliminated but controlled by good cultivation and encouragement of crops, so that weeds were smothered. At a conference in 1967 Dr Milton of The Soil Association said that benefits of pesticides had to be balanced against hazards, including spray drift. Many pesticides are toxic to succeeding plants, for they build up on the soil. They also destroy beneficial insects such as those which pollinate crops.

Not so long ago, critics would try to belittle the organic, anti-poison school by applying to it the tag 'Muck and Mystery'. Within a decade or two the situation began to alter. Masses of ordinary people began to wonder if the so-called marvels of science are all as beneficial to mankind as scientists would have them believe. Now a common target for criticism is uncontrolled chemistry (those deformed thalidomide babies are a terrible example) and the looming uncertainties of nuclear power, allied to materialistic malpractice which undermines those very foundations of life – the soil and our food.

In the words of Lady Eve, 'A great and noble task lies ahead. I am convinced that the influence of The Soil Association can play an important part in helping man to survive on this planet. This he will succeed in doing only if he learns to abandon exploitation in favour of co-operation – to become, as the late Sir Frank Fraser-Darling put it, "symbiotic instead of parasitic"; if he gives up his reliance on short-term expedients in favour of long-term ecological policy.' She herself, at the age of eighty plus, is a radiant advertisement for the health and well-being induced by organically grown wholefood and living in harmony with the land.

Note on Octavia Hill

Co-founder of The National Trust

Octavia, the eighth daughter of James Hill of Wisbech, was born in 1838 to her father's third wife, Caroline Southwood-Smith. James Hill, a man of liberal spirit, pressed for elementary schooling for every child, long before the National Schools were introduced. He also founded a lending library and fought abuses in his own town to such purpose that when the Reform Bill came into operation there was very little to be reformed in Wisbech.

Octavia's mother had been greatly influenced by her own father, Doctor Southwood-Smith, who was also an energetic social reformer. He believed that fever epidemics, then so prevalent, were due to contagion and caused by bad sanitary conditions, which he strove to have remedied. His daughter, sharing his reforming zeal, published 'advanced' articles on the necessity of promoting educational facilities for the cultivation of mental and physical well-being. These activities attracted the elderly widower James Hill, and led to their marriage when Caroline was only twenty-six.

Under such influences and example it is small wonder that Octavia grew up with public-spirited determination to help improve the lot of less-advantaged members of society. The family motto, '*Don't attempt unless you mean to put through*', sums up her lifelong attitude to work. Her own childhood was shadowed by the collapse of her father's business interests and his subsequent nervous breakdown. The comfortable family home at Wisbech had to be given up, and while older children were helped by relatives to start out in life, Octavia and two sisters were taken to a cottage in Finchley. This was provided by Doctor Southwood-Smith and situated not far from his own house in Hampstead.

The burden of bringing up her young daughters now fell almost entirely on their mother's shoulders. She gave them their schooling and taught them to be useful about the house, for now there were no hired servants to wait on the family. They were all intelligent, healthy girls who worked hard and made the most of their opportunities. When their mother obtained a post as manageress to the Christian Ladies' Guild, an enterprise set up to provide employment for women in such handicrafts as glass-painting and toy-making, the two elder daughters were already well equipped to assist her.

Octavia was barely fifteen when personal contact with the women employed in the workshop opened her eyes to the grimmer side of life around the Hills in the 1850s. Slum conditions had been rapidly created when people from rural areas swarmed into the city in search of work in developing industries. Sudden growth was unplanned and haphazard, so that proper living conditions with sanitation and adequate ventilation were seldom to be had. The River Thames was described as 'a great cesspool', and sordid gin-palaces with drunken brawling provided the sole recreation for thousands of working people.

The artistic talent which brought Octavia commissions as a designer for the Ladies' Guild attracted the attention of no less a critic than John Ruskin. Their first meeting occurred in 1853, when Ruskin was thirty-four and Octavia fifteen. He had already made a name for himself with his books *Modern Painters*, *The Stones of Venice* and *The Seven Lamps of Architecture*. In our modern universities and colleges these books are being discovered afresh. Octavia and her family read them directly they were issued, and her delight at attracting the author's attention and being offered lessons in drawing by him was intense. But it seems that she in her turn was able to expand his knowledge of social conditions.

Her contact with Ruskin continued over many years, and he used some of her designs in his books. In 1860 Mrs Hill, following the collapse and closure of the Guild workshop, opened a private school. By this time the Hills had moved to a house in Marylebone, where they soon discovered many poor people living in terrible premises. Discussing this appalling state of affairs with Ruskin, Octavia found him completely unaware that even in so-called 'better class' districts, seedy dereliction could be found alongside houses inhabited by the comparatively well-to-do professional classes. Near neighbours of the Hills were huddled together in one room, these apartments often in reeking damp basements.

Octavia could not rest until she had done something to provide improved housing for some of those unfortunate people. She was not interested in abstract political ideas, but had thought out a practical scheme for carrying out some useful reforms in her own district. Octavia had no capital, but her friend John Ruskin had inherited a large fortune from his father and was beginning to feel uneasy about enjoying luxurious comfort while others endured squalor. Impressed by his pupil's keenness and capability, he commissioned her to find a run-down property and bring it up to tolerable standards. The only stipulation he made was that the project must be put on a proper business footing and made to pay its way – which Octavia accepted without demur.

After much careful investigation of dilapidated buildings in the vicinity, Octavia acquired the lease of a row of cottages, for which Ruskin allowed her £750, with a similar sum for renovation work. In the summer of 1865, at the age of twenty-seven, she came into full control of her first scheme of improved housing. Ruskin, the legal owner, left management of property and tenants entirely in Octavia's hands, on condition that she took 'a just rent, and firmly'. They fixed the amount at a return of five per cent on the £1,500 invested.

By collecting all the rents herself, she soon became familiar with the occupants and their ways. Given better water supplies, clean walls and paintwork, neat stairs and new grates, women began to take pride in their homes. Octavia's deep concern and friendly approach encouraged and assisted the process, and she dropped a few gentle hints to the effect that in return for improved conditions the tenants were expected to take good care of the property and keep their own premises clean.

This venture proved to be a striking success, and so Octavia, again financed by Ruskin, went on to refurbish other run-down tenements. Poor though they were, people understood that such schemes could not continue unless they paid their rents promptly. The conditions originally laid down were strictly adhered to, and Ruskin received his five per cent interest. No doubt this fact spurred him to invest more capital in Octavia's housing projects. Soon she took pupils to assist her with the work. One who became very well known later on was the future Dame Henrietta Barnett.

A property off the Edgeware Road gave Octavia not only some

derelict housing to restore, but an open space as well. This had once been part of a farm and was littered with rotting timber and broken down cowsheds half buried in manure. One ancient water butt served for all the inhabitants. There was no Metropolitan Water Board at that time, and private companies delivered water when it suited them.

Octavia, who was by now experienced in the business of repairing houses, saw at once the advantage of the 'open space' – a term she herself coined. It is sufficient of itself to make her name remembered and honoured. She swept away the rotting sheds and litter, making a playground for children, neatly surfaced and railed off. The rest of the land became a small garden, planted with some trees given by Ruskin. This was the very first of Octavia's green spaces, where inhabitants could take exercise and gain a little fresh air.

People were eager to make use of it, so she began to develop the idea. The authorities were pressed to clear and open neglected strips of waste land, and presently she suggested opening deserted burial grounds for the use of city dwellers. Railways and other engineering projects had begun to encroach upon London commons, activities which she opposed with energy and foresight.

Her vigorous articles and speeches as a founder-member of the Commons Preservation Society stimulated Parliament to regulate the enclosure of common lands near cities and towns. Without this timely measure of control, there would be few left open for people today. At a meeting of the Society – soon to become the Commons and Footpaths Preservation Society – Octavia called upon her audience to join 'a few unknown heroes fighting for a great cause'.

One of the unknown crusaders, a lakeland clergyman named Canon Rawnsley, was to become a founder of the National Trust along with Sir Robert Hunter and Octavia Hill. The preservation of her 'open spaces' is still carried on to a large extent by the National Trust and its counterpart in the North, the National Trust for Scotland, which celebrated its Golden Jubilee in 1981.

Many famous gardens are now cared for by these bodies, in addition to V. Sackville-West's Sissinghurst in Kent, Tintinhull in Somerset, created by Phyllis Reiss, and Inverewe in Wester Ross, already mentioned.

Octavia Hill lived to see the seal set on this, her last public-spirited enterprise, when in 1907 Parliament passed the National Trust Act, which charged it with the special duty of preserving for the nation places of historic interest or natural beauty. She died in 1912, and all of us who belong to one or other of the Trusts, or who visit and are refreshed by the lovely places which they manage to maintain intact, should spare a grateful thought for that energetic and selfless pioneer, Octavia Hill.

Afterword

Considering the women already depicted, some of them personal friends, I am conscious of too many omissions. Anne Scott-James must be mentioned, as she is only the second woman to gain a seat on the Council of the Royal Horticultural Society, succeeding Frances Perry in 1978. Anne has gardened successfully for some forty years and is the author of several garden books.

Then there is Beth Chatto, who came to the fore as a plantswoman of discrimination during the 1970s. She cultivates unusual and interesting subjects on ten acres near Colchester and attracted attention with her first exhibit at the Chelsea Flower Show in 1976. Her nursery and garden at White Barn House, Elmstead Market, is open all the year round (except for Sundays and Bank Holidays). Beth has also recorded much valuable experience in print.

The very latest woman recipient of the coveted Victoria Medal of Honour, Mrs W. G. Knox Finlay of Keillour Castle in Perthshire, is only the second Scotswoman to be given this award, the first being Queen Elizabeth the Queen Mother.

Mary Knox Finlay received the award from Lord Aberconway, President of The Royal Horticultural Society, in London on 17th February 1981. He told the Annual General Meeting: 'When I presented a V.M.H. to Mrs Knox Finlay's late husband thirteen years ago, I suggested that in equity it should be cut in half, and half given to you, Mrs Knox Finlay. Many of us felt that, as his equal partner in the raising of your nomocharis, lilies and primulas, you were equally deserving. It therefore gives me all the more pleasure by this medal to pay tribute to you for carrying on your joint work at Keillour. You not only keep many rare plants alive; you continue to breed further rare plants – and keep them alive too.'

At one stage I hoped to find a woman gardener at a railway station, recalling platform delights which used to enhance country travel. Unfortunately these charming artefacts are almost extinct – in England, at least – and used to be a masculine preserve. There is still a fine floral display running the length of our main-line station in Scotland, which won first prize for Dunbar in the British Rail competition in 1979, but this is the labour-of-love of two men.

Then Anne Scott-James let me into the secret of an eligible garden at Shepreth in Cambridgeshire. Mrs Douglas Fuller, the wife of a railwayman, has created a real 'collector's piece' from ground beside their level-crossing house. Old-fashioned cottage plants mingle with modern varieties in mixed beds with shrubs, bulbs and alpines, while Douglas cultivates vegetables of first-class quality on a strip adjoining the line, in the best tradition of railways. The 'Crossing-House' garden is open to the public at times shown in The National Gardens Scheme booklet, issued annually from 57 Lower Belgrave Street, London SW1W 0LR.

Love of plants and gardening has led some women to write of their experiences, while others have confined their attention to horticulture. Mairi Sawyer of Inverewe refused to waste time, as she put it, on paperwork. When repeated demands for a guide-book to Inverewe came from the National Trust for Scotland, she directed me to act as her 'ghost' writer. Phyllis Reiss concentrated all her thought and energy on the lovely Tintinhull garden and in later years very seldom left it.

The writing of books, articles and lectures, which occupied my dear friend Margery Fish on winter evenings (and in summer far into the small hours) gave added pleasure to the gardener herself and to her wide-ranging public. Vita Sackville-West, who established a reputation as the author of poetry, fiction and biography before her skill as a gardener developed, turned to horticultural journalism in 1947 at the age of fifty-five, and quickly achieved the greatest popularity in this field.

A few women seem to have been garden-writers first and practical gardeners afterwards – if at all. Of Eleanour Sinclair Rohde it was once said that most of her herb gardening was done in the Reading-Room of the British Museum. Inquiries made among surviving members of her family, as well as local friends, have satisfied me that she was also a genuine working herb-gardener, with a well-earned place in these pages.

Of two other women, both writers of popular garden books in the early years of this century, I feel doubtful. How much real work did 'Elizabeth' carry out in her German Garden? On one occasion she admitted to feeling self-conscious about some digging, and hid her spade away from prying eyes. Possibly it would not have done for high-born visitors to catch the Countess von Arnim at such a menial task; but this behaviour does not suggest a really dedicated down-to-earth woman.

The writer Marion Cran published some beguiling accounts of her own garden, which in youth I found entirely credible. Then some neighbour who had seen her garden spoiled my pleasure by saying that the books were dreams of how the place might have looked if sufficient time and money had been spent on it. In his view, the author had richly imaginative ideas without the means of fulfilling them. It is just possible that Marion Cran may have been what is known as 'past it' by the time her critic came on the scene.

Mention of the time and money which she lacked brings me to the inescapable fact that these assets have always been of importance to makers of fine gardens. That is why so many women of leisure and means have found places in this book. Gertrude Jekyll may have been right when she said that the size of a garden has very little to do with its merit; but even when that size is no more than a few rods, poles or perches (or whatever the metric equivalent may be), probably full of builders' rubble and old tin cans, the owner must devote time and money to the work if a good garden is to be created. In cash terms, the cost has been grossly inflated in the last ten years.

It is true that time and money are not enough. The basic need beyond these is a genuine love of plants and the soil which nurtures their growth. It does not do to rush around with hoe, fertiliser and water-can when the weather happens to encourage outdoor activity. Plants, like babies, have to be watched over and cared for without ceasing. Even in the depths of winter there are firming-up, staking and tying jobs to be done, as well as pruning. All this becomes such an ingrained habit that the best gardeners feel unable to stop, even though advanced years and painful joints make outdoor work difficult.

Two of the longest-serving herb-growers in Britain, both former pupils of Dorothy Hewer at her Seal Herb Farm in the early 1930s, are still (1981) running their own herb nurseries. Madge Hooper owns a delightfully sheltered and fragrant garden at Stoke Lacy in

Herefordshire, which has – as she puts it – 'different little bits rambling off to make up the whole. It is a garden of herbs rather than a formal herb garden'.

Her lifelong friend, Barbara Keen, runs a herb farm at Valeswood near Shrewsbury in Shropshire. She began her work in 1932 at her aunt's house on the Welsh Border. The friends meet from time to time and discuss the awful prospect of having to give up. Then each returns home and both of them carry on as before.

Those of us who know their work and admire the vast store of herb knowledge which they have gained in some fifty years cannot bear the thought that these green-fingered women will ever have to close down their nurseries. The same applies to Carola Cochrane, who still cultivates her two Kentish acres intensively in spite of poor health and labour shortages. She carries on because she loves the job and cannot conceive of life without it.

The saddest part of a gardener's life is the knowledge that gardens are fragile and personal creations. Even the most celebrated examples, which merit being taken over by the National Trust, begin to change and lose some of their finer characteristics after the owner dies. Visitors then see plenty of well-arranged, healthy plants, neat lawns and well-weeded paths, with carefully contrived schemes of colour, and yet never quite the picture in its original glory.

'Restorers' take a hand in these works of art which, because the medium consists of living plants subject to change and decay, gives them far greater latitude than is allowed to those who preserve Rembrandt or Velasquez behind the scenes in art galleries. It is no doubt this intensely fragile and fleeting aspect of garden design which has brought its finest practitioners less regard in the halls of fame than is earned by great artists using more stable materials.

Many skilled women gardeners have not desired any publicity for themselves. They prefer to see attention focussed on their gardens. A few of my subjects refused to be photographed. Elsie Matley Moore at The Greyfriars, Worcester, stipulated 'back view only'. Mairi Sawyer, taken in a surprise attack by a young visitor, threw the print into a wastepaper basket. Retrieved in secret by a housemaid, this rare snapshot of Mairi in her seventieth year came to light after her death. Readers who may wish for more personal details of this one or that will understand that modesty and reticence have at times been unsurmountable.

In spite of a calmly appraising attitude to the manifest frailty of our creations, those of us who love gardening carry on undaunted. I have lived to see the cherished work of friends built on, neglected, or turned into commonplace areas of grass, concrete paving, and garish roses ordered by the dozen without thought. I have put in years of hard toil myself, making cherished gardens which had to be abandoned when we moved. 'How can you bear it?' People ask. The truth – trite though it may sound – is that it is infinitely better to have loved and lost than never to have loved at all.

Book List

AGAR, Madeline, *Garden Design in Theory and Practice*
AMHERST, Alicia, *A History of Gardening in England*
A RELIGIOUS of C.S.M.V., *Meditations of a Caterpillar*
ARMITAGE, Ethel, *Garden and Hedgerow*
BALFOUR, Lady Eve, *The Living Soil and the Haughley Experiment*
BLUNT, Wilfrid, *The Art of Botanical Illustration*
BROWNLOW, Margaret, *Herbs and the Fragrant Garden; The Delights of Herb Growing*
BRUCE, Maye E., *Commonsense Compost Making*
CHATTO, Beth, *The Dry Garden*
COATS, Alice M., *Flowers and their Histories; Garden Shrubs and their Histories*
COCHRANE, Carola, *Two Acres Unlimited*
COX, E. H. M., *History of Gardening in Scotland; Plant Hunting in China*
COXHEAD, Elizabeth, *One Woman's Garden*
CROWE, Sylvia, *Garden Design; To-morrow's Landscape*
Curtis's Botanical Magazine Dedications (Nelmes and Cuthbertson)
EARLE, Mrs C. W. (Theresa), *Pot-pourri from a Surrey Garden; More Pot-pourri from a Surrey Garden*
ELLACOMBE, Canon H. M., *In a Gloucestershire Garden; The Plant Lore and Garden Craft of Shakespeare*
FARRER, Reginald, *On the Eaves of the World; The English Rock Garden; The Rainbow Bridge*
FISH, Margery, *We Made a Garden; Gardening in the Shade; A Flower for Every Day; An All-the-year Garden; Ground Cover Plants; Cottage Garden Flowers; Carefree Gardening*
FLETCHER, H. R. L., *A Quest of Flowers*
GRANT, Doris, *Your Daily Food*

GRIEVE, Mrs, *A Modern Herbal*
HADFIELD, Miles, *Pioneers in Gardening; Gardening in Britain*
HARTLEY, Dorothy (Editor), *Thomas Tusser's Five Hundred Points of Good Husbandry*
HEWER, Dorothy, *Practical Herb Growing*
HILL, W. T., *Octavia Hill*
HOOPER, Madge, *Them Ole Weeds* (Stoke Lacy Herb Garden)
HOPE, Frances Jane, *Notes and Thoughts on Gardens and Woodlands* (written chiefly for amateurs)
HOWARD, Sir Albert, *An Agricultural Testament*
HOWE, Bea, *Lady with Green Fingers*
HYAMS, Edward, *The Speaking Garden*
JACKS, G. V. and WHYTE, R. O., *The Rape of the Earth*
JEKYLL, Frances, *Gertrude Jekyll, a Memoir*
JEKYLL, Gertrude, *Wood and Garden; Home and Garden; Lilies for English Gardens; Wall and Water Gardens; Roses for English Gardens; Old West Surrey; Some English Gardens; Flower Decoration in the House; Colour in the Flower Garden; Children and Gardens; Gardens for Small Country Houses* (with L. Weaver); *Garden Ornament* (with C. Hussey); *A Gardener's Testament*
JOHNSON, G. W., *A History of British Gardening*
JOHNSON, Louisa, *Every Lady Her Own Flower Gardener*
JULIAN OF NORWICH, THE LADY, *XVI Revelations of Divine Love*
KELWAY, Christine, *Gardening on the Coast*
KINGDON WARD, Frank, *The Land of the Blue Poppy; Pilgrimage for Plants*
LEYEL, Mrs C. F., *The Truth about Herbalism; Herbal Delights; Compassionate Herbs; Hearts-ease; Green Medicine; Cinquefoil; Elixirs of Life*
LOUDON, Jane, *The Mummy; Gardening for Ladies; The Ladies' Flower-Garden* (four volumes);*Botany for Ladies; The Ladies Country Companion; The Amateur Gardener's Calendar; My Own Garden*
LOUDON, John, *Arboretum Britannicum; The Suburban Gardener and Villa Companion*
MACKENZIE, Osgood, *A Hundred Years in the Highlands*
MacLEOD, Dawn, *Oasis of the North; A Book of Herbs; The Gardener's London; The Gardener's Scotland*
MASSINGHAM, Betty, *Miss Jekyll: Portrait of a Great Gardener*

178

MAXWELL, Sir H., *Scottish Gardens*
McCARRISON, Sir Robert, *Nutrition and National Health*
MORRIS, G. (Editor), *The Journeys of Celia Fiennes*
NICOLSON, P. (Editor), *V. Sackville-West's Garden Book*
NORTHBOURNE, Lord, *Look to the Land*
OSBORNE, Fairfield, *Our Plundered Planet*
PAGE, Russell, *The Education of a Gardener*
PEARSALL SMITH, Logan, *Reperusals and Recollections*
PEARSE, Dr I. H. and CROCKER, L. H., *The Peckham Experiment*
RAYNER, M. C. and JONES, W. N., *Problems in Tree Nutrition*
ROBINSON, William, *The English Flower Garden; The Wild Garden*
ROHDE, Eleanour Sinclair, *A Garden of Herbs; The Old English Herbals; The Scented Garden; The Story of the Garden; Oxford College Gardens; Gardens of Delight; Shakespeare's Wild Flowers; Herbs and Herb Gardening; Vegetable Cultivation and Cookery; The War-Time Vegetable Garden; Culinary and Salad Herbs; Uncommon Vegetables and Fruits*
RUSSELL, Sir John, *The World of the Soil*
SACKVILLE-WEST, V., *The Garden* (poem); *Country Notes in Wartime; In Your Garden; In Your Garden Again; More for Your Garden; Even More for Your Garden*
SCOTT-JAMES, Anne, *The Cottage Garden; Down to Earth; Sissinghurst – The Making of a Garden; The Pleasure Garden*
SITWELL, Sir George, *On the Making of Gardens*
TAYLOR, Geoffrey, *Some Nineteenth-century Gardeners; The Victorian Flower Garden*
WHITTLE, Tyler, *Some Ancient Gentlemen*
WILKINS, Eithne, *The Rose-Garden Game*
WILLMOTT, Ellen, *Warley Garden in Spring and Summer; The Genus Rosa* (issued in 25 parts)
WRENCH, J. T., *The Wheel of Health*

Index

Mary's Abbey, West Malling, 5, 6; Sion, 5; Stanbrook Abbey, 9-11
Corrigan, Dame Felicitas, 10
Cotswold garden – see Gardens
Council for the Protection of Rural England, 143
Country Life, 40, 42, 43, 64, 111, 150
Covent Garden market, 152
Craggs, Florence, 81, 156, 157
Craig, Edith, 91, 92
Cran, Marion, 174
Crow, William, 132
Crowe, Dame Sylvia, xiv, 111, 114, 115, 141, 150
Culpeper, Nicholas, 58
Culpeper Press, 62
Culpeper shops, 58-62, 64

D

Deanery Garden – see Gardens
Debenham, Alice, 159, 161, 163
Dennis, Doreen, 81, 156, 157
Dower House, Boughton – see Gardens
Downe House School, 144
Dyestuffs: Damson, 11; Indigofera (Indigo), 1, 79; Madder, 79; Pokeroot, 79; Tansy, 79; Woad, 1, 79

E

Earle, Captain Charles, 30, 34
Earle, Theresa, xiii, 29-34, 42, 49
East Lambrook Manor – see Gardens, also Nurseries
Elder, Madge, xiv, 154-156
'Elizabeth' (Countess von Arnim), 174
Ellacombe, Canon, 42

F

Falkner, Harold, R.I.B.A., 42
Farrer, Reginald, 55
Fiennes, Celia, xii
Finnis, Valerie, V.M.H., 147, 148
Fish, Margery, x, xiii, 28, 111, 115, 117-128, 133, 142, 173

Fleischmann, Mrs Ruby, 98
Flower Shows: Chelsea, xiv, 37, 82, 147, 148, 149, 157, 172; Temple Gardens, 32
Fraser-Darling, Sir Frank, 165
Friends' School, Saffron Walden, 119
Fuller, Mrs Douglas, 173
Furness, Flower, Lady, 131, 133, 134
Furness, Lieut-Col. Simon, 133

G

Garden Centre (Hollingbourne), xiv, 151, 152
Garden, The, 38, 40, 68
Gardening Illustrated, 53
Gardener's Chronicle, 49, 111
Gardener's Magazine, 13, 15, 18
Garden History Society, 112
Gardens: Ascreavie, xv; Badminton, xiii; Barrington Court, 125; Bowhill, xv, 155; Bramley House, 34, 35; Brympton d'Evercy, xiv, 118, 124, 125-127; Cockburn Mill, xii, 139-141; Cotswold (Quenington), 136-139; Deanery Garden, 42; Dower House, Boughton, 148; Dunbar Station, 173; East Lambrook Manor, x, 117-125, 128, 133; Folly Farm, 43; Great Dixter, 44, 45; Greyfriars, The, xii, 128-131, 134, 175; Hampton Court, xii, 4; Hamwood, 24-27; Hestercombe, 43; Hidcote, 110; Inverewe, x, xv, 8, 26, 38, 94, 95, 99-110, 112, 118, 131, 170, 173; Keillour Castle, 172; Kensington (Cecily Mure's), xii, xiv, 135, 136, 137, 139; La Mortola, 38; Lygrove, xiii; Mellerstain, xiii, 134; Mey, Castle of, xiii; Millmead, 43; Munstead, 37-39; Munstead Wood, 40, 43, 44, 45; Netherbyres, 131-135; Rowallane, x, xi; Shepreth Crossing House, 173; Sissinghurst, x, xiv, 85, 88-99, 109, 118, 153, 154, 170; Spetchley Park, 51, 52, 54; Tintinhull, x, 110-116, 118, 125, 141, 170, 173; Tyninghame, xiii, 132, 134, 135; Warley Place,

Wilkins, Miss, 143
Willis, Miss Olive, 144
Willmott, Ellen, V.M.H., ix, 29, 42, 49, 51-56, 146
Wilson, E. H., 54
Wilson, G. F., 37
Wisley – see Botanic Gardens
Woburn, xii
Wolseley, Viscountess, 29, 49, 143, 144
Women's Farm & Garden Association, the, 117, 143, 149, 150

Women's Land Army, 94, 146, 149, 150, 160
Women's Land Service Corps, 149, 150
Woodall, Edward, 37, 43
Woodlands, Cobham – see Gardens
Woolf, Virginia, 93, 98
Worcester Archaeological Society, the, 129
Wye College – see Horticultural Schools and Colleges